The

SPIRITUAL

DIMENSION

of the

ENNEAGRAM

JEREMY P. TARCHER · PUTNAM

a member of Penguin Putnam Inc.

New York

The
SPIRITUAL
DIMENSION
of the
ENNEAGRAM

⸺∾∾∾⸺

NINE
FACES
of the
SOUL

⸺∾∾∾⸺

SANDRA MAITRI

Where indicated, for purposes of analytical treatment, the author makes reference
to terms and concepts associated with Oscar Ichazo and/or the Arica Institute.
The author, however, has no connection with Mr. Ichazo or the Arica
Institute, and her interpretation and methodology are strictly her own.

Most Tarcher/Putnam books are available at special quantity discounts for bulk
purchases for sales promotions, premiums, fund-raising, and educational needs.
Special books or book excerpts also can be created to fit specific needs. For details,
write Putnam Special Markets, 375 Hudson Street, New York, NY 10014.

JEREMY P. TARCHER/PUTNAM
A MEMBER OF
PENGUIN PUTNAM INC.
375 HUDSON STREET
NEW YORK, NY 10014
WWW.PENGUINPUTNAM.COM

First Trade Paperback Edition 2001
Copyright © 2000 by Sandra Maitri

The Library of Congress has catalogued the hardcover edition as follows:

Maitri, Sandra, date.
The spiritual dimension of the enneagram : nine faces of the soul / Sandra Maitri.

p.   cm.

Includes bibliographical references and index.

ISBN 1-58542-017-4

1. Enneagram.   2. Spiritual life.   3. Personality—Religious aspects.   I. Title.
BL627.57.M35 —— 2000   99-049664 CIP
291.2´2—dc21

ISBN 1-58542-081-6 (paperback edition)

Printed in the United States of America
11 13 15 17 19 20 18 16 14 12

BOOK DESIGN BY DEBORAH KERNER

TO

OSCAR ICHAZO,
THE TEACHER BEHIND THE DOOR,

CLAUDIO NARANJO,
WHO OPENED IT,

AND

HAMEED ALI (A. H. ALMAAS),
WHO TEACHES ME TO WALK THROUGH IT

CONTENTS

———✥———

List of

DIAGRAMS

————⟨ ⟩————

FOREWORD

Before reading Sandra Maitri's brilliant book, I'd been hearing about the enneagram for a couple of years but was wary of systems that seemed to type, label, or judge. Astrology, for instance, had been a disappointment since I'd first discovered that when I told people my sign—Virgo—they'd slink away from me with mournful eyes, assuming I was fussy or frigid, and spend the rest of the evening with the hip signs, like Aquarians and Leos. When I heard I was really a Libra according to Vedic astrology, it allowed me to stretch the truth the tiniest bit by muttering "Vedic" once or twice, followed by the word "Libra" if anyone asked my sign.

Ten years ago, my friend Bess announced that astrology was passé and the enneagram was in. She said I had all the markings of "a Four," and that wasn't good. When I asked why, she replied, "Fours are dark, tragic, dramatic, and long-suffering." Before I could recover from the distressing news, Bess rattled on, "The other thing about Fours is that they always want what they don't have. They are rarely happy."

At the bookstore, I leafed through a couple of enneagram books, found descriptions of Fours that seemed familiar, but mostly my response was, "Now what? I already know these things . . ." There was a small measure of comfort in realizing that I was not alone in my behavioral skews, but comfort does not take skews away. Then I tried to figure out my husband's type, telling myself it would support our relationship, but I could never decide which he was, and would consequently accuse him of "being a typical Three—or maybe a Seven" during our fights, which did not bring us closer.

When Sandra told me she was writing this book, I asked her for the privilege of reading the chapters as they emerged. I knew that if she was writing about the enneagram, I'd understand the system with clarity and precision and its relevance to the inner journey. I was also hoping to discover that being a Four was maybe just a trifle better than the other types, though I didn't mention this to Sandra.

As an erstwhile student-turned-friend, I'd had repeated experiences of her remarkable ability to take complex metaphysical constructs and shape them into an understanding that made sense. Personal, relevant, thrilling sense. Time after time, I'd walk into her class confused or overwhelmed, and leave feeling that a piece of lush, verdant world I hadn't known existed had suddenly come alive. As her student and a student of the Diamond Approach, I learned firsthand that transformation is possible. Really truly possible.

This might sound like old news, but it was a stunning revelation for me. I'd been in twenty years of psychotherapy, had a committed meditation practice, attended dozens of workshops and retreats, and still felt hauntingly the same inside, still saw the world through the same lens of unlove that defined my childhood, i.e., "I'm always going to be separated from what I want most . . ."; "People always leave . . ."; "If only I had long legs and big hair, I'd be happy . . ." Cheery beliefs like that. No matter what the objective situation presented, I seemed to arrive at the same conclusions about myself and the world around me.

Most of us do the very same thing—and call it reality—until we are fortunate enough to encounter a person or teaching or book that sparks the longing for more. More space in us for life to unfold so that we don't have to squeeze our big starry hearts into the psyche of a two- or three- or eight-year-old.

The Spiritual Dimension of the Enneagram is one of those books, and Sandra's mind should be a national treasure. Rather than looking at the personality from inside itself and seeing what can be improved to feel better about ourselves, Sandra writes from the ground of Being, where no personality is hipper than another personality. From this perspective, there is only Being and what separates us from Being. There is no cool enneatype, which is the one piece of disturbing news.

The treasure of *The Spiritual Dimension of the Enneagram* is that it offers a way through that separation. It's as if Sandra removes the top layer of our lives, tells the secret we've been hiding for all these years. She says, "Yes, I see who you believe you are, but let me show you what (and who) is truly underneath those beliefs. Let me show you your jeweled possibilities." She presents a vision of who we are beneath the cluster of self-images and patterns we call our lives. And it's so much vaster and so much more thrilling than anything we've taken ourselves to be.

After five years of working with the practices Sandra has been taught and teaches in the book—presence and inquiry—something more miraculous than waking up with long legs and big hair has happened. The person who believed she needed those to be lovable, the child who felt separated from what she loved most, are not who I take myself to be. Fundamental ways I recognized myself—by despair, deficiency, and longing to be leading someone else's life—have been replaced by moments upon moments of settling, of openness, of contentment. The process Sandra teaches has given me my life.

Join her in the Work. Receive this gift of a book. Allow your big starry heart to open, your jeweled being to unfold.

GENEEN ROTH

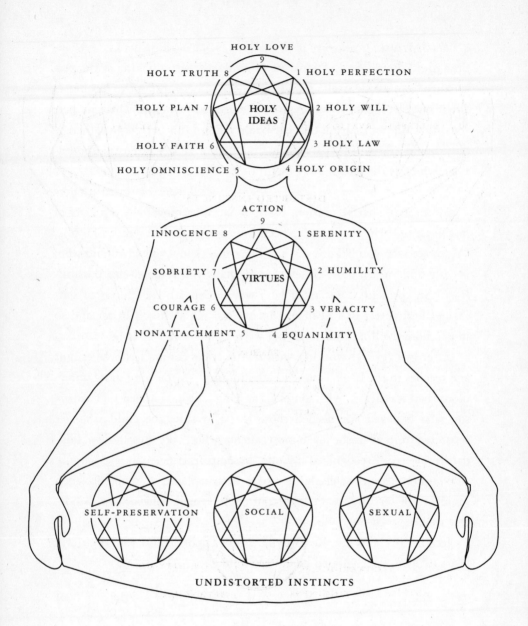

Diagram 1

THE OBJECTIVE ENNEAGRAMS

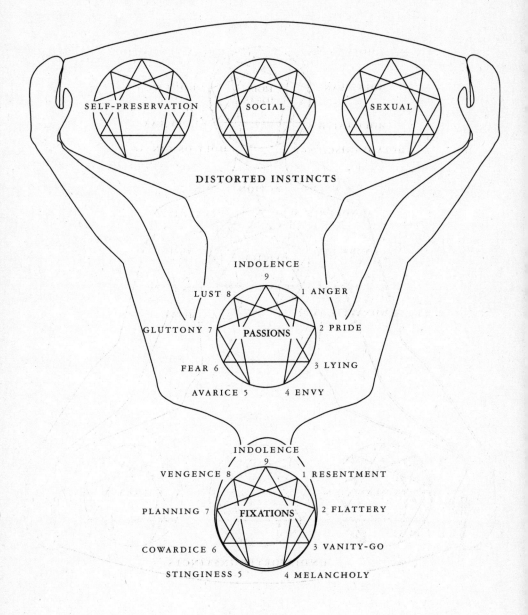

DISTORTED INSTINCTS

SELF-PRESERVATION   SOCIAL   SEXUAL

PASSIONS

INDOLENCE
9
LUST 8   1 ANGER
GLUTTONY 7   2 PRIDE
FEAR 6   3 LYING
AVARICE 5   4 ENVY

FIXATIONS

INDOLENCE
9
VENGENCE 8   1 RESENTMENT
PLANNING 7   2 FLATTERY
COWARDICE 6   3 VANITY-GO
STINGINESS 5   4 MELANCHOLY

Diagram 2

THE ENNEAGRAM OF PERSONALITY

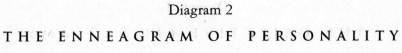

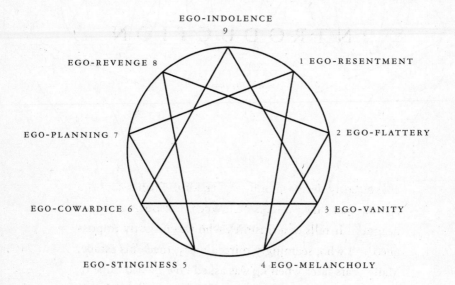

EGO-INDOLENCE
9

EGO-REVENGE 8

1 EGO-RESENTMENT

EGO-PLANNING 7

2 EGO-FLATTERY

EGO-COWARDICE 6

3 EGO-VANITY

EGO-STINGINESS 5

4 EGO-MELANCHOLY

Diagram 3

THE ENNEA-TYPES

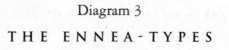

INTRODUCTION

The recently deceased Sufi teacher Idries Shah recounts a parable that I have always used when introducing the enneagram. It tells of a tinsmith who was unjustly imprisoned and who, seemingly miraculously, made his escape. Many years later when he was asked how he had done it, he replied that his wife, a weaver, had woven the design of the lock to his prison cell into the prayer rug upon which he prayed five times a day. Realizing that the prayer rug contained the design of his cell's lock, he struck a deal with his jailers to get tools to make small artifacts, which the jailers then sold and profited from. Meanwhile, he also used the tools to create a key, and one day made his escape. The moral of the story is that understanding the design of the lock that keeps us imprisoned can help us fashion the key that will unlock it.

Like all Sufi teaching stories, this one is a metaphor. It describes the condition of most of humanity: imprisoned in the labyrinth of our own ego structures. For most of us, our lives are lived within the narrow confines of what we take ourselves and the world around us to be, which, from the perspective of those not so imprisoned, is a tiny part of what is truly available to us. Particular thought patterns, feelings, and most overtly, situations repeat themselves over and over in our lives, giving our inner experience a sense of sameness. Beneath these repetitive patterns, we find fixed convictions about who we are and what the world we inhabit is like. These beliefs were formed during the first few years of life as our self-definition developed in response to our encounters with the environment and those within it, in combination with our innate predispositions. They came to shape our thought patterns and our emotional reactions, giving us a consistent inner experience of ourselves. The world that most of us inhabit, inner and outer, then, is largely a product of our past—difficult as that may be to acknowledge. The outer trappings may be more sophisticated and current than those of early childhood, but the inner core of who we take ourselves to be bears the uncanny outlines of ourselves at two or three years of age. The cast of characters that we encounter in our lives may change, but how we relate to and interact with them, how we feel about and even experience them, remains more or less constant and has the stale taste of familiarity. Although we don't see bars and walls constraining us as did the tinsmith in Shah's parable, we are truly in the prison of a holographic reality through which we filter the world around us and our very experience of ourselves.

Often we do not recognize how limited our experience of reality is— the fact that we inhabit a world that is unnecessarily confining. We may simply feel a vague dissatisfaction, a dim sense of deadness, and a lack of meaning and fulfillment, despite our best efforts to be satisfied with what society has told us should make us happy—whether it be money, possessions, position, power, fame, or relationship. For others, the sense of leading a restricted life may be more overt, manifesting itself as a painful and gnawing inner sense of inadequacy, deficiency, emptiness, or futility. Times of crisis may bring such feelings closer to the surface, giving us a glimpse of our confinement.

These glimpses are the beginning of our escape, since knowing that we are in a prison of sorts can open up the possibility of another alternative. Spiritual work throughout the ages has told us that there is more to life than we might think, that a world awaits beyond the one circumscribed by our inner constraints. The various spiritual traditions have not only articulated the extent of our captivity and their views of the dimensions of reality beyond the blinders of the ego but also have presented us with many means of escape. The story of the tinsmith tells us about one such method of gaining our freedom: understanding the design of that which keeps us locked within our cells. Without something akin to the tinsmith's prayer rug revealing the inner workings of our holographic reality—the lock that keeps us in our captivity—we often have little chance of escape.

While a number of psychological and spiritual maps delineate the realm of ego, none that I have been exposed to is as powerful as the enneagram, which I have worked with and taught for almost three decades. The enneagram of personality describes nine different personality or ego types, each with characteristic mental, emotional, and behavioral patterns. It also describes, if properly understood, how and why these patterns arise as we lose touch with our spiritual depths in early childhood. Additionally, it describes the affective and behavioral transformation each type will undergo if engaged in serious spiritual work that results in gradually reconnecting with those depths. We will speak more about these dimensions of the enneagram later because they form an integral part of truly using the enneagram as it was intended: as a tool for spiritual transformation that can help us move beyond the labyrinths of egoic reality that it describes.

The current popularization of the enneagram has focused almost exclusively on the psychological traits and patterns of the types, so this is all that most people know about the enneagram. In particular, the writings of Helen Palmer and Don Riso have introduced the enneagram to a huge number of people. Articles about the enneagram have appeared in the national press, and there are now newsletters and societies centered around it. It is being used in businesses to make personnel decisions, and it also is being used as a method of selecting an appropriate mate. While the focus has been primarily on the psychology of the nine types, all of this interest has ideally created an audience that may be receptive to its other dimensions as well. The enneagram's deeper function is to point the way to who we are beyond the level of the personality, a dimension of ourselves that is infinitely more profound, more interesting, more rewarding, and more real. It is in support of that pursuit that this book is written.

The origins of the nine-sided symbol of the enneagram are shrouded in mystery, probably because until this generation, teachings about it seem to have only been handed down orally. The enneagram first appeared in the West around the turn of the century in the work of the Armenian mystic, George Ivanovitch Gurdjieff, who said that he had learned it in the Sarmoung Brotherhood, a mystical order in Central Asia. Gurdjieff's biographer James Moore raises the question of whether the Sarmoung actually existed, and the answer to that question has never been settled.[1] In attempting to track down the origins of the enneagram, the Gurdjieffian chronicler James Webb could not find definitive traces of the figure of the enneagram as we know it prior to Gurdjieff.[2] He found only vague references that might pertain to it in antiquity, and while noting that a nine-sided figure cropped up as the frontispiece for a Jesuit text in 1665, it was composed of three equilateral triangles and was not the figure of the enneagram we use today.

Gurdjieff says a number of interesting things about the enneagram, which I will quote at some length here since they have great bearing on how to make sense of the many interpretations and ways in which the enneagram can be and is being used today:

> *Speaking in general it must be understood that the enneagram is a* universal symbol. *All knowledge can be included in the enneagram and with the help of the enneagram it can be interpreted. And in this connection only what a man is able to put into the enneagram does he actually* know, *that is, understand. What he cannot put into the enneagram he does not understand. For the man who is able to make use of it, the enneagram makes books and libraries entirely unnecessary.* Everything *can be included and read in the enneagram. A man may be quite alone in the desert and he can trace the enneagram in the sand and in it read the eternal laws of the universe. And every time he can learn something new, something he did not know before. . . . The enneagram is the fundamental hieroglyph of a universal language which has as many different meanings as there are levels of men. . . . The enneagram is a schematic diagram of perpetual motion, that is, a machine of eternal movement. But of course it is necessary to know how to read this diagram. The understanding of this symbol and the abil-*

ity to make use of it give man very great power. It is perpetual motion *and
it is also the* philosopher's stone *of the alchemists.*[3]

In order to appreciate the evolution of understanding about the enneagram and the divergences of perspectives about what it represents, it is necessary first of all to realize that, as Gurdjieff says, there isn't just one set of meanings or one level of reality that the symbol of the enneagram maps. This is important because it explains how it is that different psychological, religious, and spiritual schools use this symbol to explain radically different phenomena—although they tend to accuse each other of not using it properly if there is a divergence of phenomenon and content—and it also explains how it is that different levels of interpretation about the same phenomenon are possible. As Gurdjieff said of it in the quote above, the enneagam "has as many different meanings as there are levels of men." Being an archetypal symbol, it can be used to describe physical processes and principles, psychological ones, as well spiritual ones, and so it follows that there are enneagrams referring to and explaining many levels of things, including the days of the week and the planets in the solar system.

Gurdjieff himself used the enneagram as a model for his understanding of the functioning of the universe, and only through participating in the movement exercises he devised did he feel that the enneagram could be understood. He does not appear to have used it as a map of inner experience, as the Bolivian mystic Oscar Ichazo did when he introduced the enneagram to a small group of followers in Arica, Chile, in the early seventies.

One of Ichazo's students, who turned out to be pivotal in the recent history of the enneagram, was Chilean psychiatrist Claudio Naranjo. I was introduced to the enneagram by Naranjo in 1971 in—to the best of my knowledge—the first spiritual group in which it was taught in the United States. Before encountering Ichazo, Naranjo had studied extensively and worked with many of the Eastern spiritual traditions and Western psychological schools. He began teaching the enneagram when he returned to the States, incorporating into the theory he had learned from

Ichazo his own psychological insights based on his clinical background and his work with Fritz Perls's Gestalt therapy and Karen Horney's self-psychology. The enneagram was the central psychological tool in the group that Naranjo founded in Berkeley, California, of which I was a part. This was the first of the groups that he named SAT, which means "truth" in Sanskrit and stood for Seekers after Truth, the same name Gurdjieff had used for his early group of followers. A. H. Almaas, the founder of the contemporary spiritual path called the Diamond Approach to Inner Realization, was also a member of this group.

During the four years that the group lasted, we were taught spiritual perspectives and practices from most of the major traditions and introduced to Theravadan and Tibetan Buddhist, Hindu, Sufi, Confucian, and various fourth-way teachers (those espousing spiritual work in the context of ordinary life). The primary orientation of the group, however, had a distinctly Gurdjieffian flavor, emphasizing the overcoming of what Gurdjieff called the personality—the conditioned sense of a separate self made up of mental constructs based on the past[4]—in order to connect with our spiritual depths. To this end, Naranjo's approach was to integrate psychological and spiritual work, which at the time was a remarkable innovation. It was out of this ground that we worked with the enneagram.

We lived and breathed the enneagram, finding and giving dimension to its theory in our own experience. Naranjo's understanding of this powerful map radically circumvented our defenses against seeing and experiencing the functioning of our personalities. It led us to our personal hells—our individual experiences of deficiency at the core of our personalities, which is the inevitable result of loss of contact with our True Nature. Ego deficiency—which is probably all too familiar to many of those reading this—may feel like an inner emptiness, meaninglessness, directionlessness, pointlessness; a feeling of lacking substantiality, worth, value; a sense of inadequacy or lack. These are just a few flavors of this unpleasant state. Stripped of our previous means of avoiding this state of ego deficiency, it persisted for most if not all of us despite the plethora of spiritual practices we did and all the exciting and sublime experiences we had in the group. The SAT groups disbanded after four years, and their various members dispersed, finding other spiritual or psychological teachers, or altogether leaving what we had come to call, in Gurdjieffian fashion, the Work.

The enneagrams with which most people have become familiar are those that emanated from the teachings of Ichazo as elaborated by Naranjo, which relate to the inner experience of the human psyche. The enneagrams that they presented fall into basically two categories, the first of which relates to egoic experience—that of the personality—and the second to essential experience—that which is beyond the conditioned self, and what we also refer to as the spiritual. These two sets of enneagrams were said to be inextricably linked, but the connection wasn't clear. We were taught that what are called the Holy Ideas in the language of the enneagram represent nine different objective or enlightened perspectives on reality. The loss of them was said to lead to the fixed cognitive distortions of reality, called the fixations, which form the core of the nine personality types. How this translates experientially and why it occurs remained rather amorphous. Without understanding this, it becomes impossible to use the enneagram as a map to help us retrace our steps and reconnect with the lost realm of the spiritual, and all we can do is attempt to transcend or eradicate our personalities to experience the realm of Being. It was left for my old friend from the SAT days, Almaas, to flesh out the actual process.

Returning to Gurdjieff for a moment, he taught that what we bring to the enneagram determines our understanding of it. By itself the enneagram is simply an archetypal map, and our philosophical and spiritual orientation has everything to do with how we interpret it. What we read in it, in other words, depends upon our understanding of the territory it charts. Since the territory that this book maps out is that of the personality and its relationship with its spiritual depths, it is important to have a sense of my perspective and my approach.

The understanding of the enneagram presented in this book is grounded in the perception that the ultimate nature of all of existence—its spiritual depths—is what I will refer to as Being, the ultimate or True Nature of everything. Our individual consciousness is what I will refer to as our soul, and I see it as an individual manifestation of our divine nature, Being. Each of us, then, is a unique arising of Being. When we experience

Being within ourselves, we are experiencing the essence of who we are—what is left when all the constructs of the personality dissolve—and so are in touch with our essential nature. What I will refer to as Essence, then, is Being experienced through our individual soul.

Our souls are malleable, impressed and shaped by what we encounter in life, and this is particularly the case during our formative years before our defensive structures solidify. During this time, we develop a personality, a structured or fixed sense of ourselves and of reality, which forms the outer layer of our soul and which in time separates us from the Divine within as we progressively become identified with it. How this happens is a complex and fascinating story, and it will be told as we explore the three points of the enneagram forming its inner triangle in Chapter 1.

The work of spiritual development, as I see it, is to reconnect with the spiritual depths of our soul—our essential nature. Essence is not one static state or experience, but may arise in our consciousness as different qualities such as compassion, peacefulness, clarity, acceptance, impeccability, spaciousness, and intelligence, to name just a few, each with a characteristic feeling tone and quality of presence—even with its own unique taste and smell. These various manifestations or features of our Essence or True Nature are called the Essential Aspects.

How we apply or make use of the information about our personality and our essential nature charted by the enneagram depends upon our methodology. In a nutshell, the approach that informs this book consists simply of learning how to be fully present within our bodies, our emotions, and our thoughts, and to experientially explore and inquire into what we find. Presence and inquiry, then, are its cornerstones. Inquiry that is only mental will not produce insights that illuminate and reveal the inner workings of our soul, so this inner journey must be a profoundly experiential one. Through being present in our moment-to-moment experience with an attitude of exploration and curiosity, taking nothing that we find within our inner world for granted or as an ultimate given, the contents of our soul reveal themselves. We usually first become aware and in touch with the outermost layers of our personality, particularly our inner critic, the superego. Deeper layers of our structure emerge bit by bit as our journey progresses, and in time these begin to become more and more transparent. Gradually the various Essential Aspects of our primordial nature reveal themselves.

Putting it slightly differently, when we experientially explore the world of the personality rather than taking it as reality, we see that it is a holographic universe through which we filter our inner and outer experience. It is our own home movie, whose story line is shaped by the conclusions we came to about the nature of reality on the basis of our early childhood experiences. All that we experience is filtered—and thus distorted—through this endlessly playing and often unconscious movie, including those we encounter in our lives, who therefore have the nasty habit of falling into the roles and characters of significant people from our early life. The plot, the emotional atmosphere, and the way we respond in this movie bear the indelible imprint of our enneagrammatic type.

On close investigation, this inner reality proves to be as insubstantial an illusion as the images generated by a virtual-reality computer. Modern particle physics has shown us that matter reveals itself to be mostly made out of space when viewed with extreme magnification, and so its solidity is a perceptual illusion. So, too, with our inner world: what appears all too real in normal consciousness proves to be not so solid after all upon close scrutiny. Through developing the capacity to be present continuously, to contact our experience deeply, and to be curious about its contents, we can begin to see reality without the distortion of our inner movie. Deeper and deeper levels of reality that are not part of that drama can reveal themselves, bringing us progressively more in touch with what lies beyond and is more fundamental than the filter of the ego: reality, with a capital R, our ultimate nature and the nature of everything.

From this perspective, psychological work is inseparable from spiritual development that truly transforms the soul. Pursuing spiritual work without working on our personality typically results in a lack of resolution of deep-seated issues and a lack of true integration of our spirituality, a situation that has limited and even brought down many spiritual teachers and traditions. Conversely, most psychological work is too grounded in believing that the realm of the personality is ultimately real. When essential states do arise, the psychotherapist is usually not attuned to them or cognizant of their significance for these states to become forefront. Although true psychological insight only occurs in moments when we have a flash of understanding that profoundly touches our soul, the notion of being present to our experience does not figure into psychotherapeutic theory. As we shall see, this perspective can profoundly shift our understanding of the territory the enneagram maps in such a way that the enneagram can truly become a tool for authentic spiritual transformation.

Focusing on the enneagram itself, in the diagrams that begin this section we see the two categories of enneagrams—those relating to objective experience (as opposed to the subjective experience of the personality) depicted in Diagram 1, and those relating to egoic experience (which are referred to collectively as the enneagram of personality) depicted in Diagram 2. We will refer again and again to the information in these diagrams throughout the book, so they don't need to be absorbed all at once. Turning first to the diagram of the enneagram of personality, we notice right away that the figure upon which the enneagrams are superimposed is upside down. This illustrates the egoic condition of man, which is referred to in some of the spiritual traditions as a state of sleep; of being in darkness, ignorance, or delusion; or of seeing things upside down. This metaphor of the inverted man referring to the egoic condition can be seen in the Tarot card of the Hanged Man.[5]

We will begin with exploring what the Holy Ideas refer to, since they form the cornerstone of our understanding of the spiritual dimension of the enneagram. The nine Holy Ideas are nine different direct perceptions of reality, when it is perceived without the filter of the personality, so they are nine different enlightened perspectives. The use of the word *idea* may be misleading here, since we usually think of an idea as a mental concept. In the language of the enneagram, however, idea refers to a particular perception of reality, a vantage point from which it is seen, experienced, and understood. It is important to clearly grasp that the Holy Ideas are not particular spiritual experiences or states of consciousness but rather are views of reality freed from the prejudices of the personality. They therefore also have to do with the meaning derived from experience and the perception of the underlying thread linking various experiences. Since they refer to the various unobscured perceptions of reality, we see the nine Holy Ideas in the head region of the figure in Diagram 1.

Some of the Holy Ideas, as we will see, focus more on various generalities about reality as a whole, while others focus more on man's place within the universe. It is probably easiest to convey a sense of the Holy Ideas through elucidating each one. Some of them may seem accessible, while others may appear foreign and incomprehensible, and it is important to remember that the perspectives on reality that they describe are very profound, the subjects of the great spiritual traditions over the centuries, and are well beyond our normal view of things.

Beginning with the Holy Idea of Point Nine at the top of the enneagram, when we see reality from the vantage point of Holy Love, we see that the ultimate nature of all that exists is beneficent and loving, and that we are each made out of and are an expression of that love. Moving clockwise around the enneagram, if we perceive reality from the vantage point of the Holy Idea of Point One, which is called Holy Perfection, our take is that the fundamental nature of everything, including ourselves, is inherently perfect, good, and positive. When experiencing through the vantage point of the Holy Idea of Point Two, Holy Will, we see that the unfoldment of the universe has its own direction and momentum, and that what occurs within each of us and within our lives is part of that divine will. From the point of view of Holy Law, the Holy Idea of Point Three, we see that everything that happens is part of the changing pattern of the universe, and that nothing and no one functions separately from the movement of the whole. When experiencing reality from the angle of the Holy Idea of Point Four, called Holy Origin, we see that True Nature is the source of all manifestation, including ourselves, and that everything is inseparable from it.

From the perspective of the Holy Idea of Point Five, Holy Omniscience, we see that each of us is an inseparable part of the whole fabric of reality, and that the boundaries that distinguish us are not ultimate. When experiencing from the point of view of Holy Faith, the Holy Idea of Point Six, we see with absolute certainty that our inner nature **is** Essence, and this sustains us and gives us confidence and trust in ourselves and in reality as a whole. From the angle of Holy Plan, the Holy Idea of Point Seven, we see that there is an inherent logic and progression to the unfoldment of the human soul—including our own—whose natural movement is toward self-realization, just as a caterpillar naturally develops into a butterfly. With Holy Truth, the Holy Idea of Point Eight informing our perception, we see that Being is the ultimate nature of all that exists and that everything is made up of It, so all dualities of God and the world, Spirit and matter, even ego and Essence are fundamentally illusory.

While we can experience reality through the angle of all of the Holy Ideas, one slant is the most compelling: that of the Holy Idea of our particular point on the enneagram. According to the original theory taught by Ichazo, we are each born with all the Holy Ideas available, but are "sensitive" or particularly attuned to one in particular. Like a sensitive nerve, we seem to arrive on the planet vulnerable and susceptible around this one way of understanding life. What transpires affects our contact with this understanding, and the universal thing that happens to everyone in the first few years of life is the losing of contact with our essential nature more or less completely as we develop a personality structure. As we lose contact with Essence, we also lose contact with the particular truth represented by our Holy Idea.

We come to perceive reality devoid of its depth dimension, and because our perception of reality is incomplete, we lack a crucial understanding about it—that represented by our Holy Idea. The way we interpret this limited view crystallizes into a fixed belief about reality—a delusion specific to our point on the enneagram—which is called our fixation. This delusion about reality and human nature, then, is an understanding that replaces that of the Holy Idea, and for this reason we see the fixations in the head region of Diagram 2. Our fixation forms the basis and gives rise to a whole personality style, complete with specific mental biases, emotional reactions, and behavioral patterns. For instance, if your type were that of Point One on the enneagram, whose Holy Idea has to do with perceiving the fundamental perfection, goodness, and rightness of everything, losing contact with your essential nature in early childhood would be experienced as losing contact with what makes you and everything else perfect. This would give rise to a deep inner conviction that there is something basically wrong with you and the rest of reality—the fixation termed resentment on the diagram, which in turn would give rise to an inner emotional atmosphere of anger about all the wrongness, and a behavioral pattern of trying to fix things and make them right.

Implicit in this notion that we are born sensitive to one particular Holy Idea is its correlate: that we are born predisposed to develop one personality type. According to enneagram theory, then, we are not entirely the products of our conditioning, but rather arrive predisposed to interpret that conditioning in particular ways. The pendulum in psychological thinking has swung from the belief that our natural endowments determine the character we develop, to the belief that how we are treated in early childhood determines our character; and it is now swinging back to ascribing our character to our genetic makeup. From the perspective of enneagram theory, nature (the sensitivity we arrived with around one Holy Idea) and nurture (the effects of our conditioning) go hand in hand in shaping the personality we develop.

Each of us, then, is attuned to reality through one particular angle, that corresponding to our point on the enneagram, whether we are operating in the realm of personality or of Essence. For this reason, it seems more appropriate to speak of enneagrammatic types or ennea-types, using the term recently coined by Naranjo,[6] rather than the ego-types or fixations as he originally called them, which refer only to personality. In other words, even if we were fully enlightened, fully free from the obscurations of our conditioning, we would still be sensitive to reality in accordance with the Holy Idea of our point on the enneagram, and we would experience and manifest more of the enlightened affective state—called the virtue—of that point than of any other. Our type, awakened or asleep, remains the same.

The enneagram of personality is a map of how the ego or personality functions in its entirety, so while we are each born sensitive to one particular Holy Idea and therefore predisposed to one ennea-type, we each contain all nine types. Because of this, most people can readily understand and relate to the dynamics of all of the types. All of the types, then, are present within us, but one of them is most pronounced, and the fundamental delusion about the nature of reality that corresponds to it forms the core of our structure.

Turning once again to our diagrams of the enneagram of personality and the objective enneagrams, on Diagram 2 we see the fixations, the fixed ideas or delusions about reality that are at the core of each ennea-type, shown in the head region. While the descriptors shown on the circumference of this enneagram do not exactly correlate to my descriptions in the text, for the sake of posterity I am using here those originally given by Ichazo.[7]

The Enneagram of Passions shown on Diagram 2 in the area of the heart refers to the emotional or affective atmospheres typical of each of the types, resulting from the fundamental preconceptions about reality that are the fixations. These emotional qualities are compulsive, reactive, and charged. They form a kind of backdrop for other emotional states, a perpetual and compulsive feeling tone that typifies each type.

The corresponding Enneagram of Virtues on Diagram 1 represents the affective states resulting from integration of the perspectives of the Holy Ideas. The more objective we become—in other words, the more we experience beyond our subjective movie—the more the virtues manifest within our experience and actions as an affective tone or feel, replacing the reactivity of the passions. On a deeper level, the virtue associated with our point on the enneagram is the very quality that we need in order to experience ourselves objectively as we are. Concurrently, the more that we experience ourselves intimately in a truthful way, the more our particular virtue develops. I will discuss how this plays out more fully in the chapters on each of the ennea-types.

The enneagrams of instincts, undistorted and distorted respectively on Diagrams 1 and 2, bear a bit of explanation. The theory taught by Naranjo is that there are three instincts: self-preservation, social, and sexual, and that each of us has one that is more "passionate," or more of a central preoccupation. The passion associated with our ennea-type comes out most strongly in that particular arena of life. A pronounced self-preservation instinct refers to a preoccupation with security and survival. A pronounced social instinct refers to a preoccupation with one's social status, with friendships, and with belonging. A pronounced sexual instinct refers to a preoccupation with intimate relationship. Each ennea-type has these three subtypes, each focused around one instinct and each having a distinctive style and emphasis to their personality. In effect, there are really three versions or variations of each type, then, and these will be explored in the chapter on the subtypes. The corresponding enneagrams on Diagram 1 are simply labeled Undistorted Instincts, meaning that the more that we work through identification with the personality as a whole, the more we function objectively in these arenas of life, responding to current reality rather than to our past.

———— This book begins with exploring what is represented by the triangle formed by Points Nine, Six, and Three, which forms what is called the inner triangle of the enneagram. This inner triangle represents the archetypal process of losing contact with True Nature or Being and developing an ego structure or personality, and forms the basis for all of the other types. We will then explore each of the nine ennea-types, depicted in Diagram 3, describing the associated Holy Idea and seeing how each pattern of personality develops through its loss.[8] We will elucidate its resulting cognitive, emotional, and behavioral characteristics and its psychodynamic bias. What I hope to convey is an understanding of the processes that underlie all of these traits, beginning with the primary perceptual skew that forms a twist in the soul and leads to the manifestations of each ennea-type. Manifestations of the personality have their own logic, and deciphering it lays the ground for making sense of the personality traits themselves.

Those uncertain about their own ennea-type may wish to refer to Appendix A, in which some ways of determining one's type are explored. Determining someone's type is very much of an art, requiring a thorough understanding of the enneagram and a lot of familiarity with people whose type is quite certain. Some of the things I have learned about helping people type themselves may be beneficial in that process.

The order in which I will present the types is in the order of the dynamic movement between the points, called the inner flow in the language of the enneagram, which we see depicted in Diagram 5 and which will be focused upon in Chapter 11. While the reader may be tempted to jump to or read only the chapter on his or her ennea-type, I strongly recommend reading the types in the order in which they are presented. The

reason for this is that each type builds upon and is a response to the dilem-
mas and solutions of the type presented before it, and so an understanding of this interrelatedness is necessary for a complete picture.

Those familiar with other books on the enneagram will notice that my
descriptions of the types do not for the most part include the assets of each
type or their gradations of functionality. Writers who describe healthy and
unhealthy manifestations of each type are describing higher-functioning
ego structures and lower or more dysfunctional ones. While these are
valid and useful distinctions from a psychological perspective, we must
not lose sight of the fact that the enneagram of personality describes the
design of ego structure. Variations in prison walls do not make them any
less confining, and my orientation is helping readers move beyond these
constraints, rather than making readers more complacent about their
captivity.

Likewise, some of the various traits, emotional states, and behaviors of
each of the types may sometimes appear extreme and at the far end of normal. My experience is that even in the sanest of us, some pretty crazy
places are present, and we become conscious of them the deeper we dive
into our souls. The relative predominance of these extremes is a barome-
ter of our degree of psychological health—the more continual, the more
rigid and therefore fragile our personality structure. Nonetheless, the contents of the consciousness of each type has the same shape and manifestations.

There is often a variance between how the types outwardly behave and
their actual inner experience. For example, Fours may come across as aloof
and superior, while internally they feel afraid of exclusion and are socially
insecure. An Eight may appear bullying and confrontational, while internally feeling afraid of being weak, powerless, and helpless. I have at-
tempted to convey some of each type's inner experience and also how each
appears to others, and this disparity may leave some readers feeling misunderstood and perhaps criticized. This is not my intention, which is that
of presenting a well-rounded description of each type.

My occasional light and humorous treatment of some of the attitudes
and behaviors of the various types may strike some as wounding, which is
also not my intent. There is a fine line between taking the personality too

seriously and thus inadvertently fueling our identification with it, and discounting or being insensitive to its manifestations. I have tried to walk this line with care and compassion, which I hope I have conveyed.

Some books on the enneagram talk about the characteristic childhood and parents of each of the types, so I would like to clarify my perspective on the issue of psychodynamics. It seems to me more appropriate to describe the various ennea-types' *point of view* about their parents and what happened in their childhood, rather than asserting that this or that is what actually happened. Because each type experiences life through a particular cognitive filter, it only follows that what was forefront at the time and what remains forefront in memory are those parental qualities and childhood experiences that fit that filter. A family may have children of different ennea-types, and each will have a particular lens through which they experience the same parents—a Four will experience his or her mother as abandoning and shaming, a Five will experience her as invasive and hysterical, a Six will experience her as inconsistent, and so on around the enneagram. Personality has a characteristic sameness to it, so even though each child experiences the same parents at different ages, these parents do not fundamentally change and become radically different people as each child is born. To assert that the mother of each type has a particular set of characteristics and ways of relating, and that certain specific situations happened in each type's childhood is therefore a very dubious proposition. It is far more appropriate to speak of each type's interpretation or take on mother, father, siblings, and childhood events. Each child will focus on particular characteristics of the parents and their relationship to him or her, as well as on particular experiences that occur because of his or her predisposed sensitivity. It might be argued that each child elicits particular aspects of the parents' personalities and ways of interaction, and so the parents are somewhat different people to each child. At best, this way of looking at things means that the child's predispositions and sensitivities determine to some degree parental style, and so how a parent behaves does not entirely dictate the child's personality or ennea-type.

To convey to the reader a sense of some of the qualities and overall feel of each of the types, I have used examples of well-known people. I want to include the caveat that because I do not know these people personally, I cannot be certain that they are a particular type, and am basing my assessment on their public personas.

Included in my descriptions of each type are subsidiary enneagrams, which can be found in Appendix B. As I refer to these subsidiary enneagrams, readers may find it useful to return to the diagrams there. The traps, seen in Diagram 9, are specific notions that each type fixates upon as a solution to his problems, and are really its red herrings. The avoidances, seen in Diagram 10, are particular feeling states that each type emphatically evades. The antiself actions, seen in Diagram 11, are ways in which each type undermines and turns against its own soul. The lies, seen in Diagram 12, are characteristic attitudes and orientations in which each type deceives himself and others about reality. I learned all of these from Naranjo, aside from the Enneagram of Traps, which came from Ichazo.[9]

We will also explore what Almaas has called the idealized Aspect of each of the ennea-types. While there are perhaps hundreds of qualities of Being—Essential Aspects—one in particular is seized upon and idealized by each ennea-type. This particular quality of Being looks to each type like the antidote to its suffering and sense of lack. Although this quality is a real quality of Essence, the personality creates its own imitation of it. Each ennea-type, then, emulates the characteristics of its own idealized Aspect, creating a facsimile of it in manner, goals, and general orientation. Each type also searches for things that seem to embody the qualities of this idealized Aspect externally. Yet the personality's imitation of this quality of Essence inevitably fails to resolve the inner sense of deficiency characterizing each type. Because something external can never fill an inner sense of lack, acquiring the things that embody this quality of Essence likewise does not resolve each type's inner quandary.

For example, to an Ennea-type Six, whose primary suffering is an ongoing state of fear and doubt, inner support looks like what's needed. This Aspect is idealized: its characteristics seem to be qualities both to acquire as well as to emulate. Sixes, then, strive to feel an inner solidity, confidence, and courage that they lack; get upset with themselves about not feeling an inner foundation; and often act in ways to try to prove that they have these qualities rather than the fear and doubt that's really present. Understanding this helps us see that the characteristic defensiveness and rebelliousness of Sixes are attempts to demonstrate that they have the backbone that, however, deep down they feel is missing. It is not that attempting to acquire the particular traits of our idealized Aspect is a bad thing, but it will not bring us the satisfaction that we crave. No matter how many heroic feats a Six performs, the inner uncertainty and fear will not be banished. Understanding how our attempt to capture our idealized Aspect shapes our lives and consciousness will help us understand and eventually get in touch with what will really fulfill us: contacting the depths of who we are.

Adding another dimension to this notion of the idealized Aspect, there is a direct relationship between the idealized Aspect and the Holy Idea of each ennea-type. As previously discussed, the Holy Idea is a particular understanding about reality and the human soul with which we lose contact through the process of conditioning in early childhood. It is not, as noted earlier, a state of consciousness. The idealized Aspect of each type, however, which is a state of consciousness, seems to embody the perspective on reality of that type's Holy Idea. Each ennea-type, then, attempts to reconnect with its lost understanding about reality through experiencing its idealized Aspect. The inner logic seems to be that if I had such-and-such qualities—being sweet or bright or strong, for instance—then I would feel complete.

Using our example above may help us understand this complex linkage. The perception about reality that is missing for a Six (the Holy Idea) is that Being is our inner foundation and true support. Without this perception, reality looks to a Six like a frightening struggle for survival in which others appear as potential threats. If we knew that we had this inner foundation, we would experience a sense of support, confidence, and courage—the qualities of the idealized Aspect. So, the Sixes' attempt to feel courageous and fearless is an attempt to embody experientially what the Holy Idea of Point Six refers to: the fact that Being is what supports our existence.

At the end of the chapters on each of the ennea-types, I will discuss some of the stages of inner work and issues each type needs to confront, and how the associated virtue is both a guide in terms of inner orientation toward one's process as well as a quality that becomes stronger the more one works on oneself. Following the chapters on the types, I will cover and enlarge upon Naranjo's original theory regarding the inner flow, mentioned earlier—the dynamic relationship between connected points on the enneagram. Our study of the latter will incorporate Almaas's teaching regarding one of the primitive structures in the soul—the inner image of ourselves as a very young child— and its relationship to the idealized Aspects. Working with and digesting this material completes the picture of core issues that each type confronts in the course of truly transformative inner work and expands the material presented at the end of each chapter on the types.

Rounding out our understanding of the enneagram, in the final chapters I will describe the instinctual subtypes mentioned earlier, and discuss working with the wings, the two points on either side of each ennea-type. The descriptions included in these chapters are neither exhaustive nor definitive, but rather are intended as doorways into personal exploration and deeper understanding of these facets of the enneagram.

———— A word about gender: The English language makes it difficult to use the third-person-singular pronoun in a way that includes both genders. The old-fashioned use of *he, him,* or *his* is offensive to many women, and using *he or she* or *him or her* makes for very cumbersome reading. My solution in this book is to alternate genders in the third-person pronouns when describing the ennea-types. More men seem to be certain types, while more women are others, and so I have used those gender pronouns in the chapters describing those types. This is by no means an indication that, for instance, only women are Twos and Fours or only men are Sixes and Eights. In the chapters on the inner flow, the subtypes, and the wings, I simply alternate the gender of the pronouns. Alternating gender in my use of pronouns is not an entirely satisfying solution to a sticky problem.

———— Before turning to the material itself, let me convey a word of warning: The material presented here is very powerful and needs to be treated with great care. It can profoundly raise consciousness, and at the same time it can be deeply wounding, so how we approach and use it needs thoughtful consideration. The enneagram brings to awareness aspects of ourselves and others that the personality's defenses work overtime to keep concealed. This may feel like a mixed blessing, bringing about both a sense of relief that what has been hidden is being revealed, but it can also bring up a deep sense of unease. To really understand that much of how we have taken ourselves to be and even how we have experienced ourselves is based on a fundamental conceptual distortion can be pretty unsettling. Truly grasping the Holy Ideas experientially confronts us with how far we are from living in alignment with their perspectives, revealing the full extent of our estrangement from our depths. True change, however, is impossible without this kind of confrontation.

Ideally the material that follows should help us understand who we take ourselves to be and so begin to loosen these knots of identification. It can also help us make sense of how and why others behave, feel, and think as they do, which can open our hearts to compassionate understanding. While the information is meant to support consciousness and unfoldment, it can, however, easily be used by the personality to support itself in a couple of ways that we need to comprehend. One way is through using the material as a basis for judging oneself and others, and thus using it as a support for inner positions of right and wrong. It is extremely important not to heap value judgments and self-evaluations on top of the material presented, difficult as that may be. The material itself is neutral; what we do with it may not be. Another way is through using our identification as a particular ennea-type to create a new and improved identity, much like putting the old package in a new and more hip wrapper. In either case, nothing is being developed except reinforcements for our personality. It is probably primarily for these reasons that the enneagram was only taught orally in mystery schools until now.

The approach to the enneagram of personality presented in this book, while it includes amplifications by Almaas and myself, remains true to the original spirit and theory taught to me by Naranjo. My intention in writing this book is to convey that spirit which has to a great extent gotten lost in the popularization of this material, to honor my former teacher and the wisdom he imparted, as well as to present the enneagram as a spiritual, rather than merely psychological, tool. Perhaps the interest generated from the recent popularization of the psychological side of this material has sparked curiosity about its deeper dimensions, and perhaps this interest is an indication that we are collectively at a point where humanity can benefit from a more widespread dissemination of the wisdom of the enneagram.

It is my hope that what follows will be used in the spirit in which it was written—to compassionately support the truth of who we ultimately are. Let us, then, begin exploring the locks of our captivity, and may the understanding revealed begin to set us free.

The
INNER TRIANGLE
and the FALL

⟨⟨⟨

The figure of the enneagram is made up of an inner triangle linking Points Nine, Six, and Three, and an outer
shape formed by the linking of Points One, Four, Two,
Eight, Five, and Seven. These two forms do not intersect,
as you can see on Diagram 4 below, and so the inner triangle is a separate entity of sorts. On the level of the
enneagram of personality, the inner triangle represents factors responsible for and stages in an archetypal process—
that of the loss of contact with our fundamental or essential
nature and the concurrent development of an ego structure. Our essential nature is who we are when we experience ourselves free from the influence of the past—it is
our innate and unconditioned state of consciousness. It is
our state as infants, and coexists with our soul's particular characteristics, such as a sweet disposition, sharpness,
robustness, and so on. As babies, however, we have no capacity to know that this is our experience because self-
reflection has not yet developed.

The process of losing of contact with our essential nature is universal: everyone who develops an ego goes
through it. That, of course, means virtually every human
being on the planet, unless one is born either a saint or

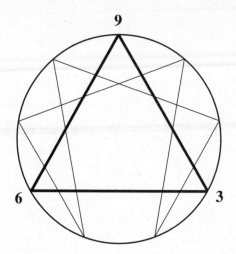

Diagram 4

THE INNER TRIANGLE

insane, i.e., never developing an ego structure. Each of the ennea-types on the triangle can be seen as "specializing" or being formed around one of the three archetypal factors in this loss. They also can be seen as high-lighting or focused around the three corresponding phases in the process of ego development. In contrast, the other points on the enneagram can be seen as further elaborations of this process. Understanding the process represented by the inner triangle not only helps us understand the ennea-gram of personality but also helps us understand what we all need to con-front within ourselves to reconnect with our essential nature. Since I am describing phases in a universal process rather than describing the three ennea-types per se, I will refer to Points Nine, Six, and Three, rather than using the names of their corresponding ennea-types.

Point Nine, as indicated by its position at the very top of the ennea-gram, represents the fundamental principle that initiates ego develop-ment: the actual loss of contact with our True Nature. This loss of contact is often referred to in spiritual work as falling asleep, resulting in a state of ignorance or darkness. The process of losing contact with that which is innate and unconditioned occurs gradually during the first few years of life, and by the time we are four years old, Essence is mostly lost to perception. This loss of consciousness of our essential nature starts the development of the scaffolding that is the ego structure.

Developing this structure is a necessary prerequisite for spiritual development, since part of the ego's attainment is self-reflective consciousness. Without it, we could not be aware of our own consciousness. Different traditions explain the reason for this seemingly inevitable and apparently regrettable process in diverse ways. Ultimately it remains a mystery, and our beliefs about the purpose behind this loss are immaterial. It is simply a given, and we can either deal with our estrangement or remain asleep to it.

A number of factors lead to this loss of contact with Essence, and the first one is identification with our bodies as being who and what we are. According to Heinz Hartmann, considered the father of ego psychology and among the pivotal post-Freudian psychoanalysts, one of the characteristics of our consciousness as newborns is that it is an undifferentiated matrix in which psychological structures that emerge later—such as the ego, superego, and the instinctual drives—are not articulated and distinguished from one another. René Spitz, roughly contemporary to Hartmann and the pioneer of analytic research into the mother-child relationship, extended this concept to that of nondifferentiation, in which there are no discriminations of any sort in our consciousness between inner and outer, self and other, psyche and soma, and, hence, no cognition.

Our understanding, based upon the experience of those who have delved into the deepest layers of their personality structure and the memories encapsulated within them, is that the infant is in a state of oneness made up of bodily sensations, emotions, and essential states. All the contents of consciousness are blended together in a kind of primordial soup. It is probable that while a child sees differentiations between things, he does not actually *know* that they are separate. He might feel the warmth of his mother's breast, for instance, and see the redness of his rubber ball, and feel the hunger pangs in his belly, but he probably does not conceptualize these experiences as different from one another. Warm, red, and hunger would all be part of the unity of his experience.

The beginning of cognition originates with the differentiation between pleasurable and unpleasurable sensations, and memory traces of these impressions gradually register in our developing central nervous system. Through repetition of these impressions, memory begins to form. The fact that our first differentiation is between pleasure and pain means that the Freudian principle of striving for pleasure and avoiding pain is the most fundamental principle underlying the ego structure.

Gradually a further differentiation begins to form: a sense of inner versus outer begins to take shape. The collection of sensations from within our body registers as a rudimentary inner sense of identity, forming the basis of our ongoing feeling of self. Through repeated experiences of being touched by the mothering person, the collection of sensations on the periphery of the body coalesce into a sense of the body's boundaries. Each human being's body is separate from every other human being's body, and so repeated contact of the environment with our skin leads to a preliminary sense of being a separate and discrete entity. This sense of separateness—of defining ourselves as being something that has edges and boundaries that are ultimate—forms another fundamental belief and characteristic of the ego structure.

The beginning of self-reflective consciousness, then, begins with physical impressions, and so our sense of who and what we are becomes identified with the body. "The ego," as Freud said, "is first and foremost a body ego."[1] This identification with the body and therefore with the fact of its discreteness as defining who and what we are disconnects us from our early infant consciousness in which everything is experienced as a wholeness—which is the same oneness as that of deep spiritual experiences, as reported by mystics throughout the centuries. In moments when this assumption of our inherent separateness is suspended, what we see is that our ultimate nature and the nature of all that exists are the same thing. When we are identified with our bodies and thus with our discreteness, instead of experiencing ourselves as unique manifestations of one thing, or as different cells in the one body of the universe, we come to experience ourselves as ultimately separate, and thus cut off and estranged from the rest of reality.

The second factor in losing contact with our essential nature has to do with inadequacies in the infant's environment. Such inadequacies involve impingements and lack of attunement and responsiveness to the infant's needs on the part of the environment, particularly the mothering person. Because infants cannot verbally communicate their needs, this lack of attunement is for the most part inevitable—the mother can only guess whether the child is hungry, having a gas pain, or emptying his bowels. Distress, which initially is physical, causes the infant to react in an attempt to relieve it. Survival anxiety kicks in, and the infant goes into red alert mode to try to protect himself from pain and remove its cause. This reaction disconnects the infant from his state of nondifferentiation in which his consciousness is completely one with Essence. When the distress passes, the infant's consciousness once again melts back into nondifferentiation.

This cycle of reaction and relaxation repeats again and again, depending upon the environment. If there is abuse or other forms of severe impingement, the reactivity will become more or less constant. Even in the absence of extreme trauma, the environment registers as more or less inconsistently supportive for all normal neurotics, and we therefore grow up more or less disconnected from our essential nature. Almaas describes below how the loss of continuous attunement and responsiveness—*holding,* in psychological terminology[2]—leads to distrust in the environment, which in turn leads to the reactivity at the core of ego development:

> *By having to react to the loss of holding, the child is no longer simply being, and the spontaneous and natural unfoldment of the soul has been disrupted. If this reactivity becomes predominant, the child's development will be based on that reactivity rather than on the continuity of Beingness. If her development is based on reactivity to an unsafe environment, the child will develop in disconnection from Being and therefore, her ego will be what becomes most developed. If her development unfolds out of the continuity of Being, the child's consciousness will remain centered in her essential nature and her development will be the maturation and expression of that nature.*
>
> *The less holding there is in the environment, the more the child's development will be based on this reactivity, which is essentially an attempt to deal with an undependable environment. The child will develop mecha-*

nisms to deal with an environment that is not trustworthy, and these mechanisms form the basis of the developing sense of self, or ego. This development of the child's consciousness is then founded on distrust, and so distrust is part of the basis of ego development. The child's consciousness—her soul—internalizes the environment it is growing up in and then projects that environment onto the world.

Implicit, then, in the ego is a fundamental distrust of reality. The failure of the holding environment leads to the absence of basic trust, which then becomes disconnection from Being, which leads to reactivity, which is ego activity.[3]

The disconnection from our original undifferentiated state creates a division or duality between ourselves and Essence, which, along with identifying ourselves with our body, gives rise to the belief in our inherent separateness. This is the genesis of the illusion of duality, the spiritual issue par excellence in which we experience ourselves and Being as two distinct things.

The third factor contributing to losing contact with Being is parental lack of attunement to our depths. The fact that we were raised by parents who themselves believed that they were ultimately discrete entities (unless we were born to totally enlightened parents) profoundly shapes our consciousness. Because of their own lack of attunement to their essential nature, our parents could not perceive, value, or mirror back to us our true depths. Since our consciousness during the first few months of life is merged with that of our mother, what she experiences of us becomes what we experience of ourselves. As Margaret Mahler has said, "Mutual cueing during the symbiotic phase creates that indelibly imprinted configuration—that complex pattern—that becomes the *leitmotif for 'the infant's becoming the child of his particular mother,'*"[4] meaning that we become what our mother perceives us to be. Not only are society and culture passed on to us by our parents, but also the entire worldview that they rest upon is imparted to us. This worldview that we absorb with our mother's milk is that of the personality, in which the physical is experienced as the only dimension of reality that is real. Because the deeper dimension of reality—that of our essential nature—is not held and mirrored back to us, we gradually begin to lose contact with it ourselves.

As mentioned in the Introduction, Essence, the nature of our consciousness or soul, has many different qualities, called the Essential Aspects. Lovingkindness, Strength, Intelligence, Joy, Peace, Impeccability, and Nourishment are just a few of these Aspects. So while the True Nature of our soul is one thing, the characteristics it manifests change, or the quality of it that we are most in touch with at a given time changes. Which quality Essence manifests depends upon the outer situation in which we find ourselves or upon what is arising in our inner process. For example, we might find compassion arising within us in the presence of a suffering friend, or we might find a sense of inner support arising when encountering our inner lack of confidence. As in the Sufi story of the mullas who each touch a different part of an elephant in the dark and so each have a different sense of what an elephant is, each Aspect presents a different quality of our True Nature but are all parts of one thing. While the face Essence presents may differ, it remains nonetheless one.

While it appears that the infant experiences many different qualities of Essence, particular ones become prominent at specific developmental phases. For example, during the phase called symbiosis by Mahler, which lasts from about two to six months, the Aspect most dominant is that of ecstatic love, characterized by a melting sweetness and the sense of being united with everything. It is during this phase that both the infant and mother feel merged with each other, and it is this blissful sense of union that adults unconsciously seek to recapture through falling in love. As the infant begins to separate physically from the mother through crawling at around the sixth or seventh month, she also begins to form an inner sense of discrimination between herself and mother, a "hatching" out of the symbiotic orbit. The Aspect that corresponds to this subphase of differentiation is characterized by an energetic expansiveness, a sense of strength and of capacity. As the child begins to explore her world, delighting in being able to touch, taste, and manipulate all the fascinating people and objects in it, another Aspect becomes prominent. This one is characterized by a sense of delight and of endless and goalless curiosity about all that one encounters.

As the child moves through each stage of ego development, a corresponding Aspect is predominant at that time. Any disruptions or traumas that occur during that developmental stage—of which even the most well-adjusted have many—affect our relationship to the associated Essential Aspect, weakening our contact with it. These disruptions become part of the history stored in our bodies and souls.

This loss of contact with our depths is called the fall in some of the spiritual schools. It does not happen all at once as some teachings seem to imply, but rather it occurs gradually during the first four years of childhood, as we move through the stages in which particular Aspects are dominant. Disruptions and lack of mirroring of these Aspects, as previously discussed, cause them sequentially to become lost to consciousness, some gradually and some abruptly. Eventually a sort of critical mass is reached, in which the whole of the essential realm fades from conscious awareness. Because Essence is the nature of the soul, the fall is not an actual *loss* of Essence—rather, we simply lose touch with it. This is an important discernment, because it means that the essential realm is present all the time; we have just "forgotten" it or screened it out of awareness. It is here in each moment and is inseparable from who and what we are, but it has gone into our unconscious. This understanding is the basis of some spiritual teachings that say that we are already enlightened. This is, however, of little comfort to most of us, since the essential realm does not emerge into consciousness just because we mentally know it is there.

One way, then, of looking at spiritual development is as a matter of making conscious the unconscious. In normal consciousness, the essential realm is covered over by the deepest strata of the personality, which is composed of contents that have been repressed from consciousness as well as contents that have never reached consciousness, such as the instinctual drives, and memories and fantasies related to them. Freud, who formulated the notion of the unconscious, perceived it to contain certain functions of the ego and superego which are not conscious, as well as what he called the id. His concept of the id was that it "contains everything that is inherited, that is present at birth, that is laid down in the constitution—above all therefore, the instincts, which originate from the somatic organization and which find a first psychical expression here [in the id] in forms unknown to us."[5] The essential realm, which is present at birth, would be, interestingly enough, encompassed by Freud's own definition of the id, although Freud did not theorize or write about the spiritual dimension.[6]

As Essence sinks into the cauldron of the unconscious as part of the id, one Aspect at a time, we gradually lose contact with this precious part of ourselves—in fact, with what makes us precious to begin with. This understanding is formulated by Almaas as the theory of holes, for reasons that will become clear momentarily. As each Aspect is "lost," we feel that something is missing and so experience a sense of lack that we interpret as deficiency: "Something is missing in me and so something is wrong with me." It is as though there were holes in our consciousness where something integral ought to be, and this sense of empty places may feel quite literal. We may even have the impression that there are holes in various parts of our bodies, although we know that everything is physically there. As more and more of these holes result from the loss of Essential Aspects, the balance becomes tipped toward a general sense of emptiness and deficiency, which then forms the core of most people's inner experience, whether consciously or not. This state of ego deficiency, which can feel like a sense of being valueless, worthless, small, and weak, of feeling completely helplessness, impotent, inadequate, ineffective, and suspended without support, forms the deepest layer and therefore the deepest experience of the personality. It cannot be otherwise, since the personality is a sense of self lacking its ground—Essence—and so can *only* feel deficient.

This first phase, losing contact with one's essential nature which initiates the formation of the personality or ego structure and results in the state of deficient emptiness at its core, is represented by Point Nine on the inner triangle. At the risk of confusing the reader by adding another level of complexity, it is interesting to notice that the three factors I have described as contributing to the loss of contact with Essence—identification with our bodies, reactivity and loss of trust in the environment, and the essential realm not being reflected back to us—correspond to the three corners of the inner triangle, so we have a triangle within a triangle. Identification with the body correlates to Point Nine, reactive alarm to our needs not being fully met by our early caregivers correlates to Point Six, and our parents' lack of contact with and thus reflection back to us of the realm of Essence correlates to Point Three. In what follows, we will see why I have made these correlations.

In Diagram 3, Point Nine and its adjacent points, Eight and One, form the "indolent" corner of the enneagram, meaning that all of these types—Ego-Indolence (9), Ego-Revenge (8), and Ego-Resentment (1)—have as an underlying connecting thread "falling asleep": losing contact with Essence, and becoming externally directed. The idea is that being asleep to one's True Nature and not trying to awake from the sleep of unconsciousness is laziness—not doing what really needs to be done.

Following the direction of movement within the triangle, the next stage in the development of the personality is represented by Point Six. This corner of the enneagram, Point Six (Ego-Cowardice) and its adjacent points—Seven (Ego-Planning) and Five (Ego-Stinginess)—is the "fear" corner, representing the fear within the soul resulting from the disruptions in the holding environment that caused it to move away from Essence and, in circular fashion, the fear that arises due to this loss of contact.

The deficient emptiness left in the wake of the formation of the holes is far too painful for the infant's consciousness to tolerate, and triggers the fear that she will not survive this loss. This fear of ceasing to exist if the loss is experienced forms a layer of tension and constriction around any given hole, and collectively feels like a ring of terror at the base of the personality structure. This ring is a level of fear in which we feel disconnected, lost, and profoundly at risk, and which can more accurately be described as primal terror. It is a contraction of the soul, and expresses itself in the patterns of tension or armoring in the body. The whole of the structure of the personality is ultimately one big contraction—a rigid holding—that is synonymous with this primal fear crystallized in the soul.

This layer of fear becomes particularly apparent in the process of retrieving contact with Essence, as we experientially move beyond the outer strata of the personality and begin getting close to the underlying state of deficient emptiness. It is this layer of fear that is the archetype of signal anxiety, the sense of impending danger that we feel as something stored in the unconscious starts making its way into awareness, and which mobilizes the ego's defensive systems to keep this content sealed off from consciousness. Signal anxiety, then, is a superficial manifestation of this primal layer of fear. It is, as previously noted, paradoxically the same fear that catapulted us out of contact with Essence in the first place, since, as we have seen, disruptions in the holding trigger reactivity that disconnects us from abiding in Being. We will return to the fear corner when discussing the process of reconnecting with our essential nature.

In the face of the fear of not surviving, the infant attempts to restore some equilibrium in her emerging psychic economy; and as we move into this part of the process of ego development, we are dealing with what Point Three represents. To cope with what feels like life-threatening fear, she covers the holes through losing consciousness of them and the fear surrounding them. Once she loses consciousness of these empty places in her psyche, she also sets about trying to fill them, since although they have become repressed, her soul knows they are still there. She tries to fill them by getting from the outside something that feels like what is missing, a process that becomes more elaborate and refined as she becomes older. Initially, for example, a warm bottle or her "blankie" might substitute for the loss of sweet loving contact. By adulthood, this filling of holes can take the shape of seeking worldly success to fill the hole of powerlessness, seeking recognition or accumulating priceless things to fill the hole of valuelessness, doing something considered societally important to fill the hole of worthlessness, climbing mountains to fill the hole of weakness or impotence, seeking a partner to fill the hole of feeling unlovable, and so on.

Sectors of the personality in turn develop, corresponding to each hole. The memory traces that we described earlier coalesce into self-representations, or inner images of ourselves. These self-representations contain within them the memory of the loss of contact with each Aspect, the belief about ourselves that the loss gives rise to, and the emotions that arise as part of this sense of self. In time, these self-representations form parts of an overall self-image, an inner picture of ourselves, much of which remains unconscious. We take ourselves to be someone who is weak or unlovable or lacking perseverance or brilliance or whatever quality we have lost touch with inside of ourselves.

The external persona that we present to the world, which is often referred to as self-image, is just the outermost manifestation of this inner picture of ourselves. The ennea-types of the "image" corner of the ennea-gram, whose names—as we see in Diagram 3—are Ego-Flattery (Point Two), Ego-Vanity (Point Three), and Ego-Melancholy (Point Four) all share a focus and preoccupation with image—both with what is presented externally as well as what is imaged internally. This is a superficial mani-festation of a deeper process of identification with inner pictures of our-selves—our self-image.

This self-image eventually becomes consistent over time—we are such and such a person who has such-and-such qualities, characteristics, and abilities—largely determined by the particular holes and inherent charac-teristics forming our sense of who we are. This sense of self, as object re-lations psychologists explain, develops in conjunction with a sense of "other." The repeated impressions and experiences registering as memory traces in the infant's developing consciousness eventually fuse into a sense of what is us and what is not us, of other—originally mother or our pri-mary caretaker as infants. This original internal picture or concept of the other, our object-image—which forever bears the imprint of our mother—forms a template through which we experience the whole of the outer world. So just as the development of our self-image is closely linked to what our parents perceived and mirrored back to us, our sense of those other than ourselves replicates those who did this early mirroring. For this reason, our friends and lovers have the peculiar habit of reminding us of our parents, and even our deepest concepts of the Divine have the often distressing characteristic of reminding us of mother.

These mental structures of self and object-images, which define who we are relative to the world around us, act as filters that keep our awareness focused on and identified with the surface of who we are, rather than with our depths. This identification with the surface is closely related to the lack of parental perception of our deepest nature discussed earlier as one of the factors responsible for the disconnection from Essence, and rep-resented here by Point Three. As Almaas says,

In time, there will be no essence in the person's conscious experience. In-stead of essence or being, there will be many holes: all kinds of deep deficien-

cies and lacks. However, the person will not usually be consciously aware of his perforated state. Instead, he is usually aware of the filling that covers up the awareness of these deficiencies, what he takes to be his personality. That is why this personality is considered a false personality by people aware of essence. The individual, however, honestly believes that what he is aware of is himself, not knowing that it is only a filling, layers of veils over the original experiences of loss. What is usually left of the experience of essence and its loss is a vague feeling of incompleteness, a gnawing sense of lack, that increases and deepens with age.[7]

When the sense of incompleteness and lack that Almaas described above moves us to ask whether there isn't more to life than the meaninglessness and inner emptiness that we feel, when we finally exhaust the hope that the answers to our problems will come from external solutions, when we stop trying to be a particular way so that we can get what we think will be fulfilling, and when we cease attempting to fill our inner emptiness or divert ourselves from facing it, we may finally begin the great reversal of the wheel of life: facing our inner world and our consciousness—which really determines what we experience—directly and truthfully.

If we understand that our sense of incompleteness is the result of having lost contact with our depths and that this contact is obscured by layers of psychological structure, it follows that all we have to do to connect with our spiritual roots is thread our way back through these structures to what lies beyond them. Because these structures that form the personality develop in response to holes, they mimic the qualities of Being that are lost to consciousness. Therefore what we have to do to regain contact with our depths is to retrace, in effect, our developmental steps. This entails being present in our immediate experience, which means fully contacting and feeling our bodily sensations, our emotions, and our thoughts—and being curious about and inquiring into what we find. Whatever is based on a mental construct—and that is what our self and object-images are—will, under experiential investigation, dissolve and ultimately reveal the hole of Essence that this fabrication is filling. Whatever is inherently real will expand and become more prominent in our consciousness.

Letting go of our defenses of self-deception, denial, and avoidance, we find that at the beginning of inner work who we take ourselves to be is the false personality, which, as we have seen, is only something filling the overall hole of loss of contact with our True Nature. We begin the Journey, then, at Point Three, which represents here the identification with the surface of ourselves, the personality. It also represents all of the supports for the personality—everything that we look for from the outer world to fulfill us, including relationship, wealth, power, status, knowledge, and so on. Broadly speaking, it symbolizes the filling of our holes, whether through mental constructs or outer accoutrements, which only serves to disconnect us more completely from the depths that truly sustain—and are implicit in—the surface of ourselves and our lives.

The personality is characterized by a number of qualities that distinguish it clearly from our essential nature. One of its chief characteristics is that it is rigid and static, so our ongoing sense of self varies little from moment to moment, and we respond to what life presents us with based on our subjective sense of self rather than based on what the situation demands. Our experience of the present moment is filtered through the layer of pictures discussed earlier about who we are and what the world around us is—our own inner movie—pieced together from elements of our distant past. It buffers us from what is happening, distorting and causing us to misinterpret what we perceive, so that we are indeed responding to the past and not the present. This may manifest in the simplest of ways as when, for instance, we are faced with a situation in which we need to be assertive about our needs, but we don't express them because we actually experience ourselves as someone who cannot and should not. This rigidity arises most poignantly in intimate relationships when we can't believe that the other person really loves us—believing ourselves to be fundamentally unlovable—or that the other must not *really* be as wonderful as we thought if we realize that he or she actually does love us. Another common example is when we get a big promotion or a lot of recognition for our accomplishments, and think that there must have been some mistake.

One of the common threads in all of these examples is that they assert a self-image based on lack, reflecting the deficiency that forms the personality's deepest layer. This is why when we get what we have most wanted—what we thought would *really* fill that hole—if we have not already found something wrong with what we got or convinced ourselves that we can't *really* have it, the fulfillment is fleeting at best.

It is important to understand that the self-image has so structured our consciousness that we are not dealing with something volitional—with conscious mental ideas that we have some choice about—but rather with unquestioned, mostly unconscious convictions about who and what we are, and who and what others and the world around us are. People may come and go in our lives, but the parts that we assign them to in our inner movie vary only slightly and are for the most part elaborations of those of significant people from our childhood. The life situations in which we find ourselves have the devilish habit of repeating themselves. When we really begin to apprehend our situation in our identification with the realm of the personality, we begin to appreciate the magnitude of our confinement in our self-image.

By bringing consciousness to our bodies, experiencing and fully allowing whatever sensations, emotions, and thoughts that arise within our consciousness, we move deeper into ourselves and start feeling more in contact with ourselves. This shift of focus from outer directedness to inner exploration in and of itself begins to take some of the wind out of the personality's sails. As we begin exploring the terrain within us, one of the first things that we typically encounter is our inner "shoulds" that come from our internal critic, the superego. This voice inside of us, which is the internalization of composite authority figures from childhood, was the final layer of the personality to develop, and so it is the first that we encounter. As Freud's name for it in the original German—the *Über-Ich*—implies, its function is to oversee the *Ich,* our sense of "I." It preserves the status quo of the personality through its injunctions and admonitions, telling us what to do and how to be, what is all right within ourselves and what isn't. It evaluates our experience into good and bad, right and wrong, okay and not okay, and so on. It keeps alive the hope that if we only become "better," we will get the fulfillment we are seeking. Because of this, our superego blocks the unraveling of the personality structure that the experiential inquiry I have been describing facilitates, because it dictates what should and shouldn't be occurring within us.

One of the first orders of business on our inner journey, then, is learning to defend against the superego. This is essentially a matter of feeling the suffering inflicted upon ourselves through judgment and criticism, as well as recognizing that this approach to ourselves is completely counterproductive. We need to see that the means here—criticizing and judging ourselves—determine the end: a perpetuation of the inner sense of deficiency.[8] The superego of each of the ennea-types has a particular flavor, as well as a particular relationship to what is experienced as oneself. We will explore this as we discuss each of the types.

As we learn to defend against the superego, staying with the contents of our consciousness—regardless of what arises—becomes easier. Following the thread of an issue, reaction, or physical contraction will lead us through the related psychological structures and their history to the hole in our consciousness where contact with the associated quality of Essence is missing. An example might be useful to help understand this process.

Let's say that you have an issue about material support in your life. You never seem to have enough money to cover your needs, and you feel angry and jealous when you notice others around you being able to take expensive vacations, buy houses, and so on. Emotionally you notice that you feel deprived and needy as you experience your state when this issue is up for you. You realize that you always seem to have felt like this, and many memories of your childhood may arise, perhaps seeing other children getting things from their parents that you didn't. You might remember your mother simply not being there for you, not meeting your needs emotionally or materially.

Deep pain arises, and you notice that the pain is coming from a contraction at the base of your belly. As you allow the pain, you might glimpse an emptiness that seems to be centered there, and fear arises of feeling this fully. Staying with this fear and attempting to understand what feels scary brings up memories of overwhelming fear about not surviving because your mother wasn't attuned to what you needed, and you realize that you feel about one year old. You see that you really couldn't tolerate this hole when you were that young, but realize that you are now an adult and that it will be okay to feel it. As you feel the hole, the contraction in your belly relaxes, although the emptiness feels terrible. It seems to go on forever, and your mind tells you that it is pointless to pursue this. You realize that this hole has been there as long as you can remember, and feels very familiar, part of your sense of who you are, although it has been very much in the background. You see that you have felt it was useless to really experience it, and so you walled it off and actually pushed it out of sight.

Facing it now, it feels like the bottom has dropped out and that you will fall forever if you go into it. Seeing that this is an assumption, you check it out experientially, and find yourself in the middle of the hole. You suddenly realize that instead of falling, you are floating, and that it feels like something is holding you up. When you inquire into what is holding you up, you feel a strong sense of a presence that feels supportive and steady. At first it feels outside of you, but as you stay with the experience, you notice that this presence is actually inside of you. In fact, you feel the presence of this support in your belly exactly where the emptiness was before.

This is a hypothetical example of moving through the hole of essential support. In it, we can see how a problem in our day-to-day life, especially one that comes up again and again, is the manifestation of lacking contact with one of the qualities of our essential nature. Disturbances on the surface have a direct connection to what is going on in the depths, and ultimately only contacting these depths will substantially alter the surface. We can also see in this example how an attitude of open-ended inquiry into our experience can lead us to and through the hole at the root of the surface turbulence.

Every hole, like the one in our example, is surrounded by fear; and following the map of the inner triangle, we are at Point Six when we confront it. As discussed earlier, this blanket of fear is both apprehension about experiencing the hole as well as the reactive alarm in the soul that created the hole in the first place. Inevitably a conviction is implicit in the fear that it will be intolerable to feel the hole fully. This might manifest as being afraid that we will go crazy, fall apart, disintegrate, fragment, disappear, or die. The more fundamental the hole is to one's personality structure, the greater the fear will be. What will disappear, dissolve, disintegrate, and so on is the sector of the personality that forms the layer over the fear. We will, in other words, move beyond the personality when we go beyond the fear, and although this is what we profess to want, it is also what we are most afraid of because we have come to believe the personality is who we are and *all* that we are. Implicit in the fear is a contraction away from the hole, and paradoxically, it is this pulling away that gives the hole its feeling of deficiency. As long as we reject the hole, it feels bad. The moment we accept it and open up to it, what felt like a lack becomes a spaciousness imbued with the very quality of Essence that seemed missing. Following our map of the inner triangle, this movement beyond the fear into the deficient emptiness and beyond it to the spaciousness of Essence is moving through Point Nine.

This process of moving through the structures of the personality represented by Point Three, through the layer of fear that surrounds each hole at Point Six, and through the deficient emptiness to Essence represented by Point Nine will have to be gone through many times for a substantial disidentification with the personality to occur. Just as a critical mass of holes in early childhood tipped the inner balance from identification with Essence to identification with the personality, a critical mass must also be reached on the Journey of Return. Repeated experiences of moving through our holes and contacting our essential nature will finally shift our identification from the personality to Essence. How long this takes is entirely individual, dependent upon many factors that include the severity of childhood trauma and the extent of inner motivation to go through whatever it takes to face the truth of who we are.

This work of reconnecting with our essential nature is not easy nor is it quick. But for those moved by an inner flame to discover the depths of themselves, it is a necessity. In the words of the thirteenth-century mystical poet Jelaluddin Rumi,

You've been fearful
of being absorbed in the ground,
or drawn up by the air.

Now, your waterbead lets go
and drops into the ocean,
where it came from.

It no longer has the form it had,
but it's still water.
The essence is the same.

This giving up is not a repenting.
It's a deep honoring of yourself.[9]

ENNEA-TYPE NINE: EGO-INDOLENCE

Ennea-type Nine is the "mother" of all ennea-types, to borrow a turn of phrase from that infamous Eight, Saddam Hussein. As we saw in Chapter 1, Point Nine represents the principle of losing contact with our essential nature, and because this estrangement from our True Nature is common to all egos, all of the other types can be seen as differentiations of this fundamental archetype of personality. To put it differently, this personality type is the one most purely anchored in issues relating to the forgetting of our real self—the falling asleep to our deepest nature—and the other types are variations or embellishments of this basic principle at the heart of the ego.

Briefly summarizing the characteristics of this ennea-type, Nines shun calling personal attention to themselves. They do not come across as big personalities, and instead may seem nondescript or indistinct. They place others before themselves, and have a hard time being primary in their own and other people's attention. Preferring to give others the limelight, they see themselves as less important and consequential, and tend to fade into the background. Rarely asserting themselves, they like keeping things harmonious and pleasant, and have difficulty doing or saying anything that others might find offensive, uncomfortable, or controversial. So they shun confrontations, rarely express negative feelings or opinions, and focus on the positive. They are excellent mediators, able to see everyone's point of view, but often have difficulty discerning and expressing their own. They have difficulty figuring out and attending to what is really essential for themselves personally. This can run the gamut from neglecting their inner life, to not paying attention to their feelings and thoughts, to not taking care of what they need to in their lives.

Externally directed, they may be very active or inclining toward laziness, but in either case they leave themselves and their own personal needs out of the picture. They tend to get lost in the details of life, and have trouble discriminating what really needs their attention. Inclining toward inertia, they have a difficult time getting moving and, once moving, have difficulty changing course and stopping. They tend toward muddledness and can be a bit chaotic, but in a pleasant and inoffensive kind of way. Inner feelings of worthlessness, unimportance, and inadequacy form their central sense of deficiency, and they soothe themselves with comforts and diversions to numb out these painful feelings. Energetically Nines are solid and stable, dependable and kind.

Just as the central orientation of the personality type associated with Point Nine is the most fundamental—forgetting ourselves—so too is the Holy Idea of this point. The Holy Idea of each point is, as we have discussed in the Introduction, a particular way that we perceive reality when all of the subjective veils of the personality are absent. Each Holy Idea is a way of seeing the nature of reality from a slightly different vantage point, all of which are enlightened views of it and all of which are equally true. Each ennea-type is sensitive to the Holy Idea associated with it, which means that it is the most unstable; and when each type loses contact with Being, so too goes its Holy Idea. As we will explore in detail in discussing each type, the loss of its Holy Idea creates a basic blind spot for each type.

The particular perspective on reality—the Holy Idea—that Ennea-type Nine is especially sensitive to is called Holy Love. Holy Love is the perception that reality, when seen without the filter of ego, is inherently loving and lovely, delighting and delightful, pleasing and pleasurable, full of wonder and wonderful. Holy Love points to the fact that Being is both the source of love and love itself, and that all of existence is a manifestation and embodiment of that love. Holy Love does not refer to the feeling of love itself, but rather to the perception that Being or True Nature is inherently positive and affects us in favorable ways. Almaas calls this characteristic "nonconceptual positivity," and as he says, it is difficult to convey in words, since it is something beyond our usual comparative notions of positive versus negative, or goodness versus badness. It does not imply that everything that happens is positive but rather that the fundamental nature of all of creation is beneficial and propitious. Hinduism refers to this characteristic of reality as *ananda,* or "blissfulness," and it is the basis of the *bhakti,* or "devotional" spiritual paths, which invoke and cultivate this uplifting characteristic of Being.

Holy Love is neither an emotion, then, nor is it an essential state. This may be a bit difficult to grasp, but might become clearer from the following quote of Almaas in which he describes the perception of Holy Love in various Essential Aspects, or states of consciousness:

> *Holy Love is a clear and distinct quality of the very substance and consciousness of each essential aspect. Holy Love is seen in the positive, uplifting, and blissful affect and effect of each aspect. It is the sweetness and softness in Love. It is the lightness and playfulness in Joy. It is the preciousness and the exquisiteness of Intelligence and Brilliancy. It is the purity and the confidence of Will. It is the aliveness, excitement, and glamour of the Red or Strength aspect. It is the mysteriousness and silkiness in the Black or Peace aspect. It is the wholeness and integrity in the Pearl or Personal Essence. It is the freshness and the newness of Space. It is the depth, the deep warmth, and the satisfying realness of Truth.* [1]

Holy Love is the perception that our essential nature, regardless of which of its qualities is forefront at any given time, is innately beautiful and that the experience of it is always a positive experience. So on a personal level, since our essential nature forms the nucleus of all that we are, Holy Love tells us that we are therefore fundamentally beautiful and lovable, and our inseparability from Being is what makes this so. True Nature, in other words, suffuses our souls and our bodies with beauty and lovableness, and is what makes us beautiful and lovable.

When we experience Being directly, without the filter of our conceptual mind, the effect it has upon us is of a sense of meaning, of value, of benefit, of fulfillment. Our souls relax, our hearts open, and we experience a sense of well-being in such moments. We are responding to the inherent characteristic of reality that Holy Love describes—its pure positivity. As Almaas says,

> When you objectively apprehend reality . . . you cannot help but feel positive toward it. In this experience, there are no positive or negative categories that your mind has divided things into. There is no polarity here; this nonconceptual positivity is beyond all polarities. The nature of reality, then, is such that the more it touches your heart, the more your heart feels happy and full, regardless of your mental judgments of good or bad.[2]

So the closer we are to our depths, the more in balance and in harmony we feel. This is because Being is, from the angle of Holy Love, fundamentally positive and affects us as such. This explains why being in touch with the truth of our experience and revealing ourselves as we are makes us feel good, even if what we are getting in touch with or expressing is something we don't like seeing or disclosing about ourselves. We are moving deeper into ourselves, and so our souls are closer to and more infused with the goodness of True Nature. Being more deeply in touch with ourselves just feels better than not being in touch. Without this characteristic of Holy Love, we would not feel motivated to travel any spiritual path. Contact with Being affects us in an agreeable, beneficial, and constructive way, making the struggles and difficulties of becoming more conscious worth our time, energy, and devotion.

In the course of working on ourselves, we learn in time that when we stay on the surface of ourselves, which is to say when we are identified with and operating from our outer shell—our personality—we suffer. The more asleep we are to the reality beneath our shells, the less we feel that life is fulfilling, meaningful, and pleasurable. Or, in the language of the enneagram, the more fixated we are, the less we partake of the loving nature of reality, for we have lost our connection with Holy Love. Our suffering is not the result of being alone or of being in the wrong relationship, is not because we don't have enough money or because we have too much of it, or because of anything of the sort. Nor is it because our outer surface doesn't look as pretty as we think it should or because our personality isn't as pleasant as we think it might be. We suffer because we are living at a distance from our depths—it's as simple as that. The more our souls are infused with Being, the better we feel and the better life seems to us, no matter what our outer circumstances happen to be.

This brings us to another nuance in our understanding of Holy Love, which has to do with its universality. The inherent goodness of reality is not localized somewhere—it is implicit in the fabric of all that exists. It is not a commodity that exists out there someplace, waiting for us to get in touch with it. It does not reside in a particular person, nor is it dependent upon a particular situation. It is not a separate something that is outside of ourselves. It is the nature of everything that exists, and we don't see this to the extent that we experience life through the veil of our personality. It may seem that the goodness or beneficence of reality is something that comes and goes, that it is something we have in one moment and lose in the next, and that is only accessible to us in certain situations and so is about those circumstances. For example, it may seem that we only feel the goodness of life when someone loves us or gives us attention, or when we get a promotion or a raise. Or, in the early stages of a spiritual journey, we may only get in touch with our essential nature and experience ourselves as wonderful and lovable when we are meditating or in the presence of our teacher, and so the positivity of our nature seems like something that is ephemeral. This is only a stage—eventually we come to see that the beauty and wonder of Being is not a something that resides in someone else or even that it is a thing inside of us somewhere, but rather is the nature of everything and so is everywhere. From this perspective, we see that there is in fact nothing but Being—it is not something we need to acquire or, at a certain point, even connect with. The Journey, then, transforms into something else when there is no longer the sense of it as a movement from here to there and when we recognize and abide in the goodness and splendor of Being.

Without this perception, we might still perceive that there is benevolence in the universe, but we don't see that it is the nature of everything, including ourselves. When we lose contact with Holy Love, we lose contact with its boundlessness, and it seems to us that the goodness of reality can be in one place and not in another. So the positive becomes conditional and fleeting—it arises only in particular situations and it is here one minute and gone the next. Likewise, one person can appear lovable and another not.

This sense of the restrictiveness and the conditionality of the goodness of life makes possible the delusion of Ennea-type Nine, which is the loss of perception of being made of love and so inherently lovable. To a Nine, others appear lovable and seem to partake of the benevolence of life, while she does not. This is the fundamental perceptual distortion of Ennea-type Nine, upon which rest all the characteristics of this type. It is a distortion that might be difficult to see as such, since it is fundamental to all personality types. If we consider, however, that the very substance of our bodies and our consciousness is the expression and embodiment of Being, whose central characteristic is Its positivity, how can we be anything but innately lovable? How can our lovability be determined by how our bodies look, who loves us, or how much we have?

Along with the loss of contact with Essence, then, which as we have seen takes place in gradual stages over the first three to four years of life, Ennea-type Nines lose the perception of Holy Love. For a Nine, the process of losing contact with her essential nature results in the belief—the fixed cognitive perception or fixation—that who she is is not inherently lovable, valuable, significant, meaningful, or worthwhile. So the loss of contact with or turning away from Essence is also a disconnection from experiencing herself as precious and worthy of all the positive things that life has to offer. She experiences herself as outside of the goodness of life, not part of its fabric. This fundamental fixed belief is the underpinning of all the resulting mental constructs, emotional affects, and behavioral patterns of this type.

From the perspective of the forces in early life that shaped a Nine's psyche, her psychodynamics, the lack of holding and mirroring of her True Nature in infancy is interpreted by her as meaning that who she is fundamentally is not worth being with and attending to. This deduction—albeit at its roots a nonconceptual one—arises because of our soul's inherent knowledge of her inseparability from that core: If Being, which is who we fundamentally are, is not held and valued, we interpret this as indicating that we are not valuable, lovable, worth being with, and so on. Filtered through a Nine's blindness to Holy Love, the perception—and thus experience—of her childhood is of not having received much unconditional love, care, or attention. Whether or not she was physically or emotionally neglected, the impression of not being personally attended to is strongly imprinted in every Nine's soul, since what is most real was indeed not sufficiently paid attention to: her essential nature. Something almost completely universal—the lack of attunement to True Nature—is thus taken very personally by Nines. Although never actually put into words, they come to the conclusion that "Because my parents are not attuned to my depths, which is who I am, I must not be important and so it is clear that I am fundamentally insignificant."

Nines in turn forsake their inner depths, turning their consciousness away from Being in imitation of their early caregivers. It is important to note that Being does not go away—it simply slips into the unconscious. Since Being is who and what we are, one cannot turn away from it without turning away from oneself, so Nines gradually start turning a deaf ear to themselves and expect that the world will also. Interestingly enough, the ear is the part of the body associated with this type, and so they not only characteristically fail to listen to themselves inwardly but often tune things out and miss what is being said.

The "deafness" of Nines is at heart a loss of attunement to the realm of Essence, as we have seen. So just as they believe that they can be to varying degrees negligible and forgettable, they have, with losing contact with Essence, forgotten themselves. This self-forgetting, which is the hallmark of this ennea-type, manifests from the depths to the outermost surface of the personality: from the forgetting of Essence to simple forgetfulness in daily functioning. Self-forgetting basically describes a Nine's relationship to herself. For this reason, on the Enneagram of Antiself Actions, which you will find in Appendix B, self-forgetting appears at Point Nine. This enneagram refers to each ennea-type's characteristic relationship to what we experience as self—our soul—as discussed in the Introduction.

With their depths forgotten, an underlying attitude of "What's the point of paying attention to myself? There's nothing of value in here anyway," permeates the behavior, thoughts, and feelings of Nines. They end up feeling that they are nothing special and that there is nothing remarkable about them. The inner is neglected and forgotten, and the outer seems to be all that is worth paying attention to. Outer expression and experience appear far more consequential than what is going on internally, which in comparison seems insignificant and unimportant. They become more outer rather than inner directed, synchronizing with and responding to what is needed by the environment and by others, rather than responding to inner promptings. The needs of others drown out their own, which by comparison feel less important and of a much lower priority. Their self-importance in time becomes based on responding to and serving others rather than themselves.

In the process, the spiritual ground, which gives our outer expression and functioning meaning and significance, is lost, so the outer husk of life becomes a shallow and lifeless shell. This loss of contact with the spiritual dimension of ourselves, our essential nature, is of course the situation for those identified with the personality, and that means at least 99 percent of humanity. Living a life that is more than a shell is beyond the conception of most people, so living the husk of a life and forgetting that there is anything more is a cultural given. So part and parcel of becoming a civilized human being is this process of becoming like everyone else: losing contact with our depths. This process of human adaptation or conditioning, which from a spiritual perspective is one of falling asleep and of self-forgetting, is exemplified by this ennea-type.

When True Nature is not held and reflected back to us, we not only turn away from it, mimicking how we are being related to, as we have seen, but we also add interpretations about why this is happening. These notions are not conscious or even conceptual at their inception since they are formed before we have the capacity to think, but they nonetheless color and flavor the whole of our relationship to ourselves. More cognitive beliefs and attitudes about ourselves and the world we inhabit, which develop later, are rooted in these preconceptual "interpretations." For Nines, the experience of their deepest nature not being held by the environment is not only interpreted as meaning that who they fundamentally are is not worth contacting, is not inherently valuable and lovable, and is ultimately forgettable, but also results in the felt sense that there is something fundamentally *lacking* about them. This very painful feeling of lack carries the sense that there is something missing, something unformed or undeveloped, something defective, or something embryonic that has become twisted and deformed. For Nines, this is the sense of self that surrounds the hole where contact with True Nature has been lost, and forms their fundamental sense of deficiency. Each ennea-type has a characteristic deficiency state upon which the personality is built, but all of them are variations on that of Point Nine: the basic inner sense that something is lacking or inadequate about oneself.

In all the types, this sense of deficiency is the often unconscious basis of our inner picture of ourselves—our self-image—which in turn shapes our experience of ourselves. A Nine sees and experiences herself as someone who is fundamentally missing some parts, didn't arrive with all that was needed, is lacking something crucial, is stunted or misshapen, as though something basic never developed fully or even at all, or perhaps was never there to begin with. There may even be the sense for a Nine of her soul being stillborn or dead. Obviously this deeply painful sense of deficiency is a reflection of the truth that she is indeed missing something crucial: contact with who she really is beyond this self-image, which is based on insufficiency.

Our self-image does not arise in isolation, as we saw in Chapter 1. Our sense of self, which begins to form in infancy and is rooted in the body, is based not only on internal sensations but also develops through contact with the environment on the surface of our skin. So our sense of who we are always arises in relation to what is other than us, i.e., what is beyond our body's edges. Our self-image, then, exists in counterpoint to an object-image, a conceptual picture of "other." The other for Nines appears to have what they don't: others arrived with all their parts intact and are inherently lovable and valuable. Compared to others, Nines feel acutely inferior: not as good, complete, or worthy. This sense may have developed through having had a parent who appeared to the Nine as special and gifted in some way, or who simply took up a lot of psychic space because of being highly emotive, mentally unstable, or very outgoing. In relation to that parent, she became background, functioning as a backdrop. Again, as discussed in the Introduction, it is important to remember that this may not have been the main characteristic about that parent or even one that was especially strong. But because of a Nine's particular sensitivity, this was the one that she picked up on and responded to.

Having had a sibling who appeared more central in the family dynamics, one who was more assertive or who had special qualities or special problems, is a common variation. Another is that of growing up in a crowd: being one of many children or other relatives in the home, so the Nine ended up feeling lost in the shuffle. Her role or function in the family may have seemed like all that mattered, and so anything strictly personal about the Nine seemed unimportant and forgotten. Regardless of who the object was (or were) that the sense of self arose in relation to, this primary relationship forms the template for all subsequent experiences of self and other. In a nutshell, relative to other, a Nine feels not only inferior but also inconsequential.

A Nine develops, then, a sense of invisibility and a deep resignation about ever being center stage and loved or valued in her own right—both by others and also within her own consciousness—leading to a pervasive self-abnegation. Nines assume that they will not get love and attention, and also that they do not deserve it, since they have lost their innate sense of value and worth. This resigned self-abasement manifests in many ways: they have great difficulty with attention being focused upon them, with taking up their own space and other people's time, with asking to be seen or heard, much less loved, and tend to shun anything that would bring them to the fore or call attention to themselves. They melt into the background, rarely expressing themselves in a group. Because reality has a peculiar way of conforming to our beliefs about it, even when they do assert themselves and speak up, their assumption that they will not be received is often, in fact, confirmed, and they are ignored. It is as though they generate a field around them that says, "Don't pay attention to me—I am not important." They are thus easily overlooked and not considered by others; this reflects and reinforces their basic assumption about themselves. Ironically, many Nines are physically imposing, mesomorphic of body type—large, round, and sturdy looking.

Each ennea-type defends against experiencing its core deficiency state because it is incredibly painful and because it appears to be the bottom line—the ultimate and unalterable truth about oneself. This belief that something is fundamentally lacking or wrong with us, like all of the convictions that shape our personality, is not, once again, simply an intellectual idea—it is a felt experience and so appears to be the truth. It feels so true that it seems ridiculous even to suggest that it is simply an assumption. Because it seems to be reality, the energy of the personality goes into keeping one's consciousness away from this painful sense of deficiency, and all the defenses one uses feel necessary and justified. Experiencing it seems as if it would only confirm it, and why question something that appears so unshakably true? All of the defensive strategies and defense mechanisms of the personality are at their core marshaled against this deficient experience of self.

Nines defend against their fundamental sense of being deficient and unlovable in a very straightforward way: they simply push it out of consciousness. A numbing or deadening of inner awareness and a shift of attention from inside oneself to outside seem to be the best ways of dulling their inner pain. This lulling of oneself into psychic sleep is the defense mechanism of Point Nine, which is called narcotization. Unfortunately, we cannot pick and choose which aspects of inner experience we want to render unconscious and which we want to retain, so the result is that much, if not all, of the inner life of a Nine fades into unawareness. The narcotizing of self can manifest visibly: a Nine's eyes may look dull, dead, or glazed over. It also manifests behaviorally in the form of a predilection for distractions that divert her consciousness away from herself. One Nine I know has to have the TV or radio on at all times, even when falling asleep at night, and wears a Walkman whenever out for a walk. Burying herself in crossword puzzles, games like Trivial Pursuit, afternoon talk shows, the newspaper, or getting lost in trashy novels are other forms of diversions that a Nine might use to distract herself.

What results is a characteristic inner experience of being in a morass, a dense foggy state, in which nothing is very defined or discriminated and everything feels murky and diffuse. A lack of vitality and vibrancy and a sense of numbness, boredom, deadness, lethargy, and heaviness pervade. Naranjo used to describe female Nines as "swamp queens," which nicely describes the feel of this inner landscape—languid and stagnant. It also conveys the feeling tone that is the passion of this ennea-type: indolence, as we see on the Enneagram of Passions in Diagram 2. Characteristic of this marshy inner terrain is this indolence, a quality of laziness and stuckness that exerts for this type an inexorable kind of gravitational pull. It may take the form of procrastination and lethargy, having difficulty rousing herself to accomplish the task at hand, or of doing everything except the one thing that really needs to be done.

Part of the fuzziness of a Nine's inner terrain is often due to her inability to tell what direction to move in or which action needs to be taken. It is like bumping around in the darkness, bumbling along following the line of least resistance, rather than clearly perceiving the appropriate course to take and following it. An inner sense of chaos and disorder, which may be reflected outwardly in messiness and clutter, is the more superficial manifestation of this inner state. What may appear to others as procrastination may be a Nine's need to order what she perceives as the chaos around her and bring clarity to her environment before she can settle down to the task at hand, reflecting her attempt to come to grips with her inner disarray. The guidance and orientation that only contact with self can provide have been tuned out; a Nine's inner knowing either doesn't break the surface of consciousness or is ignored.

This indolent atmosphere, which could also be described as one of laziness and heedlessness, has many levels and nuances to it, as we are seeing. The indolence might express itself in an obliviousness to what needs attention or action, or if there is a sense that something needs to be done, a lack of discrimination or difficulty determining what exactly it is; a difficulty assessing priority of importance; and/or losing her focus and contact with herself in the details of the task or inadvertently substituting another one for it. A Nine who is facing a crucial deadline on a project, for example, might find herself cleaning the entire house or going through all of her files with the initial idea that this is necessary to do first so that she can really concentrate on the task, and then becoming so absorbed in all the things she finds herself ordering that she forgets the project entirely and runs out of time for it. Her difficulty prioritizing what needs to be done reflects her characteristic trouble with discrimination and organization— she simply has difficulty discerning what needs to be done and in what order to do things. If it is clear what needs to be done, the indolence might show up as simply not having the energy for it and just not doing it.

The indolence characteristically manifests outwardly in Nines as heedlessness about their appearance and about diet and exercise (with a resulting tendency to be overweight), as well as in other forms of self-neglect. Lacking attunement to their physical and psychic limits, some Nines overextend themselves, mostly in the service of others' needs, to the point of collapse. Other Nines underextend, preferring comfort and indulgence to bestirring themselves. Or a Nine might focus on, and indeed obsess about, one particular aspect of maintaining her health, like dietary supplements for example, while making really poor choices about what she eats and neglecting to exercise. A symptom might be focused upon rather than the cause: attention may be lavished on a sore ankle, for instance, without associating that difficulty to excess weight or inappropriate shoes.

Ultimately, however, the central issue of a Nine's indolence is not related to either outward doing or physical neglect. This is an extremely important point to grasp, since it explains why some Nines can be workaholics, while others seem to do little with their time. What is personally significant is what is most neglected by a Nine, and ultimately her laziness is about paying attention to and cultivating contact with what is most real within herself: at its heart, this laziness is fundamentally being unconscious to and remaining unconscious to her essential nature.

As mentioned earlier, a Nine's characteristic of forgetfulness not only manifests in losing sight of her depths—her True Nature—but can also manifest as more superficial absentmindedness. Nines tend to be simply forgetful. They don't remember things, what they need to do slips their minds, and they lose track of what they embark upon by becoming easily distracted by irrelevant things. The forgetting is at root a Nine's attempt to dull herself to her inner sense of being unlovable, negligible, and valueless; so while it may feel problematic, it is ultimately a defense against what feels intolerable to experience. This forgetfulness exacerbates the feeling of disorientation, of lostness in the inner morass, and consequently also amplifies the sense of being stuck or paralyzed that Nines often feel quite helpless to do anything about.

This stuckness, which can feel like having her feet embedded in wet cement or, alternatively, of sinking into quicksand, is connected with the characteristic inertia of Nines. In physics, inertia is defined as "the tendency of a body to resist acceleration; the tendency of a body at rest to remain at rest or of a body in motion to stay in motion in a straight line unless disturbed by an external force."[3] Inertia is not the sole domain of Nines; it is fundamental to the perpetuation of the personality, regardless of one's type. It is a maintaining of our conditioned patterns of thought, feeling, and behavior, a preservation of the grooves in the soul, imprinted through experiences in our distant past. These patterns form the fabric of the personality, and the inertia that maintains them may feel like a leadenness when experientially contacted, weighing us down and dulling our senses.

In Nines, this inertia typically appears as having great difficulty initiating action or, once moving, in changing direction. Like the elephant, the animal associated with Point Nine, they are slow to get moving and, once in motion, have a hard time stopping. In other words, once their course is set or their routine becomes habitual, these patterns are not easily altered, and Nines obstinately hold to them. They can be tenaciously stubborn, digging their heels in and refusing to change their minds or their course of action. This manifests most poignantly in a determined clinging that many Nines have to their deep sense of being inferior and deficient: often no amount of evidence to the contrary seems capable of dislodging this embedded belief.

Her superego supports her sense of deficiency. Like much else in the inner world of a Nine, it is often amorphous and not a clearly differentiated critical and judgmental inner voice. Initially it may feel like more of a depressing and minimizing feeling tone, an assertive, although passive, push to stay invisible and not take up too much space. Evidence of her superego will be seen in the shame she feels about having needs and difficulties, as if they shouldn't be there, and for having any anger or aggression. Her superego demands, in a vague and not too evident way, that she is responsible for keeping the environment happy and safe, and pushes her to take care of others. As a child, she might feel compelled by her inner demands to befriend the new kid at school or the sick one that the other kids ostracize. Often this is a way of minimizing the pain of another so that she will not be reminded of her own sense of not being loved or lovable. Her superego pushes her not to upset anyone, to stay middle-of-the-road, so that even as a rebellious teenager, she makes sure everyone feels good about her.

Transitions are difficult and threatening, so Nines tend to avoid any changes in relationships, work, life direction, and so on. The universal characteristic in the personality of clinging to the familiar is exemplified here. They like stability and support the status quo, resisting change and innovation. Preserving what we called in the sixties the "Establishment"—the prevailing sociopolitical order—is the domain of Nines. As a whole they tend to be conservative and orthodox, politically and otherwise, entrenched in tradition, custom bound, and resistant to change. This is not to say that Nines are never revolutionaries, but when they are, they are very doctrinaire, adhering to and supporting their new Establishment, becoming in effect conservative radicals.

It is often difficult for Nines to discriminate what values they personally hold, following instead the line of least resistance in conforming to those of their culture or subculture. This is why consideration/mechanical conformity appears at Point Nine on the Enneagram of Lies, the enneagram charting the characteristic ways each type forsakes its own truth, and which you will find in Appendix B. A Nine's lie is in considering others and not herself, as discussed earlier, and mechanically conforming to the prevailing currents. Because of this tendency, Nine-ness is associated with bureaucratic and robotic behavior and institutions in which the motions are gone through with little personal engagement. Not to make waves, Nines fit in, conforming to the role assigned to them and following the program seamlessly.

They become cogs in a larger wheel, oiling any squeaks by shutting them off from awareness and so attending to their niche without complaint. Deadened to their inner world and caught up in outer functioning without questioning it, life for a Nine can become institutionalized, mechanical, and robotic. The stereotype of the nameless and faceless bureaucrat typifies this quality, buried in red tape and busy with paperwork, insisting on protocol even when it makes no sense, with nothing real or relevant being accomplished. The U.S. Postal Service and the Internal Revenue Service are frequently thought of in this way. At first glance, this robotic tendency may seem at odds with the laziness and disorganization mentioned earlier as typifying this type. On closer inspection, we see that a Nine may have one area of life in which she is a stickler for detail and fulfills her function seamlessly, but the rest of her life may be in a state of disarray, or there simply may not be a rest of her life to speak of. Anything personal or individual may be neglected or shunned as unimportant. The versions of communism embodied in the former Soviet Union and in China (two of the cultures associated with Point Nine) exemplify this perfunctory way of life, in which the individual's value is derived from how smoothly he or she functions in the overall machine of state and in which personal opinion or wishes are subsumed in the collective momentum.[4]

Mentally a Nine's inertia manifests as stubbornly holding on to what is familiar and known, and a tendency to be dogmatic and opinionated. Once they have landed in a conceptual groove, their minds become closed and resistant to influence. Their mental laziness reveals itself in literal-mindedness and matter-of-factness, taking things at face value rather than being attuned to subtleties. It is also seen in losing sight of the idea behind an action, procedure, or policy and simply automatically performing it.

Set in their ways, obstinate, and inflexible, Nines may be perceived by others as bland, unexciting, or undynamic, but the flip side is that they also seem very solid and rocklike: dependable, implacable, persistent, and consistent. Rarely erratic or explosive, Nines are steadier than the other ennea-types, and give the impression that they can always be counted on—and indeed they usually can be. Since their evenness and dependability result from absenting themselves from priority and deriving a sense of value and worth from outer activity, these qualities are a mixed blessing at best for a Nine.

Closely connected to the inertia of Nines is their avoidance of discomfort. Comfort is very important to them, and they invest much time and energy into making themselves both physically and emotionally comfortable. Their defense mechanism of narcotization discussed earlier is a psychological attempt at comfort. Behaviorally they tend to collect things that will make their lives superficially more pleasant, pouring through catalogues filled with gadgets to make life run more easily and smoothly. Water beds, heated swimming pools, motels, remote controls, and Jacuzzis are examples of the kinds of things Nines relish since they reduce physical exertion and thus discomfort. Devices and contrivances that promise comfort are part of the quest for diversion that is characteristic of Nines, as is their typical love for amusements, pleasantries, trivia, and minutia. Ultimately all of the gadgets and entertainments are distractions from their painful sense of deficiency and unlovability. This is the pain that must be soothed and anesthetized through diversions and ease.

Because they rarely rock the boat and try to make others just as comfortable as they would like to be, it's very pleasant to be with Nines as a rule, although you might come away hungry for something to chew on or engage with, wondering, Where's the beef? They seem to be peaceful, untroubled, and calm. They are compliant, amicable, cordial, and genial and, for the most part, easy to be with. While you may not find out what is really going on inside them, you will feel cared for and soothed. Exemplifying this, Ed McMahon, the former *Tonight Show* sidekick, fulfilled this function in counterpoint to Johnny Carson's more mercurial temperament. Walter Cronkite was for decades a calming presence in American homes, reporting on the often turbulent events of the sixties and seventies on the CBS televised evening news. Today we have Rosie O'Donnell, actress and talk show host who has been dubbed the queen of nice on television in the afternoons. While these last two exemplars may seem at odds with the picture of Nines as lazy, it is important to remember that the indolence of a Nine is something much deeper than whether or not they outwardly get a task done.

The most uncomfortable thing to a Nine is conflict, and so they avoid it at all costs, as we see on the Enneagram of Avoidances, found in Appendix B. Upsetting the prevailing flow of things, or lack thereof, might be uncomfortable, and so it is decisively shunned. Rather than clash with others, they appease and placate. They have difficulty confronting others, especially about being overlooked, unconsidered, not listened to, and so on, and will often talk themselves out of their ruffled feelings or simply distract themselves from feeling hurt rather than risking locking horns with another by bringing up a difficulty. In this regard, Lady Bird Johnson comes to mind, serving as a foil for her volatile Eight husband, LBJ. Edith Bunker, the television character in the series *All in the Family,* fulfilled the same placating role with her Eight husband, the bigoted and abusive Archie.

Because keeping the peace is so important, they are good mediators and peacemakers, finding ways to smooth things out, which can drift into smoothing things over. Beyond the motivation to maintain harmony, they also mediate well because they can see things from many angles and are able to understand everyone's point of view. Dwight D. Eisenhower, Supreme Allied Commander during World War II and two-term U.S. president, exemplifies this Nine-ish forte as we see in the following biographical excerpt:

> *Eisenhower's rapid advancement, after a long army career spent in relative obscurity, was not only due to his knowledge of military strategy and a talent for organization but also to his ability to persuade, to mediate, and to be agreeable. Men from a variety of backgrounds and nationalities, impressed by his friendliness, humility, and persistent optimism, liked and trusted him.*[5]

Nines are said to have the most objective perception of all the types, being able to set aside any personal bias and see what is going on around them clearly. This is another dubious blessing, since it is based on self-forgetting: What is difficult for them is knowing where *they* stand and what *they* feel, since their tendency is to be outwardly rather than inwardly at-tuned. Keeping their perceptions—especially critical ones of others—somewhat vague and fuzzy ensures that they will not be hurtful toward others, as they assume being sharp and clear would be. Even if they are in touch with what they think and feel, they rarely put their thoughts and feelings forward because of the risk of a challenge. Psychodynamically this avoidance of conflict may have its roots in not wanting to upset or stand up to an inattentive parent for fear of losing what little love and attention they seem to be receiving. The laid-back and hang-loose Polynesian cul-ture exemplifies this comfort-loving and conflict-avoiding side of Ennea-type Nine.

As discussed in the Introduction, the personality structure and behav-ioral patterns of each ennea-type mimic a particular quality of Being, or state of consciousness, which is called its idealized Aspect. This replica-tion can be seen as the soul's attempt to shape itself into an embodiment of the lost Holy Idea. Because the soul has lost contact with her essential roots, this embodiment is of necessity a fake. Through this simulation, the soul attempts to recapture the lost Holy Idea, which in the case of Ennea-type Nine is the perception that the universe is inherently loving and that, as a manifestation of it, she is inherently lovable. The quality of Being that Ennea-type Nine emulates is called Living Daylight in the Di-amond Approach. It is called this because that is what it feels like when we contact this particular presence: warm and life-giving sunlight. We feel held in a sweet and gentle presence that is totally loving, beneficent, and well disposed toward us. We feel that we can relax and let go, and that we will be held and supported by a universe that is suffused with goodness, and that is inherently kind and life affirming. It is the gentle and loving presence that pervades and sustains all of creation, which in some traditions is referred to as Cosmic or Divine Love, and in the theis-tic traditions is what is meant by the concept of God.

The simulation of Living Daylight can be glimpsed in all of the per-sonality traits of Ennea-type Nine. As a whole, the cognitive, emotional, and behavioral style of this type is an attempt to be a person who is lov-ing, holding, supportive, kind, and gentle in a very unobtrusive and inconspicuous way. The stability and solidity, the impartiality and congeniality, the emphasis on comfort and harmony that are characteristic of this type all are simulations on the personality level of this dimension of reality. Since Living Daylight is the experience of Being as supportive ground, the Nine stance in life of unobtrusively staying in the shadows is an important part of this replication.

Not only does the personality attempt to emulate the idealized Aspect but this quality of Being is also idealized in the sense that it looks like the solution to one's difficulties and deficiencies. Each ennea-type, therefore, can be seen as an attempt to *have* as well as an attempt to *become* the idealized Aspect. That particular state of consciousness will be sought, either directly or through manifestations that seem to embody it, whether in the form of another person or an object. So Nines not only attempt to "look" like or shape themselves into a facsimile of Living Daylight but also believe that if they were loved and held, and if they were treated like an implicit part of the whole (whatever they take that to be), their problems would be over. The love and holding, as well as the sense of inclusion that they seek, might appear to reside in social or intimate relationships, in having a comfortable and easy life, or in cozy pleasantries and diversions.

The real resolution, however, will not be found in these places. It lies in moving beyond identification with the realm of the personality and reconnecting with the realm of Being. This will require for a Nine cultivating the virtue associated with this point, action, which we find in Diagram 1 in the enneagram in the heart region of the figure. As mentioned in the Introduction, the virtue not only manifests itself the freer one becomes from identification with one's personality, but also is what is needed for this disidentification to happen. The following is Ichazo's definition of the virtue of action:

> *It is essential movement without interference from the mind, arising naturally from the body's need to function in harmony with its environment. Action is the normal attitude of a being in tune with his own energy and with the energy of the planet.*[6]

Real action, then, which is based on authentic harmony and an internal as well as an external responsiveness, necessitates for a Nine a radical change of focus. First and foremost, it implies becoming present and conscious of what is going on inside herself. It means changing her focus and orientation from her actions and interactions to the source out of which functioning arises—her consciousness or soul. The more conscious we become of the state of our soul, which is our inner experience, and the more we inquire into what is shaping it, the more transparent the shell of the personality becomes. Eventually it becomes so thin that we can experience the realms of Being beyond it. This is a waking up from the sleep of unconsciousness, and a remembering of the depths within that the Nine has forgotten. This is true action, action that is essential in both senses of the word.

Action, in the sense it is used here, is the opposite of the passion of indolence. So rather than engaging in nonessential activities—doing things that are distractions or unnecessary—or not doing anything at all, real action is the capacity to discriminate what really needs to be done and doing it. The more freedom a Nine has from the grip of identification with the personality, the more able she becomes to do what is really important. This might mean simply paying attention to her physical or emotional needs or, on a deeper level, doing what it takes to make the unconscious—which includes the essential realm—conscious.

The elephant, the animal associated with this point as mentioned earlier, is relevant in connection with the virtue of action. In Buddhist iconography, the Bodhisattva Samantabhadra (in Sanskrit) or Fugen (in Japanese), who represents spiritual practice as compassion, sits on an elephant throne. This symbolizes that true kindness toward oneself is having the steadiness, solidity, patience, and inner power—like an elephant—to work on oneself in a committed and determined way.

For a Nine, this radical shift in focus—from outside of herself to what is going on within—is a huge step and is the key to her unfoldment. Taking this step will require questioning some of her basic beliefs about herself, most specifically the assumption that she is not worth considering and paying attention to. It is a knee-jerk reaction for a Nine to disregard herself and simply to go along with the prevailing flow of other people's desires, preferences, and actions. Throughout her work on herself, this tendency to absent herself and overlook herself will arise in ever more subtle ways, and she will need to repeatedly notice it and inquire into why she is doing it.

Making this internal shift—which is really taking action to reverse the inertial pull of her personality in keeping her awareness away from her inner life—will require facing her tendency to distract herself. There may be endless crises in her life or ceaseless demands at work that seem to require her to stay busy juggling things so that she can't pay attention to herself. She will have to be willing to let all the plates that she keeps spinning fall in order to make herself primary in her own consciousness. Blaming others and life in general for her difficulties and trying to get satisfaction on external terms will have to be seen as the diversion that it is. She will have to face her tendency to seek gratification and answers outside of herself, a tendency encapsulated by the "seeker" on the Enneagram of Traps, which we find in Appendix B. The traps are the characteristic ways each type distracts their attention from the real issue. She will have to pay attention to what is going on inside rather than staying focused on what is happening outside, no matter how enticing keeping all those balls in the air seems to be.

Her superego vigilantly wants to keep this shift in attention from happening, however, so she must defend against her inner attacks on herself just to have the space to pay attention to herself. Her superego wants to protect her at all costs from coming into conflict with others, which looks like the inevitable result if she pays attention to her own desires, feelings, and inner promptings. It berates her and tells her to be good and not make waves by going along with the prevailing external flow, cautions her against making too big a deal about herself, and admonishes her that taking up too much space might be dangerous. To defend against these attacks, her desire to know who she is beyond her indolent shell will have to become stronger than her desire for comfort. This is a reciprocal process, as the more she gets in touch with her essential self, the more her inner strength will rally to defend her soul. She will discover that true ease and comfort reside in Being and not in indolently forgetting herself.

Really grappling with her habitual tendency to ignore and neglect herself and defending against her superego will rapidly confront a Nine with her profound sense of worthlessness, valuelessness, and unlovability.

Deeper still, she will encounter the felt sense that she is fundamentally lacking and inadequate, the deficiency state at the core of her personality. She will need to unearth, examine, and inquire into why she believes this about herself and how this central belief became the foundation of her sense of self. As she allows and feels into this extremely painful sense of inadequacy and of inferiority, memories both conceptual and preconceptual that gave rise to and supported this sense of herself will surface and need to be digested. The resulting object relations—her inner sense of self and other—will need to be seen in operation externally, and she will need to bring to consciousness these internal constructs.

Simultaneously taking real action will mean connecting with and fully inhabiting her body. Rather than skipping over and minimizing her inner sensations, she will need to become attuned to them and pay attention to them. Making deep experiential contact with her body will bring up all of the years of neglect, and probably much grief will be experienced. The more that she fully abides in her body and focuses her attention within it, the more she is at the same time contacting as well as supporting a sense of her own inherent value and self-worth. Also, the more she pays attention to her body, the more she will begin noticing and listening to her emotions, and the sharper and clearer her mind will become. She will increasingly feel more alive and more a part of life. Eventually, as she keeps focusing her awareness within, what she senses will be the entirety of her soul.

The more present she becomes, the more she will become aware of her absence of contact with her essential nature, which may feel like a huge hole in her soul. As she allows herself to feel into this hole and to be curious about it, rather than escaping from it into sleepiness or distractions, she will find that what she had experienced as a deficient emptiness changes. As she progressively opens to it and explores how it really feels, the negativity and feelings of lack will transform. The emptiness becomes a spaciousness, and over time all of the qualities of Being will gradually arise in her consciousness as she makes this inner descent over and over again. For a long time, it will seem to her that Being comes and goes, until a sort of critical mass is reached in her soul, and her identity shifts from her personality to Being. Then Being will feel like the ground of her experience, and she will see that it was she who came and went, losing and gaining consciousness of what was there all the time.

Eventually, the shell of her personality will become more and more transparent to Being, and as this happens, she will find herself experiencing, embodying, and manifesting the quality of Being she has tried to emulate, Living Daylight. Her inner experience will gradually change from feeling deficient, unloved, unimportant, and overlooked to feeling sustained, taken care of, and inseparable from a beneficent universe filled with love and blessings. When this happens, she will at long last fully know herself to be truly a manifestation and embodiment of the love of the Divine.

CHAPTER 3

ENNEA-TYPE SIX:
EGO-COWARDICE

Those of this ennea-type are characterized by fear. While fear may be present in those of any ennea-type, here it is the central factor that distinguishes this type. Sixes doubt their perceptions, question and second-guess themselves, are suspicious, lack certainty and confidence, and much of their psychic energy is directed toward coping with their anxiety. They are the paranoids of the enneagram, convinced, whether consciously or not, that others are out to get them, undermine them, or otherwise threaten them. While the underlying internal dynamics are the same, there are two distinct styles of Sixes: those who are overtly fearful and those who are counterphobic, intent on proving that they are not afraid. While some Sixes may be phobic in some areas of their lives and counterphobic in others, one overriding style is usually predominant and apparent in their manner.

In phobic Sixes, their fear and insecurity are obvious. They tend to be furtive in manner, obsequious to authority figures or those they consider more powerful, have difficulty making decisions and taking decisive action, ask others for advice and guidance, and may be blindly loyal to a faith, cause, or leader. There is often a kind of stuttering quality to their actions—one foot forward and one foot back—and often to their speech pattern as well. Counterphobic Sixes, on the other hand, mask their fear through trying to behave in ways that will overcome it, or will demonstrate to themselves and others that they are not, in fact, insecure. They are risk takers and daredevils, seeking out situations that are challenging and that test their mettle in an effort to prove their strength and confidence.

Sixes have lost touch with the particular perspective on reality—the Holy Idea—that would allay their fear and doubt. This particular view of reality that Ennea-type Six is the most attuned to has two names because it has a twofold meaning. The first is Holy Strength. Holy Strength is the perception that the nature of our soul is Essence. It is the recognition that who we are is not the body or our thoughts or our emotions but rather a presence or Beingness that has many qualities and has progressively deeper dimensions of profundity. This presence is seen here as the ground of the soul, and hence what both gives it strength and is its strength.

Without the recognition of Essence as the inner nature of what we are as human beings, we experience ourselves as lacking a foundation, and so feel ourselves to be fundamentally weak and helpless. We are left identified with the body and its instincts, and therefore experience ourselves as mostly hairless animals with large brains as our only protection. The body is subject to disease and death, and if we take ourselves to be our bodies, we are indeed in a very precarious situation. Without recognition of Being, our lives are ephemeral and fleeting, and lack enduring meaning. The more we are in touch with Being and perceive it from the angle of Holy Strength, the more we know our True Nature to be indestructible and imperishable, immune to the vicissitudes of the body. While we may experience physical suffering, if we are grounded in recognition of our depths, even that becomes bearable. Perception of our essential nature can give us the fortitude to withstand what might otherwise seem unendurable.

The more we perceive our essential nature, the more we know ourselves to be ultimately embodiments and expressions of the Divine. While this is true for all of the manifest world, as humans we alone have the capacity to recognize our deepest nature. This gives us a unique place in creation and is another aspect of our strength and thus is another nuance of what Holy Strength means.

The effect that this recognition has upon us is what is meant by the second Holy Idea associated with this point, Holy Faith. The recognition that our inner nature is Essence gives us faith. The use of the word *faith* here needs some explanation if we are really to understand this Holy Idea, since the way it is used is different from our usual understanding of it. In normal usage, faith means that we believe something is probably true even though we have not directly experienced it and have no real proof of it. Our faith, then, is intellectual or intuitive rather than experiential. We also use *faith* in the sense of being faithful—being loyal to God, to what we see as our duty, or to another person. Here, as a Holy Idea, faith means that we know our inner nature to be Essence based on our direct contact with it and our soul's integration of that contact. This faith is not the result of believing this to be the truth on the basis of someone else's experience or some religious or spiritual doctrine.

This experiential knowledge gives rise to the unshakable certainty that Essence is our nature regardless of whether or not we are feeling in touch with these depths in the moment. We simply know in a way that cannot be doubted—in our bones as it were—that our inner nature is Being. When we perceive in this unquestionable way that who we are is Essence, our souls have undergone a radical transformation. The way we experience the world and ourselves is dramatically different from how it was prior to this shift in consciousness. We are no longer believers and seekers but have become identified with Being as who and what we are. This, then, is a particular way of conceiving enlightenment—seen through the angle of Point Six. The enlightened view of reality that Holy Strength and Holy Faith focus on, then, is that the nature of our souls—of who we are—is Being. When we experience ourselves objectively, without the veils of the personality, this is what we know to be true.

Many people embark on spiritual work and plod along the Path for a long time without feeling that they have experienced fundamental change. For real transformation to occur, which means a shift in our soul's center of gravity from the personality to Essence, we need to know ourselves as Essence in a way that is beyond doubt. All of the faith we have in any spiritual teacher and teaching is not enough to change radically our sense of who we are, nor are all of our mental concepts of what objective reality looks like enough to shift our orientation. Our souls transform only through direct experience.

It is also not enough to directly experience someone else as Essence or even the whole universe as an embodiment of Being for our sense of who we are to become fundamentally changed. We must experience directly that our *own* soul is Essence for us to really integrate Holy Faith. As Almaas says,

> We are making the distinction here between an experience of Essence that doesn't feel like you, that feels like something alien, or something imposed on you, or induced or transmitted by someone else, and the experience of Essence as your own inner reality. This is an enormous distinction. Many people experience Essence and believe that they are just feeling their spiritual teacher or that they have been hypnotized, and this implies a lack of recognition of Essence as their nature.[1]

If present, this direct knowing of Essence as our nature serves as a solid foundation for the soul. If absent, which is the situation when Sixes are identified with their personality, the lack of this ground creates all sorts of insecurities and fears. In conjunction with the loss of contact with Essence in early childhood, Sixes lose the recognition that it exists as their inner nature and that it is what sustains them. This loss of contact with and loss of recognition of Essence may sound like the same thing, but it is not: you can experience yourself as disconnected from the depth dimension within, and yet still know with certainty that it exists. While you may not currently be having an essential experience, you still remember and know that you have had such experiences in the past. Without this Holy Idea, that knowing is gone. Those experiences feel as though they never happened or as though you made them up. You and your world are therefore experienced as devoid of Essence and so devoid of all that makes humanity able to rise above egocentricity and survival concerns to become loving, altruistic, generous, and noble. Humanity, including yourself, is experienced without these higher impulses and values, and so you see it operating from purely instinctual and animalistic motives. At the extreme, the world appears as a Darwinian jungle in which everyone is simply struggling to survive and in which the strong triumph over and destroy the weak. Love and holding are ephemeral, and life is primarily a matter of endurance.

This, then, is a Six's interpretation of the inevitable lack of total holding in infancy because of his sensitivity to the Holy Ideas of Holy Strength and Holy Faith. The soul of a Six seems constellated around and frozen in reactive alarm to early unmet physical needs, to impingement, or to an atmosphere of physical danger. This state of apprehensive guardedness in anticipation of the next trauma, which a Six feels hopelessly unprepared for, drowns out everything else. The environment was perceived by him as untrustworthy or unpredictable, and the young Six's parents were viewed through this unstable lens. He may have had an alcoholic parent whose behavior seemed to change apparently at random; or a parent subject to unpredictable fits of rage, triggered by something apparently insignificant. One of the parents may have had dramatic mood fluctuations, or there may have been great variations in the quality of attention the child received. The main caretaking parent may have felt insecure about handling the infant Six's body or fulfilling his needs, or this parent may have simply had a timid personality. One parent may have been a stern authority figure, demanding absolute obedience and permanently intimidating the young Six. Regardless of the actual parents' reality, these were the factors focused upon and left as imprints because of the Six's sensitivity to Holy Faith and Holy Strength. The "interpretation" made by the child's developing consciousness was that one or both parents or the environment as a whole couldn't be consistently depended upon to fill his needs, which feels life-threatening to a totally dependent infant and young child. The soul, then, becomes and remains fixated around survival anxiety and the fear of physical death. The inability and helplessness to meet his own needs, coupled with a seemingly undependable other, become imprinted and form the core of the sense of self of this ennea-type.

This take on reality, which solidifies in early childhood, shapes the soul of a Six and mushrooms into a whole worldview that Almaas describes as cynical. Without Holy Faith there is indeed a form of faith, but it is the conviction that the universe is basically unloving and unsupportive and that human beings are ultimately self-serving and self-aggrandizing, caring nothing for the consequences of their actions on others. It's a dog-eat-dog world, and regardless of whether a Six puffs himself up in an attempt to prove that he is one of the strong in the struggle or outrightly considers himself to be one of the weaklings, this is the way reality looks to him. Despite his fluctuation between hopefulness and doubt, this cynicism— the belief that human conduct is inherently self-serving and based on self-interest—becomes consciously or unconsciously firmly set in his soul. In such a world, there is little trust in human nature, except the "trust" that others are out to get you if you stand in the way of their self-gratification.

Without the perception of one's true ground—Essence—there is little in one's own nature to trust either, and so the Six is left without a foundation and can only feel hopelessly inadequate in the struggle of life. Left with only his wits as survival tools in what appears as a threatening world, and lacking the perception, much less contact with, anything inside that is of real support, this inner sense of insufficiency is the only possible result. This sense of not having what it takes in the skirmish of life—the helplessness in the face of an unpredictable and undependable other—is the Six's deficiency state and, as touched on earlier, forms the core sense of self. You experience yourself here either consciously or unconsciously as one of those at risk of not surviving—one of the runts of the litter, the weak, the ill prepared, the defenseless, the inept, the feeble, the wimps. Others appear more strong, powerful, tough, intelligent, savvy, skillful, capable, and definitely more self-assured.

This cynical perception of the world and inadequate sense of self in relation to it form the fixed mind-set—the fixation—of Ennea-type Six, denoted as cowardice on Diagram 2. Out of it arise all of the behavioral, emotional, and cognitive patterns characteristic of this type, as we shall see.

Focusing on what we've seen about how a Six's orientation toward reality is constellated around reactive alarm and survival anxiety, we can see that what becomes predominant is the level of pure physical instinct, the animal part of the human soul. This level, which forms the ground of the personality regardless of ennea-type as we saw in Chapter 1, is the particular preoccupation of Sixes. Focusing upon it obscures what lies beneath it, if we conceive of consciousness topographically, which is the realm of Being. Out of this ground of animal instincts arises not only the self-aggrandizing and self-serving orientation that Sixes experience as threatening in others but also the Six's drive to survive this threat. The instinctual level, then, becomes *both* the enemy and the savior, and embedded in this contradiction lies the heart of the conflict and uncertainty that forms the terrain of the Six landscape.

It is a vicious cycle: inner affects, impetus, and perceptions that could be constructive and supportive are doubted and invalidated since they might arise from the dangerous part within—the instinctual and animalistic. So the shadow of doubt blocks all impulse, making it something to question rather than to act upon. While Sixes often act impulsively and reactively out of their fear, any spontaneous inner contents are suspect and are picked apart by the mind and rendered lifeless.

The result of all this behavior—which at its heart is self-protective—is, ironically, to undercut the very ground a Six is standing on. It is a form of self-castration, which psychologically means rendering oneself impotent or depriving oneself of vitality. Not only is this self-castration a psychological one, manifesting in all kinds of personality traits that are self-undermining, but it also sabotages a Six's contact with the spiritual dimension as well. The invalidation of internal experience and inhibition of impulse undermine a Six's capacity to give credence to his process, which is the only way for his experience to deepen and eventually reconnect him with the essential dimension underlying it. We see this in self-inhibiting appearing at Point Six on the Enneagram of Antiself Actions, Diagram 11, reflecting how this undercutting of impulse sabotages his soul's unfoldment.

This internal weakening of self is the basis of the castration complex defined by Freud that is typically found in this type: the usually unconscious fear of physical harm or loss of power at the hands of an authority figure. Psychological understanding holds that if castration anxiety is extreme, it will manifest as a narcissistic overestimation of the penis in both sexes. The part of the body associated with Point Six is, naturally, the genitals, and one often has the feeling around Sixes that they are alternately defending or displaying their genitals through their actions. In this we see an obvious physical displacement of a psychic sensitivity.

Although a universal phenomenon, what is referred to in the Diamond Approach as the genital hole is particularly relevant here and might be called a specialty of Point Six. The genital hole is the experiential sense of an absence where you know your genitals to be. It is one of the first ways people typically experience on a physical level their lack of contact with Essence. Staying with this sense of a hole will lead us to an experience of spaciousness, as though one were in deep space. This space is the ground out of which all the Aspects of Essence arise. This understanding gives another level of meaning to castration since without contact with the spiritual dimension, we actually experience ourselves as being without genitals.[2]

Without perceiving the ground of Being, and at the same time rejecting—while being rooted in—the primitive instinctual realm, the world is an uncertain place lacking a real foundation. Things are therefore inherently unstable and insecure. Others, seen through the lens of cynicism, are not to be trusted and so cannot be counted on. While they may outwardly appear kind, loving, and supportive, Sixes watch suspiciously for the other shoe to drop and the true state of affairs to be revealed. The most insidious uncertainty, however, is inward. Because there is little inside to trust, a Six lives—to a greater or lesser extent depending upon his degree of fixatedness—not only with a state of uncertainty but also with difficulty being sure about almost anything. This includes what he feels, wants, experiences, or thinks. Doubt pervades everything, manifesting in hesitation, indecision, vacillation, indefiniteness, irresoluteness, oscillation, and skepticism. Because they are not sure where they stand or what they feel, decision making can become obsessive and fraught with the fear of making the wrong choice. They stutter—vocally or not—blocking themselves and making it difficult for their action to flow unimpeded by this self-doubt. Inevitably this makes it very difficult for Sixes to take decisive and unequivocal action. When they do come to a conclusion and act on it, second-guessing and worry about having done the wrong thing follow quickly. Their movement—whether physically or just metaphorically—is therefore jerky, like the animal associated with this point, the rabbit.

The pervasive inner affective state, the passion of Ennea-type Six, is fear, as we see on the Enneagram of Passions in Diagram 2. In psychological language, fear is defined as a conscious response to a realistic external danger, while anxiety is defined as a response to a danger that is internal and unconscious in origin. For the majority of Sixes, the two appear pretty much synonymous, since internal threats are experienced as external ones through the defense mechanism of projection, which we will discuss shortly. The fear and anxiety that Sixes experience as a pervasive ongoing emotional atmosphere is anticipatory—about what might arise internally or externally. Sixes, in fact, are rarely afraid in the actual situations they are frightened of, and so the fear is clearly based on ideation.

Freud is once again relevant here for our understanding about the nature of the anxiety of this ennea-type. The fact that many of Freud's theories are so pertinent to the psychology of Sixes may be because he might have been one himself.[3] Freud's later theory about anxiety differentiated between two kinds: the first, which he called automatic anxiety, arises from what he called traumatic situations, in which the psyche is flooded with excessive stimulation that it cannot come to grips with and so experiences as overwhelming. This kind of anxiety arises primarily in early infancy, before the ego structure has begun to coalesce. The following quote paraphrasing Freud from Charles Brenner, M.D., a psychoanalyst and former head of the American Psychoanalytic Association, gives us the flavor of this type of anxiety:

> A young infant is dependent on its mother, not only for the satisfaction of most of its bodily needs, but also for the instinctual gratifications, which, at least in the early months of life, infants experience chiefly in connection with bodily satisfactions. Thus, for example, when an infant is nursed, not only is its hunger sated. It also experiences simultaneously the instinctual pleasure which is associated with oral stimulation, as well as the pleasure of being held, warmed, and fondled. Before a certain age an infant cannot achieve these pleasures, that is, these instinctual gratifications, by itself. It

needs its mother to be able to do so. If, when its mother is absent, the infant experiences an instinctual need which can be gratified only through its mother, then a situation develops which is traumatic for the child in the sense in which Freud used this word. The infant's ego is not sufficiently developed to be able to postpone gratification by holding the drive wishes in abeyance and instead the infant's psyche is overwhelmed by an influx of stimuli. Since it can neither master nor adequately discharge these stimuli, anxiety develops.[4]

The second, and more relevant form for adults, is the signal anxiety, which we touched upon briefly in Chapter 1 in discussing Point Six. Here, anxiety arises in anticipation of a traumatic situation rather than as a result of it and initiates the mobilization of the personality's defensive functions so that the situation will not become traumatic. Objective external danger will trigger this anticipatory anxiety and will cause us to take defensive action, while situations of psychic conflict that feel dangerous will cause the defensive functions of the ego to ward off the impulse or feeling that threatens to emerge into consciousness. Using the example above, signal anxiety would arise at a later stage when the child anticipates his mother leaving, because he would associate the departure with potential trauma like that described above.

Freud also delineated a series of situations dangerous to the developing ego structure of a child, all pertinent at specific developmental phases, and all, as we shall see, particularly pertinent to the psychology of Sixes. The first dangerous situation is the loss of the mothering person, the child's caretaker and love object. Later the danger becomes the fear of losing her love, followed developmentally by the fear of castration. Finally the fear of the latency period—between six and twelve years of age—is that of punishment by the internalized parental figure, the superego. The anxiety associated with each of these phase-specific dangers may and indeed does persist into later phases. This includes adulthood, in which seemingly adult concerns and worries belie these primitive anxieties buried deep in the unconscious. For Sixes, any and all of these dangerous situations seem current, if only in the unconscious. The quality of fear and anxiety in a Six may vary from an ongoing inner state of agitation and worry to outright terror, depending upon the degree of neurosis, but to whatever extent he is identified with his personality, fear will be present.

The passion of fear is inextricably tied to the Six's defense mechanism of projection, mentioned above. It is defined as "a mental process whereby a personally unacceptable impulse or idea is attributed to the external world. As a result of this defensive process, one's own interests and desires are perceived as if they belong to others, or one's own mental experience may be mistaken for consensual reality."[5] Because of this defense, it is often difficult for a Six to discern what is objectively going on in someone else, and what of his own unconscious is being experienced as belonging to another.

Most often, aggressive and hostile feelings and impulses are projected by Sixes, and in turn fuel their fear of a malevolent world. Criticism, judgment, and rejection are some of the less overtly aggressive but nonetheless undercutting projections favored by Sixes. The unconscious "reasoning" of the soul for projecting aggression is that it was experienced early on as threatening, and so having it inside oneself means having something dangerous inside. So the Six's way of getting rid of this internal threat is to disavow it through projection. Also, experiencing himself as aggressive would challenge a Six's core identity as a frightened weakling; and even though that sense of self is painful, it is nonetheless familiar, and thus ironically safe, territory.

Unallowable feelings of love and sexual attraction, such as homosexual impulses or attraction to someone who is unavailable, off limits, or uninterested, often undergo a transformation in the process of projection. The love object then appears hateful or cruel, tormenting and demeaning the Six, who can then consciously feel hatred and fear of the unconsciously desired object, and can thus successfully defend against intolerable desires. Another typical variation of this mechanism in Sixes is the surrendering of power and authority to an idealized other, to whom the Six is unswervingly loyal and devoted, and who then may become experienced as malevolent, persecuting and castrating the Six. We will explore this type of projection more thoroughly when we focus on the Six's relationship with authority, a particularly loaded area for this ennea-type.

The defense of projection, then, protects a Six from unacceptable inner feelings, thoughts, and impulses that threaten to become conscious, as well as from the anxiety that would accompany their emergence into awareness. This anxiety becomes transmuted into fear through projection—fear of an external other or the world at large. Unacceptable id drives—instinctual and other unconscious impulses—are experienced outside of himself, which supports and reinforces the Six's fundamental cognitive distortion produced by the loss of contact with the Holy Idea—that the world is a dangerous place filled with thinly veneered self-seeking animals. Projection, then, is fundamental to shaping a Six's experience of others and the world. The inner sense of having no stable and solid ground to stand on, which has its roots in the loss of Holy Strength and Holy Faith, leads to a profound inner sense of uncertainty and insecurity, as we have seen. Through projection, this becomes displaced onto others and onto the world at large, which then become seen as unreliable and untrustworthy. The world for a Six becomes frightening and precarious as much through projection as through early imprinting. Where one begins and the other ends may be impossible to figure out.

Projection leads us in turn to the subject of paranoia, central to the psychology of this ennea-type. Paranoia is defined by Webster's as "a tendency on the part of an individual or group toward excessive or irrational suspiciousness and distrustfulness of others that is based not on objective reality but on a need to defend the ego against unconscious impulses, that uses projection as a mechanism of defense, and that often takes the form of a compensatory megalomania."[6] At the extreme, paranoia is a form of psychosis in which you believe that you are being persecuted, singled out for abuse, maligned, even poisoned by one person in particular, a group, or the world at large. While normal neurotic Sixes may at times have such feelings, it is more appropriate to talk about a paranoid *attitude* when describing Sixes who are not at the dysfunctional end of the mental-health continuum. This paranoid attitude is one of hypervigilance and hypersensitivity to slights and attacks, suspiciousness, and a general sense of mistrust. Almaas refers to this paranoid quality in Sixes as "defensive suspiciousness."

Not only does a Six's paranoid attitude lead to feeling victimized, persecuted, and bullied, but it also leads to treating others this way in the form of scapegoating. Particular individuals or groups of people may become seen by Sixes as the source of their problems, particularly their sense of weakness and impotence. This is clear in the two cultures associated with Point Six, Germany and South Africa. The rise of Nazism in Germany can be seen as the response of a defeated and weakened country in the aftermath of World War I, in turn disempowering and attempting to destroy those who seemed to them prosperous and powerful, symbolized by the Jewish intelligencia. In South Africa, the white minority shored itself up by officially relegating blacks and those of mixed race to inferior status—theoretically separate but equal, but in fact having no political power in their own country.

Implicit in paranoia is a doubting attitude, which is itself the effect of fear on the mind. When paranoia is dominant, everything is questioned by a Six through the lens of doubt. This questioning is not an open examination, an actual indecision, or a careful weighing of the facts of a situation, but rather a biased one. There is a skepticism about it, a predisposition to disbelieve, a suspiciousness. This bias is, of course, based on the cynical perspective that the world is a dangerous place filled with self-serving people who would just as soon undercut you as support you, and that this is the bottom line of reality. David Shapiro, in his description of the paranoid style, which well delineates the extreme of Enneatype Six, discusses this biased suspicious thinking as follows:

> *A suspicious person is a person who has something on his mind. He looks at the world with fixed and preoccupying expectation, and he searches repetitively, and only, for confirmation of it. He will not be persuaded to abandon his suspicion or some plan of action based on it. On the contrary, he will pay no attention to rational arguments except to find in them some aspect or feature that actually confirms his original view. Anyone who tries to influence or persuade a suspicious person will not only fail, but also, unless he is sensible enough to abandon his efforts early, will, himself, become an object of the original suspicious idea.*[7]

As Shapiro notes, paranoid people will search relentlessly through the data available to them to confirm what they suspect, asserting and even believing that they are simply trying to get to the truth of the situation. They are very keen observers, but with the underlying agenda of searching for a clue that will confirm their suspicions. What is observed, then, is misconstrued to fit the picture that they already have about how things are. For example, a Six who is convinced that you do not like him, despite all of your assurances to the contrary, will be hyperalert to any action on your part that might be construed as rejection and will undoubtedly in time find confirmation of what he fears. Underlying his hyperalertness is his desire to feel safe and supported so that he can relax, letting down his vigilance, even if momentarily.

While the inner dynamics are the same, as mentioned at the beginning of this chapter, there are two very different behavioral styles of Sixes. A Six may manifest both of these styles of behavior at certain times and in particular life situations, moving back and forth between them. One style, however, tends as a rule to be the dominant one in his personality. The first is the phobic type: a Six who feels his fear acutely and becomes paralyzed by it, like a deer caught in the headlights. This style of Six is timid, indecisive, hesitant, compliant, insecure, and constantly trying to stay safe and out of danger. Diane Keaton, probably a Six, often appears in roles that exemplify this indecisive and insecure side of Sixes, while her friend Woody Allen turns the neurotic and paranoid side of this type into comedy in his films. Phobic Sixes look and act frightened, their souls frozen in fear.

The second type is counterphobic: a Six who tries to act as though he is not afraid. This type of Six actively seeks out risky situations to prove that he is not frightened or weak. This is the daredevil, tightrope walking between skyscrapers or placing his head in the mouth of a lion, scaling an impossible peak or hunting down a violent criminal, pumping and puffing his body up or making split-second decisions speculating with vast sums of money, flying an experimental fighter jet on a dangerous sortie or snow boarding off a cliff. Sylvester Stallone and Arnold Schwarzenegger exemplify and portray in the movies the bodybuilding version of counterphobic Six, while Harrison Ford, Willem Dafoe, and Clint Eastwood often portray adventurers and heroes contending with and barely escaping dangerous predicaments. Linda Hamilton, in her *Terminator* roles, is a female version. Counterphobic Sixes can be megalomaniacal, obsessed with appearing heroic, grand, and omnipotent—the Napoleons and Hitlers of the world. Despite all of a counterphobic Six's attempts to prove he is not afraid—or perhaps because of them—his obsession with fear stands out as his motivating drive.

The superego of these two varieties of Sixes has a slightly different flavor. In both cases it is authoritarian—imperious and overbearing—and demanding total conformity. It reinforces his basic sense of himself as deficient and just plain not having what it takes in the game of life. In phobic Sixes, his domineering and bossy inner critic berates him for being so fearful, such a weakling, and for having no backbone. In counterphobic Sixes, his superego gets projected onto others whom he experiences as judgmental and critical, undermining and threatening him. His superego demands that he be tough and strong and, like a phobic Six, castigates him for his fear. A Six's relationship to his superego mirrors his relationship with authority figures, as we shall see.

In relationship to authority figures, these two styles behave differently on the surface, and yet are really coming from the same place deeper down. Both have a hyperattunement to who has power, rank, authority, and clout and who doesn't—to who is the boss and who is the peon, in other words. With little internal sense of a center of strength, power, and guidance, Sixes project that authority outside of themselves. Because of their internal insecurity and lack of a sense of inner foundation, on the one hand they see that missing authority outside of themselves in the form of an individual, organization, or belief system. The phobic type is devoted, dutiful, and fawning in relation to whoever or whatever they consider this external authority. They are hero-worshipers and devoted followers. The stereotypical ingratiating sycophant and the faithful and obsequious servant to whom it would be unthinkable and frightening to step out of that role are examples of this type of Six. They want this authority to provide the certainty and decisiveness that they lack; they want someone to tell them what to do and what is right and wrong; they want a creed, cause, or faith they can believe in wholeheartedly and be loyal to; they want a pillar that will give them a sense of strength and solidity and will infuse their lives with a sense of meaning, a sense of living for something larger and grander than oneself; they want something or someone to whom they can be devoted and dutiful. In short, a phobic Six wants someone or something that will provide him with security, and this is what both lures him and is his pitfall, as we see on the Enneagram of Traps, Diagram 9.

On the other hand, this hero-worshiping puts Sixes in a subordinate and submissive position, having turned over all of their inner guidance, judgment, and power to this authority, and this in time feels like a castration. They have indeed castrated themselves, but, again because of the defense mechanism of projection, it seems to them that they are the persecuted victims of the authority. Therefore, like everything else, even a phobic Six's relationship to authority is ambivalent.

This brings us to the counterphobic Six's relationship to authority. The counterphobic type is rebellious, defiant, and obsessed with remaining autonomous, to the point of not recognizing or acknowledging any external authority. Here we see the archetypal rebel without a cause, resisting authority to ward off real or imagined undercutting and anticipated castration. Moving along the continuum further, a counterphobic Six may try to portray himself as the authority, wanting others to follow and idealize him, as discussed earlier in our examples of Adolf Hitler and Napoleon Bonaparte. Cult leaders like Jim Jones also exemplify this counterphobic extreme. This is a counterphobic Six's attempt to reclaim his inner authority by proving to himself that he has it because he wields so much power and influence over others. He tries to find security—his trap, as we saw above—through being revered, feared, and followed by his loyal devotees.

The phobic Six's need to follow blindly something or someone whom he perceives as greater than himself and to whom he can subordinate himself and the counterphobic Six's need to rebel against or become the authority are reflected in the word *idealization* at Point Six on the Enneagram of Lies, Diagram 12. In all these relationships to authority, we see the projection of the qualities of a Six's real strength—Essence—onto such a figure. Someone or something needs to be held up and seen as ideal, strong, and powerful; and someone else needs to be smaller than, be afraid of, and serve this ideal. This is a Six's central object relation, regardless of which side of it he identifies himself with.

Both the phobic and counterphobic relationships to authority were manifested in Nazi Germany. Hitler, the counterphobic paranoid who demanded total allegiance and obedience, received it from a culture that many perceive as historically looking for strong leaders to follow blindly. Ursula Hegi explains German behavior in the Nazi era in her novel *Stones from the River:*

> *Only a few of the people in Burgdorf had read* Mein Kampf, *and many thought that all this talk about* Rassenreinheit—*purity of the race—was ludicrous and impossible to enforce. Yet the long training in obedience to elders, government, and church made it difficult—even for those who considered the views of the Nazis dishonorable—to give voice to their misgivings. And so they kept hushed, yielding to each new indignity while they waited for the Nazis and their ideas to go away, but with every compliance they relinquished more of themselves, weakening the texture of the community while the power of the Nazis swelled.*[8]

Even the phobic type of Six, appearing so acquiescent and deferential on the surface, nonetheless has a hidden deviant tendency, which may be subtle or more overt. It can manifest as a passive aggressiveness—saying you are going to do something and then simply not doing it, for example. It may also take the form of asking everyone's advice about something, and then rejecting all opinions in rebellion to being "coerced" by others. Facing this tendency is not easy for a Six. Even for a rebellious Six, experiencing himself as disloyal or forsaking what he perceives as his duty is profoundly avoided. He might be a gang member, engaging in activities that the rest of society considers deviant, but he will see himself as loyal to his comrades.

Deep down, because Sixes cannot be completely and always in agreement with those they hold as authority figures—cannot be fully dutiful—they experience themselves as deviant and delinquent, and they believe that they are deficient because of it. Their devotedness belies their underlying lack of authentic faith, as expressed eloquently by the mid-twentieth-century Christian theologian Reinhold Niebuhr: "Frantic orthodoxy is never rooted in faith but in doubt. It is when we are not sure that we are

doubly sure."[9] There is profound shame about not being fully in alignment with whoever or whatever they consider an authority, and so Sixes
avoid this inner sense like the plague. The sense of being different, outside of the norm, disloyal, or shirking in his duty is almost intolerable for
a Six. For this reason, deviance/delinquency appear at Point Six on the Enneagram of Avoidances, Diagram 10, since these are the experiences a Six
most wants to avoid.

The great spiritual teacher Jiddu Krishnamurti, who was probably a
Six, focused his work on and developed a whole spiritual teaching around
one's relationship to authority. He taught rejection of all outer authority
and of any defined practice including formal meditation. Raised to become a world messiah by the Theosophist Annie Besant during the early
years of the twentieth century, he abandoned the role, refusing to be set
up as a figure for disciples to follow. His statement of dissolution of the
order that he was to be the head of declared in effect that "truth is a path-
less land, and you cannot approach it by any path whatsoever, by any religion, by any sect. Truth, being limitless, unconditioned, unapproachable
by any path whatsoever, cannot be organized; nor should any organization
be formed to lead or to coerce people along any particular path."[10]

Nowhere is the quality of Essence idealized by Sixes—the idealized
Aspect of this ennea-type—more obvious than in a Six's relationship to
authority. For a Six, the quality of Being that seems to be what is missing
in themselves and that looks like the answer to their problems is the one
characterized by steadfastness, solidity, certainty, definiteness, concrete-
ness, perseverance, resoluteness, determination, substantiality, and sup-
portedness. This is the Essential Aspect called the White or Will in the
Diamond Approach. It is one of the *lataif,* subtle centers described in the
Sufi system, which are doors into the essential realm. The *lataif* also include the Red or Strength Aspect, which we will discuss when exploring
Ennea-type Eight; the Yellow or Joy Aspect, which we will explore when
discussing Ennea-type Seven; the Green or Compassion Aspect; and the
Black or Power Aspect.

The experience of Will is feeling the presence of Being as a steadfast
and unswerving inner support. It may feel as if we are standing on or actually are an immense and immovable mountain, and when we experience

it, we know that our essential nature is always present and that it alone is unshakable. Because the personality is a mental construct, when we are identified with it our soul has no real foundation or ground. Unlike Being, the personality needs to be constantly shored up and reinforced; we need others to give us emotional support and affirmation to uphold our sense of who we are. Being, in contrast, is what is present when we fully relax and stop trying to make anything happen, and when we let go of all of our beliefs and positions. The presence of Will gives us a sense of confidence in ourselves and in our capacity to persevere in any enterprise we embark upon. Ultimately it is the confidence in our ability to persevere in discovering our deepest truths, to travel our inner terrain resolutely and find out firsthand who and what we really are.[11]

In the case of the phobic type of Six, the outer authority figure appears to be the embodiment of Will, while a counterphobic Six attempts to become the embodiment of it himself. The phobic Six's devotion, faithfulness, dedication, reliability, and constancy are always in relation to an other who appears as their anchor, their support, and their foundation—the incarnation of Will, in short. The counterphobic Six's heroism and risk taking are attempts to act as though he were the manifestation of Will. In either case, the personality is shaped in such a way that it mimics the characteristics of real Will.

The confidence and security of Will are the primary qualities that the Six personality attempts to replicate and embody, but this solution requires mental, emotional, and physical tension to maintain. To contact and embody these qualities fully in a real way such that his soul can fully relax and unfold with a sense of safety, a Six must make sustained contact with his inner depths. To do this, he needs the virtue associated with this point, courage, as we see on the Enneagram of Virtues in Diagram 1. The more he faces his inner reality without being swept away by fear and without doubting his experience, the more he also develops courage. Courage is actually what he needs to be able to confront memories and parts of himself that feel terrifying and life threatening, and courage is what manifests the more he is able to do this. Sixes mistake courage for outer acts of bravery, while the deepest manifestation of courage is being able to face and question fundamental concepts of self and other embedded in the texture of the soul.

Ichazo defines the virtue of courage as "the recognition of the individual's responsibility for his own existence. In the position of courage, the body moves naturally to preserve life." In contrast to the Six's tendency to look for security outside of himself, then, in the form of a person, cause, or creed he can be devoted to—or if counterphobic, who he can spend his energy rebelling against or becoming the one others follow and thus support—his orientation needs to shift first of all to self-reliance. If true transformation is to take place within him, he needs to let go of anything he is holding on to for security and be willing to face himself courageously as he is. Some of the highlights of what a Six's inner journey needs to address follow.

In the spiritual and psychological arenas, facing himself will mean acknowledging and trying to understand his needs to swallow unquestioningly the teachings he has embraced and to conform unthinkingly to them. He will find that this tendency is based on doubt rather than certainty: his own doubt about having any more to him than his personality. Despite his immense loyalty and dedication to his teacher or teaching, he does not really believe that *his* nature is Essence. He feels that the closest he can get to True Nature is proximity to those who seem to embody it. He does not have real faith in the essential realm based on his own experience, as we discussed concerning the Holy Ideas, but rather he clings out of fear to blind faith in what another tells him. Courage, then, first of all means facing this reality about himself unflinchingly. As he does this, he will quickly get in touch with how little he actually does know with certainty about himself and about others, and how much his mental orientation is one of suspiciousness and doubt. He will see that this is a very positioned and fearful bias, arising out of his sense of himself as small, weak, and defenseless. Even if he is counterphobic and has gone to great lengths to prove how fearless and tough he is, if he is really honest he will see that he has been defending against this deeper frightened layer underneath.

He will get in touch with his lack of faith in his own perceptions, his doubt and his distrust of himself. There is history here for him that needs to be explored about what childhood events contributed to his lack of trust. He may find an authoritarian undermining parental figure or an unconfident and insecure one. He may have been told repeatedly that he didn't know anything and that he was undependable. He may find that the frightening situations he had to face in early childhood were so scary for him that he could not trust his perceptions. For some Sixes, the reliance in early childhood on people whom they feared yet needed created great inner ambivalence and doubt, an inner uncertainty about what the reality really was.

As he explores this, his fear will undoubtedly arise. He will need to get in touch with the sense of self and of other that gives rise to this fright: himself as a weakling, the runt of the litter of life, unequipped and defenseless against a life-threatening world filled with brutal and malevolent others. He will need to experience and understand how this way of holding things got established and understand why he feels so inadequate. He may find, if a phobic type, that it was historically not okay for him to be strong and that he was required to be submissive and malleable. Or, if counterphobic, that he had to be far tougher than he really felt and that it was not okay for him to express his fear. In either case, it is unlikely that his fear was really held in his early environment, and to really transform it, he will find that he is the one who must now allow it and question its basis and whether he really does need to be so afraid.

He will have to face his drives and impulses, his aggression and his strength, and discover whether they are really parts of himself that he and others need to be afraid of. Contacting them will put him in touch with his capacity to be strong and not cower in the face of danger, and this in turn will bring up his fear of losing someone outside to whom he can relate to either subserviently, rebelliously, or as an authoritarian. He will, in short, be faced with his aloneness as he lets the inner object relations dissolve and begins to experience his soul without these veils. Being afraid of others has still kept him in relationship with them, if only in his own mind, and whether problematic and ambivalent or not, this has kept him from fully facing himself. His superego will try to keep him from this level of inquiry, threatening him with losing all of his security.

Getting in touch with and inquiring into his fear will take him to its heart: the fear that he is only an empty shell with no deeper reality to him. This will bring him to his lack of contact with his essential nature, and he will see that his fear forms a ring around the places in his soul where this loss of contact feels like a hole or a gap. Facing the emptiness in these holes will require all of the courage he can muster, and he will eventually see that the most frightening thing is not the emptiness but the anticipation—the fear itself—of what might or might not be there. In time he will be able to move courageously into these empty places in his soul and find that rather than being deadly and devouring abysses as he had feared, if fully allowed the emptiness becomes a spaciousness. As he experiences this, his soul will begin to relax as he sees that there has really been nothing to be frightened of within—which was the root of his fear.

With repeated descents into his inner world over time, out of the spaciousness will arise all of the various qualities of his True Nature. The more that he has the courage to make these inner forays, the more he will contact his ground, which in turn will give him a sense of inner security and confidence in himself. Bit by bit, he will reclaim his depths and find his foundation within. Rather than being a believer and a follower, he will know Essence firsthand, and out of this experiential contact with himself, he will know that who he is fundamentally is absolutely unshakable and indestructible. Rather than being one of the faithful, he will know Essence to be his strength and will see that it is something he does not need to preserve or protect or be afraid of losing. His faith, at long last, will be real.

E N N E A - T Y P E
T H R E E :
E G O - V A N I T Y

The quintessential image type, Threes are characterized by an overriding concern with how they present themselves, how they look, and the impact that they have on others. This is the proverbial self-made man or woman, creating themselves and pulling themselves up by their own bootstraps. They are chameleonlike, taking on the colorings needed to make a positive impression. It is often difficult to discern what they truly feel or even who they truly are, since they seem to become whoever they need to in order to present the image necessary to achieve the result that they wish. They tend to change their presentation depending upon the situation and who they are with, so that often others have very different experiences and impressions of the same person.

They are driven and goal oriented, and value success in the particular domain in which they are invested more than anything. Achieving what they set out to do takes precedence over every other concern, whether they be physical constraints, those of class or economic origin, or the feelings of others or even of themselves. They often drive themselves mercilessly in their pursuit of accomplishment, and may be perceived by others as ruthless, calculating, and possessing a steely determination. Threes are pragmatic and matter-of-fact, doing whatever it takes to get the job done, including using manipulation and deception. While sometimes consciously duplic-itous, Threes often do not know what is really true for them, since they of-ten feel the emotions and have the attitude that they think is appropriate for their situation.

Threes are doers, and the perspective on reality that they are sensitive to—their Holy Idea—has to do with activity. As with Point Six, there is more than one name for the Holy Idea associated with Point Three on the enneagram. Two of them, Holy Law and Holy Harmony, are perceptions about reality; and the third, Holy Hope, refers to the effect upon the soul as these understandings about reality are integrated. All three nuances of this Holy Idea concern the dynamic aspect of Being, the fact that it is not static but rather is ceaselessly unfolding, and this effulgence is the uni-verse of which we are a part. This dimension of Being is called the Logos in the Diamond Approach. So this Idea is related to the functioning of re-ality and has many shades of meaning—more than most of the other points—which I will briefly describe. In a nutshell, this Idea tells us that reality as a unified whole is constantly unfolding and that the actions, changes, and movements of each of us are inseparable from the shifts of that wholeness. If we consciously participate in this ceaseless unfoldment, which means that if our fixations, which rigidify the soul, relax, our con-sciousness will naturally move deeper and deeper toward our depths, our essential nature; and we will experience more harmony, inner and outer. This progressive movement closer to the ultimate truth of our nature is the potentiality of the human soul.

Let us look at each of the particulars of this Idea in more detail. Holy Law is the understanding that the universe as one whole and unified en-tity is constantly in a state of change. The perceptions that all manifesta-tion is a unity and that all of us are ultimately different cells in the one body of the universe are the focus of the Holy Ideas of Points Eight and Five, Holy Truth and Holy Omniscience, respectively. Here, at Point Three, we understand that this unity is always in motion and does not hold still. The whole substance of reality in all of its dimensions is per-petually in flux, like a great ocean whose surface is made up of the movement of many different waves and whose depths are made up of many currents. All of the shifts and movements of the various forms are part of the unfoldment of the whole.

This is a very difficult perception for most people to grasp. It challenges some of our fundamental beliefs about ourselves, regardless of ennea-type. First of all, it challenges our notions of cause and effect, since from the unobstructed view of Holy Law we see that nothing and no one is separately affecting or making anything happen. Everything that happens is part of the fabric of the universe unfurling itself. So nothing happens in isolation from the whole of that fabric, and no one initiates action of her own accord, nor do we cause things to occur separately from the momentum of that whole. It is easier to understand that we are inseparable from the oneness of the universe than it is to understand that we actually do nothing in isolation from the dynamism of the whole of reality. We will discuss this more a little further on.

Perceiving the dynamism of Being—the fact that it is a presence in constant flow—also challenges our notion of time, something I will discuss more fully in Chapter 10 when we explore Holy Plan, which deals with the pattern of this dynamism. Understanding Holy Law also calls into question any of our notions of God as an entity outside the fabric of the universe, since clearly this is not possible. It also shows us that it makes no sense to conceive of this separate entity, God, who at some point in the distant past created the world. When we see that the universe is one whole thing that is constantly arising, we see that the creation is occurring all the time. This is also something I will discuss more fully in Chapter 10. Our ideas about life and death change if we understand Holy Law, as we see in the following quote of Almaas:

> To understand that the totality of the universe is constantly renewing itself radically changes our notion of death. Personal death is simply Being manifesting at one moment with a particular person as part of the picture, and in the next moment without that person. From this perspective, all the issues about death change character. Death disappears into the continual flow of unfolding, self-arising change.[1]

So all that exists is a manifestation of Being, forms arising and sinking back into the mystery of the Absolute. Out of nothing, something arises. This is the creativity of Being, expressing Itself in all of the forms of the world, including our own bodies and souls. Not only is Being manifesting Itself in all of us and all that surrounds us but Holy Law tells us that It is also revealing Itself. All of the loveliness of the physical world—all of the stars, galaxies, and planets, all of the beauties of nature, and all of the creatures of the earth including ourselves—is Being revealing Itself in all of its magnificence. Its inner nature displays Itself in all of its grandeur in the world of form. The world of manifestation, then, is the expression of the constantly self-revealing creativity of Being.

When we perceive the harmonious interplay of all of manifestation, we are in touch with Holy Harmony, the next nuance of this Idea. It tells us that what may appear as conflicts and incongruities among the various parts of the whole that is the universe only look that way when seen from the surface. Since the unfoldment of the universe is the movement and dynamism of a oneness, none of the parts can be fundamentally at odds with each other. They are all part of the same harmonious outpouring.

It also refers to the understanding that there is a magnetic pull upon the human soul which, left unimpeded, will draw us toward the depths in which this unitive, and thus harmonious, functioning is apparent. If the soul is supported in developing and unfolding, in other words, it will naturally be drawn toward its Essence, which is its inner truth. Spiritual development, then, is really a matter of nondoing and of removing the obstacles and logjams that impede the flow of our souls. Most people experience movement and change, but it usually stays within more or less narrow confines, as discussed in the Introduction, which gives our lives a sense of staleness, sameness, and stuckness. Expanding our consciousness, then, when seen from the angle of Point Three, is a matter of increasing the movement or the flow of our souls so that we experience more of the various dimensions of the universe. The final goal of spiritual work, then, is not a particular state but rather a capacity to move from one state to another freely and easily. This gives us a sense of momentum and of dynamism, reflecting that of Being as we attune to it.

The more we open to the flow of our souls, the more we experience our consciousness and in turn our lives as more harmonious. This brings us to Holy Hope, which describes the effect upon us of integrating Holy Law and Holy Harmony. The closer we move toward our depths, the more we feel in alignment with the universe, functioning harmoniously within its unfolding pattern. This proximity to our deepest truth delights the heart since we are answering its call to connect with its greatest love. Like an irresistibly attracted lover, the human soul is drawn like a magnet to its Beloved, Being. As we move closer to It, the world we inhabit becomes one of beauty, grace, and harmony.

Another meaning of Holy Hope is that this innate pull to connect with and realize our True Nature is humanity's deepest potential and its salvation. To the extent that we are in contact with our depths, to that extent we understand that we are functioning as parts of a larger body, and this affects us by giving our souls a sense of optimism about ourselves, the world, and the whole of the universe.

Turning to the loss of the Holy Idea, we will return to Holy Law. The major implication of Holy Law is that nothing in the universe occurs in isolation and that the actions of one part affect and are linked to the actions of all other parts of the whole. Therefore, no one and nothing can function independently of the whole body of the universe, so it is not possible to have laws that apply to only one part. Because Ennea-type Threes are sensitive to this Holy Idea, as they lose contact with Being, they also lose this understanding and come to feel very much like independent operatives, separate entities acting and doing autonomously, unrelated to the functioning of everyone and everything else. They come to believe that they are laws unto themselves, beyond the morals, strictures, and principles that govern others. This ultimately estranged sense that they can function separately from the whole is the fixed and fundamental belief about reality, the fixation of this ennea-type, and is described by the word vanity on the Enneagram of Fixations, Diagram 2. (Ichazo's secondary term *go* refers to the Three's characteristic of always being busy—on the go.)

With the loss of the perception of Holy Harmony, Ennea-type Threes, who experience themselves as separate players in life as we have seen, can be oblivious to the ramifications and effects of their actions on others or on the world as a whole. We see this today in the mind-set that disregards environmental consequences if personal gain is at stake, losing sight of the fact that if the ecosystem degenerates, there will be nothing more to profit from and no place to enjoy what one has acquired. Perhaps it is seen more directly in the mind-set of the person who supports "good causes," only to behave in cutthroat ways toward her most immediate business associates, and so simultaneously feeling virtuous while personally acting dishonestly. While characteristic although not confined to Threes, this kind of insular thinking is only possible with the loss of knowing oneself to be part of a greater whole in which the actions of each part affect the totality. Climbing to the top of the heap at the expense of other people may feel like a personal triumph—which it usually does to a Three—but it can hardly be seen as success if the whole system is taken into account. Such a Three-ish definition of success does not make any ultimate sense: one part of the whole profits to the detriment of another part of itself.

Without the sense that you are part of the unfoldment of the whole fabric of reality and that your inner nature is made up of the same presence as everyone and everything else, you are left, like Atlas, to hold up your own separate little world. This is reality for a Three. You are on your own, fundamentally unrelated to everyone and everything else, and actually surpassing Atlas, it's up to you to create as well as maintain your own universe. There is no activity, unfoldment, or development unless you make it happen. If you don't generate yourself and your life—worse than nothing happening—you and your world will fall apart. So you have to be constantly active, ceaselessly busy both internally and externally, and hence the nickname of this type, Ego-Go. Whatever happens in your life is up to you, there is no sustenance beyond what you actuate, and there is no salvation beyond yourself. There is, in other words, no Holy Hope. The self who does all of this is the soul identified with the personality, cut off from consciousness of Being. To a Three who is identified with his personality, there is nothing deeper, and it's the only ground she has to operate from.

I have lumped together the sense of self-creation, an internal cognitive function, as well as the Three's sense of instigating external events, and what this linkage implies bears looking into more deeply. It is easy to understand a Three's belief that if she doesn't make things happen, nothing *will* happen, when we think of external action. Most of us, identified as we are with our personalities, take it for granted that we cause things to happen, that our actions determine what ensues in our lives, and that in this respect we are masters of our fate. Stepping outside of the perspective of the personality, however, one sees that this is not the case. Being acts *through* us. This is one of the most difficult things for most people to understand, and perhaps using our previous metaphor will make it easier to grasp: we are each individual manifestations of Being, separate waves arising and passing away on the surface of the great Ocean. The movement of each individual wave is not self-generated nor is it separately decided upon; it is part of the movement of the whole sea. In the same way, all that occurs is part of the movement of the larger fabric of reality. From this angle, the differentiation between inner and outer doing—a differentiation based upon whether action is physically manifest or not—breaks down. One implication of this is that our thoughts and emotions are every bit as much a part of this movement as physical actions are, an understanding reflected in the often-misunderstood notion of karma.

External doing is always driven by inner doing when we are identified with the personality. The inner doing of the personality is what is called ego activity in spiritual language. It is the ceaseless generation of psychological content, which is based upon our identification as a particular person, and it also supports that identification. It supports our sense of who we are, in other words, and is what I referred to as self-generation or self-creation. Sometimes consciously, but most often unconsciously, we are continuously generating internal pictures of ourselves that have been shaped by our history. These pictures, as discussed in the Introduction, are like holographic images, complete with feeling tones, affective texture, physical tension patterns, and other sensations, and are based on our beliefs. We might experience ourselves as someone who is misunderstood, or someone who others are not inclined to like, someone who never does things right, or someone who has a hard time initiating action; or more positively, as someone who is brighter than others, someone who is very kind, or someone who is strong. As also previously discussed, these pictures of ourselves, which form our self-representations, arise in counterpoint to our sense of what is other than us, forming the object relations that are the building blocks of the personality. As also discussed, embedded within and responsible for the dynamic of producing these object relations is the fundamental drive behind ego activity to avoid pain and experience pleasure.

Ego activity is ceaseless in the personality, and until we experience moments in which it stops, we have little idea of how tiring and wearing it is. Even when we are asleep, our unconscious is busily processing the day's experiences and anticipating those of tomorrow in the form of dreams. Only in deep sleep does this activity stop in the ordinary person, and as experiments of sleep deprivation have shown, without this respite, we become psychological wrecks. This cessation of ego activity is the goal of many kinds of spiritual work, and such experiences are what are called enlightenment experiences, because it is only when we experience ourselves without this activity that we experience ourselves completely beyond the personality. In such moments, we know our nature pristinely, without any filters of the past, and we experience ourselves as Being.

Once we know that Being is our fundamental nature, a further stage is the realization that the sense of "I" that our ego activity has been so busy creating and supporting is not necessary for us to function. Because our sense of self developed simultaneously with our capacity to function, the two have become inseparable in most people's minds. Eventually, as we continue to develop spiritually, we see that we can function without producing inner pictures of ourselves. We learn that we do not have to remind ourselves of who we are to drive the car or do our taxes, for instance. Letting go of our historical self, with the holographic movie whose theme is a life lived within object relations, we contact reality directly, responding to the present instead of the past. We feel simple and empty in a positive way, deplete of preconceptions and emotional reactions. Then we can begin to live a life in touch with and informed by Being, knowing consciously that we are individual manifestations of it. We experience ourselves as waves of the great Ocean, ourselves one with it. Our place and function within the body of humanity is evident, and we live our lives in a harmonious way. This is the development of the Essential Aspect called the Pearl in the Diamond Approach. It is the state of embodying and living a life informed by Being. This is a very deep level of development, since it means not simply having transcended the personality. It means having thoroughly worked through identification with our psychology and no longer consciously or unconsciously identifying with the personality as defining who and what we are.[2] Obviously this is no small task and is a level of development embodied by very few.

This quality of Being—the Pearl—is the one that this personality type mimics and idealizes, and so it is its idealized Aspect. Let us pick this understanding apart. Ego activity and the internal image of self that it generates, as well as external actions that are motivated by it, are central to the psychology of Ennea-type Threes, as we have seen. This activity is a reflection and an imitation of the creative and dynamic characteristic of Being. So in their attempt to reconnect with the lost Holy Idea of Holy Law, which has to do with this generative functioning of Being, Threes attempt to mold or shape themselves into a person. Rather than generating the whole universe, as Being does, here the activity produces a personality based upon a self-image. Threes are deeply identified with this internal image of self, produced by their ego activity, as well as with the external activity directed by this "I." Rather than experiencing herself as an individual manifestation and expression of Being, which is the experience of the Pearl, the Three feels this "I" as supreme. This "I" is an imitation Pearl, a fake embodiment of God, so to speak, and that is exactly what the ego self is.

Threes act as though they are the generative principle, the creative aspect of God, in other words, since in their own apparently separate universe, that is how it seems. Threes, then, try to take God's place, creating themselves and their lives in accordance with their own inner dictates. This is the consummate vanity, in the theological sense: relating to the separate "I" as though it were the acme. Looking at it from a slightly different angle, the personality, the outer surface of who we are, becomes central. The shell, the husk of ourselves, is all that remains, with all of the emptiness at the core that this image conjures up, and it is this shell that feels primary. It usurps the place and the function—as well as the functioning—of Being.

From a psychodynamic point of view, the loss of the Holy Idea has, as we have seen, left the Three with the sense that she is not part of the fabric of the Whole but rather a separate actor who must create a reality and a life. From a historical vantage point, she has reacted to the lack of holding in her early environment with the attitude that "I'll do it myself." The sensitivity of Threes to their essential nature not being seen and reflected by the environment, filtered through the loss of the Holy Idea, creates the interpretation they must *do* to survive and to be loved—that their value is rooted in their ego activity and arises from their role and achievements. So the take on their childhood is that their survival was up to them and that they were loved for their accomplishments and not for themselves. Sometimes there was physical deprivation in the past of a Three, or she had to take care of herself as well as other siblings at a very young age because of an absent, overextended, or simply neglectful parent. These kinds of backgrounds, filtered through the loss of Holy Law, lead to the "self-made man," clearly a Three archetype, in which someone from destitute roots pulls himself up by his own bootstraps to achieve phenomenal wealth and fame. Sometimes the deprivation a Three has experienced is not physical at all—many Threes are of course born into affluent and powerful families. In these cases, the neglect is more of an emotional withholding in which conforming to the family's ideals and the Three's achievements were all that seemed to receive much notice. Nannies or a kindly grandmother might have taken the place of mother, who had other, presumably more important, things to do. The message that filtered through the Three's sensitivity was that she was a showpiece valued only for her role. Regardless of the childhood circumstances, the message Threes get is that their survival and their value lie in their performance and achievements, and their personality becomes focused around image and action.

As the name of this ennea-type—ego-vanity—indicates, the issue of vanity is central to the psychology of Threes. The word *vain* is defined as "having no real value, meaning or foundation,"[3] and this graphically describes the soul, cut off from awareness of Being, in which the shell of the personality is experienced as preeminent. Indeed, one's real foundation—which alone can give a true sense of meaning and value to one's life—is missing. This is the deepest level of the vanity of Threes. Vanity is also defined as "inflated pride in oneself or one's appearance, attainments, performance, possessions, or successes; hunger for praise or admiration; the ostentation of fashion, wealth, or power regarded as an occasion of empty pride or a vain show."[4] These are more superficial manifestations of the fundamental vanity of Threes, that of the personality usurping the place of Being, and we will explore them in detail.

The superficial itself—the surface, what is seen, what is presented—is of utmost importance to Threes. Appearance, in other words, is everything. How one's shell looks and functions matters profoundly, since having the perfect image and performing flawlessly is what a Three values. The presentation is more important than what lies behind it; the image one presents is the end in itself. The form matters more than the substance here. Translated in personal terms, what matters to a Three is how she looks, what she achieves, and what she has. The animal associated with this ennea-type exemplifies this: the peacock, who, like a Three, exhibits and struts his beautiful plumage to impress. Threes' sense of self and of self-worth is inextricably linked up with their image, and it is difficult for them to see or to experience themselves as anything separate from it. What a Three presents is, to them, who they are. So the central preoccupation for a Three is to master the perfect image. This shaping of her soul into an image is reflected on the Enneagram of Antiself Actions as self-imaging, which appears at Point Three, as we see on Diagram 11. This shows up visually: there is often something masklike about a Three's face, having usually a broad, flat, and often sometimes even plastic quality to it.

To so value your image, you must see yourself through the eyes of others. Preoccupation with image, then, implies relationship: how you look, what you achieve, and what you have are all relative to others. The image that Threes try to shape themselves into perfectly is based on what others value and idealize. This image is not a personal one arising from inner values or ideals—although these are taken on as part of the image—but rather one arising from the values and ideals of one's family or culture. Threes try to become this ideal, at least on the surface, and how well they achieve it determines their degree of success in their own eyes. The overarching image a Three takes on changes as her milieu changes, and she adjusts it to achieve her ends and to be accepted by particular individuals. They are in this sense chameleons, taking on the colorings of their environment, so there is little that feels unique, creative, or original about Threes. As personifications of collective ideals, Threes are often very charismatic, mesmerizing, and captivating. A striking example of this was President John F. Kennedy.

In psychological terminology what I have just described is the process of identification, and it is the defense mechanism of this ennea-type. In identification, "various attitudes, functions, and values of the other are integrated into a cohesive, effective identity and become fully functional parts of the self compatible with other parts."[5] What a Three identifies with, they take themselves to be.

Physical beauty, wealth, and power are generally what Threes consider important because these are things most people consider important. Beauty contests, fashion shows, the movie scene, executive boardrooms, venture capital groups, junk bond trading, the advertising industry, and even the tabloids are all typical Three venues. The entertainment industry abounds in Threes. Stars of previous decades who are most likely Threes include Richard Chamberlain, Farrah Fawcett, Cheryl Ladd, Robert Wagner, Don Johnson, Diana Ross, and Tom Selleck. More currently, we have Cindy Crawford, George Clooney, Pamela Anderson, Leonardo DiCaprio, Whitney Houston, and perhaps Holly Hunter. Kristy Yamaguchi, the Olympic ice-skater, is probably also a Three. Threes are the cheerleaders and pom-pom girls, the class president and homecoming king and queen, the California girl, the supermodel and movie star, the corporate CEO, the slick Wall Street trader, and perhaps most graphically, the advertising executive. Image consciousness is the packaging and marketing of oneself, the selling of oneself like a product. The proverbial snake oil salesman and used car dealer are less savory Three archetypes.

There are many variations in what image a Three takes on, depending upon her social milieu. If involved in the religious right, for instance, a Three will try to look and act pious and zealous. If involved in politics, a Three will try to present the most politically correct face—aided by spin doctors, the masters of image manipulation and itself a Three phenomenon. If involved in spiritual work, a Three will try to manifest seamlessly the spiritual ideal of her tradition. And it is in this arena that image consciousness becomes most problematic, because experiences of Essence and True Nature only serve to expose and highlight the falsehood of a Three's front. Threes can be successful for a time in presenting a spiritually correct veneer, but in time reality must expose the sham for there to be true transformation. A case in point is Werner Erhard, the founder of est, who was dubbed the supersalesman of consciousness. He created a popular spiritual empire and made a fortune offering weekend courses that promised "getting it," i.e., enlightenment. While what he preached emphasized truthfulness and familial reconciliation, his downfall was precipitated by his being exposed as overtly abusive to his wife, and in the course of investigations about it, his dubious financial dealings also came to light.

In addition to shaping themselves into a cultural ideal, image consciousness also operates more subtly in Threes. They are very aware of how they are coming across to others, and will modify what they are presenting to make the impact and achieve the result they want. Threes will suppress feelings, thoughts, and even sensations that don't seem appropriate to a situation in order to present the correct image. Because of this tendency, those who know them may all experience them quite differently, since Threes present to each something of themselves that the other person will like. With someone who values personal sharing, they will become emotionally disclosing, while with someone who values a business-like attitude, they will be precise and hard-nosed. Becoming all things to all people, Threes often feel that no one really knows them.

Threes often feel somewhat impersonal to others. There is a lack of emotionality about them, a mechanicalness visible behind even a show of emotion. This is because their emotions are those of the image—those they think they should feel—rather than those coming from a deeper inner source. There is also something cool about Threes, a kind of beautiful but untouchable and impenetrable facade. You have the sense that they are not personally relating to you but rather are relating to the image that you form of them. It is very difficult for them to tolerate being seen in a bad light by others. They will go to extremes to dispel a negative image another forms of them, even if it involves fabrications and duplicity, a subject we will explore in a few moments.

They seem perpetually adolescent and youthful, with a boyish quality in the men and a cute ingenue quality in the women, which we see exemplified in Tom Cruise, Robert Redford, Brooke Shields, and Christie Brinkley. They tend to have sunny dispositions, presenting themselves as self-assured, buoyant, and confident. But this positive face is not based on a true optimism about life or trust in the goodness of humanity or of reality and is instead founded upon an anticipatory leaning toward personal success. There is nothing airy-fairy about their bright-eyed demeanor, since behind it lies the conviction that there is no hope or help beyond themselves and their own efforts. They are pragmatic, practical, matter-of-fact, facing reality coolly, with no complicating emotional reactions or moral compunctions, so that they can expediently meet and master the challenges life presents to them.

Success—a very important word for Threes—is defined here by how successful your image is, how seamless your performance is and what it has gotten you, as well as who you have impressed. Reaching your goals is far more important than personal relationships—unless they are the conquest (as in landing that famous/wealthy/powerful person) or are stepping-stones toward some accomplishment. There is a driven quality about Threes that causes them to overexert, often neglecting themselves physically and emotionally in ordered to achieve something. They will subordinate eating, sleeping, and any feelings that might arise to the task at hand. It is very difficult for a Three *not* to be active. Relaxing—unless it becomes a project in and of itself—is not easy for Threes. Achieving things gives them a sense of value and meaning, so not doing means losing that. It also means that their world might crumble and put their survival in jeopardy. This is the typical workaholic syndrome, although it is important to remember that, while typical, overworking is not the sole domain of Threes. It is also important to note that not all Threes are successes, but they all strive to be.

The drive of a Three is at its roots an attempt to offset and avoid their core deficiency state, which usually lies buried in the unconscious: feeling like a failure. There are a number of reasons why Threes feel that they have failed. First, they fundamentally believe that their only value arises from the image they present and from their accomplishments, which means that who they *are* feels worthless to them. The soul knows that its outer mask and activities are only the external, and so there is a deep sense of personal failing that nothing else about oneself seems to be of worth. This might manifest as the belief that they failed to hold their mother's love based solely on who they were rather than on what they could do. So the failure may be felt as not having been enough of a person to make mother care. Deeper still, we see that implicit in this sense of failure is a helplessness that is intolerable to Threes: it is the sense of not having been able in childhood to make the environment hold them and also of not having been able to get their essential nature mirrored. This sense of help-lessness can only have life if we believe we could have affected these things, which in fact none of us has any control over. Behind this is an even deeper sense of helplessness and failure for Threes: the sense that they have not managed to stay connected to their depths. To the soul of a Three, believing as they do that it is all up to them, this is their ultimate lack of success, and all of their outer achievements are at root an attempt to nullify this fundamental sense of failure.

Feeling helpless, like a failure, or being unsuccessful in achieving a goal is avoided at all costs, even if it means lying to oneself and others—a subject we will return to. We see this reflected on the Enneagram of Avoid-ances, Diagram 10, which you will find in Appendix B, with failure ap-pearing at Point Three. On the other hand, no success ever feels as though it is real or enough, since it is the image that is responsible for it. So the cycle continues of driving oneself on to greater and greater triumphs, none of which ever really brings a sense of satisfaction to a Three's soul.

In their drive for success, Threes can be relentless and ruthless. They often do not care who they use or step on to get where they are going, since the goal is far more important to them than another person. They are acutely conscious of who has the most beauty, wealth, power, and suc-cess; and they are unabashedly competitive about surpassing their rival and getting to the top. They are unequivocally ambitious and will toler-ate no obstacles, inward or outward, in realizing their aspirations. There is nothing like a good contest or challenge to sharpen up their edge. They can be calculating, cutthroat, cunning, and heartless, exhibiting a steely determination to get what they want. This was graphically portrayed by the character of Gordon Gekko played by Michael Douglas in the film *Wall Street,* and also by Al Pacino's portrayal of the devil as a slick executive in *The Devil's Advocate.* To this end, they may badmouth others in subtle and not-so-subtle ways, slyly pushing the competition to the side. It is not that they are cruel or vindictive but rather that they are focused on winning and on triumph, and will allow no one and nothing to stand in their way, compelled by their inner imperative to avoid failure.

A Three's superego exhorts her to do more and more, to be more efficient and faster at what she does, and above all else, to succeed in her ambitions. Her superego uses the threat of failure against her, convincing her that if she lets up, she will surely be a failure. Pushing and driving her onward, her superego is far more heartless and merciless toward her than she could ever be toward anyone else. Physical or emotional fatigue are not things her superego considers adequate reasons to stop her ceaseless activity, much less the simple human need for unstructured downtime. How she feels does not matter to her inner critic, only what she accomplishes, mimicking the message she internalized from her parents. Her superego also attacks her viciously for being phony, fake, insubstantial, and boring. So while insisting that she conform to the image others will approve of and like her for, she berates herself for her superficiality. Caught in this double bind, the focus on activity gets reinforced.

Her superego contributes to her all-business-and-no-nonsense orientation, centered on the product rather than the process. Quality is subordinated to quantity, and effect takes priority over affect. To a great extent, Threes' sense of personal value is measured by how effective, competent, and productive they are, and they judge others using the same yardstick. Efficiency is a Three's trap, as we see on the Enneagram of Traps, Diagram 9 in Appendix B. They often project inefficiency onto others, believing that they can do things better and faster than anyone else and not trusting others to get the job done. So they often end up trying to do it all themselves, whatever the task at hand happens to be. They often don't imagine that anyone could or would assist them, believing it's all up to them. They try to do everything quickly, getting as much accomplished as possible, and often do many things at the same time. So things are rushed through, often not done thoroughly, and quality gets sacrificed.

Modern life, which is progressively taking on more and more of a Three-ish character, is replete with things designed to increase our efficiency. Fast-food restaurants are springing up all over the planet, where you can order and eat without leaving your car. Packaged meals, modern versions of the TV dinners of the fifties, are a staple in many people's lives. Institutional cafeterias and take-out meals satisfy our physical needs while not slowing us down. We have cellular phones to carry everywhere with us so that we can always reach others and be reached, and televisions and even computers are now available in cars so that we miss nothing that is going on. This proliferation of technology that keeps us constantly in contact with the rest of the world is an interesting facsimile of the interconnectedness that is missing in a Three's consciousness.

Prefabricated houses, utilitarian and functional, can be assembled quickly, creating instant neighborhoods. Malls and supermarkets make shopping for a variety of things efficient and quick. And freeways get us wherever we are going rapidly, sacrificing the quality of the journey for speed. Many of these innovations of contemporary life are American, our culture being an uneasy blend of One-ish morality and puritan ethics, and Three-ish amoral expediency and personal ambition. The rest of the world emulates and often outdoes our packaging and promotion of the image and our headlong rush to success. Clothes and shoes with designer labels prominently displayed carry the Three message that you are what you wear. The wrapping substitutes for the substance, the surface for the depth. Silk flowers and plastic lawn animals imitate and replace life. Karaoke bars let you pretend that you are actually singing the song.

Pretense, falseness, and shallowness are words that often arise describing the feel of a Three, and this leads us to exploring the passion of this ennea-type, lying, as we see on the Enneagram of Passions in Diagram 2. The deepest lie a Three tells herself is that the personality is paramount; and in supporting it, she deceives both herself and others about what is truly real—real about herself and real about the nature of reality. This level of deceit is of course common to all those who are identified with their personality, which is most of humanity. It is the most dangerous form of deception because we believe it.

Although lying to themselves about who they really are is the deepest lie, many other varieties of lying are particular to Ennea-type Threes. There are outright lies that a Three is consciously telling—about her feelings, her past, her motives, about what really happened, what was said and by whom, and so forth. These lies are about getting the job done, getting what she wants, and impressing others as well as avoiding defeat or being perceived as failing, negligent, inefficient, or inept. There are the "little white lies" that are so much a part of conventional life, like "I never got the message that you called," or "Don't you look wonderful," when that is not at all what happened or what a Three feels. There are those in which the truth is stretched, twisted, or varnished to give it a different look. There are exaggerations, inflations, and embellishments of the truth. Things are fabricated and trumped up to create a particular impression or picture. Particular aspects of the truth may be highlighted, blown up, or enlarged upon, distorting the overall impression. All of these shades of lying are for a Three about creating and preserving a particular image both to herself and to others, which she feels she must do, and much of the prevarication is unconscious—she often actually believes she is telling the truth at the time.

This is another area that makes inner work very slippery for a Three. They very often do not know where the truth leaves off and the lie begins. The biggest deception is a self-deception about her inner reality, and hence self-deception occupies Point Three on the Enneagram of Lies, Diagram 12. It is sometimes difficult for Threes to separate out what they think they *ought* to feel, think, or believe, and what is actually the case for them. The identification with their role or function may be so complete that there is no internal space for any disparities. Unlike the other two image types, Ennea-types Two and Four, a Three's identification with her image is so total that she believes it is who she is. We might say of Threes what Holly Golightly's manager says of her in *Breakfast at Tiffany's,* "She's a *real* phony." Like perpetual method actors who never leave the stage, Threes become the role they are playing, forgetting that it is only a performance and believing it is who they are. This inextricable linkage between self and image, and self and function is another variety of lie. A Three may be so successful at convincing others that she is deeply religious or profoundly spiritually realized, gathering around herself numerous devoted followers, that she believes it herself and begins to think that she is beyond the mores and strictures that apply to others. If a Three's arena is business, she may be so influential and revered that she skirts the edge of the law, putting together deals or having affairs that she honestly believes will not, and cannot, have personal consequences.

The body part associated with Point Three is the thymus gland, and understanding its significance may help us comprehend something about what is necessary for a Three to evolve spiritually. The thymus is an organ of the lymphatic system located just behind the breastbone. While little is known about the actual functioning of the thymus, it is very important for the human immune system and needs to be present at birth for an infant to be healthy. It is most active in utero and during childhood; and as part of the immune system, it helps to distinguish "nonself" or foreign tissue and to attack malignant cells, fungal and viral infection, and bacteria.

Translating this in terms of consciousness, this tells us that discriminating what is oneself and what is nonself is crucial for a Three's development. A Three must first of all turn inward, no easy task for one whose sense of self resides in her reflection in the eyes of others and who subordinates inner experience to outer achievements. She needs to stop long enough to begin to face her inner truth—herself as she is—and this is where the virtue of Point Three, veracity, comes into play. We find it on the Enneagram of Virtues in Diagram 1. Ichazo's definition of veracity is as follows: "A healthy body can only express its own being; it cannot lie because it cannot be anything other than what it is." The word *veracity* has a few different meanings, all of which are relevant to the transformation and development of a Three. It means devotion to the truth, the power to convey or perceive truth, accuracy in the sense of conforming to truth or fact, and something true. In the following, we will discuss some of the highlights of a Three's inner journey to becoming an embodiment of truth.

For a Three to become veracious in the sense of being devoted to the truth, which is one definition of spiritual work, she will have to see how she lies to herself. This is the beginning of being truthful. The first level of lie she will have to confront is her belief that she is what she does. Only by understanding how dependent her self-esteem is upon her performance can she seriously begin to step off the stage and deal with her inner life. This will mean facing how little value she has to herself if she is not achieving something, which in turn will reveal the underpinnings of that attitude—the formative factors in her early childhood that left her with the conviction that she has no inherent value just as a person. She will probably have to reexperience how little real contact and love touched her soul as a child, and how the majority of attention she received was for her accomplishments, not for what she was feeling or even thinking about. She will see that just as her inner life received little notice or value from her parents, so, too, she ceased paying attention to her inner world. Inquiring into this will probably bring up a great deal of grief and pain for having so completely turned away from her soul.

The more she pays attention to herself, the more she will begin to perceive the extent of her identification with her image. She will discover how little of a gap there is between the face she presents and anything else going on inside of herself. This is a particularly painful juncture for a Three. It brings up feelings of superficiality and shallowness, and is fertile ground for her superego to give her a very difficult time. It has probably already been on her case for slowing down to look at herself in the first place. Here it attacks her for being so insubstantial and empty. If she can defend against its attacks and persevere in exploring her inner reality, she will see how extensive her identification with familial and cultural ideals has been. She will see how profoundly she has molded herself into the form of those ideals, to the extent that there is little left of her outside of that shape. She may find that she does not really know what she herself wants or feels outside of what she thinks she should, and more troubling still, that she does not even know how to begin asking herself those questions.

The degree of inner emptiness that will arise as she faces the extent of her identification with her image is profound. Because so much of her psyche and her life force have been invested in the image, there is so little else of her soul left for her to turn toward. So a yawning abyss faces her as her soul begins to let go of the investment in this façade. Because of this, Threes may have the most objectively painful inner journey of all of the ennea-types. If the image is a lie, what else does she have? This is a very difficult inner confrontation. She also doesn't feel that she can really rely on herself in this part of her inner terrain, because her sense of what is real and what is the truth is so changeable and untrustworthy. This is a problem that follows her throughout her inner work: discerning what is really true for her and what is the spin she has given things. So just like her holding environment as a young child, which felt profoundly unsupportive to her and left her with the belief that the only holding she will ever find will come from her own hands, she finds herself at this juncture to be undependable as well.

The other problem that dogs her process is her knee-jerk tendency to want to see results right away. She wants what she is discovering about herself to be useful—she wants her development to help her in her work in the world or in her relationships. She tends to try to package it and market it so that she will make some kind of profit from it, either materially or in the form of accolades for being so spiritually evolved. Most of all, she wants some payoff, rather than having to face the chasm of her inner emptiness, which looks distinctly unrewarding.

The emptiness brings up the dreaded feelings of defeat, the sense that despite all of her best efforts, she could not shape herself into God. This is the heart of her vanity as we have seen—her belief that she could bring about through her own efforts all of the plentitude and fulfillment of Being. On the face of it, that may sound like a ridiculous self-expectation, but for a Three, it is not. It is how she really feels deep down—the source of her feelings of failure and helplessness—whether conscious or not. Somewhere in her inner journey, this impossible demand on herself will have to emerge into consciousness and be seen for the absurdity that it is. She will see how all of her ceaseless doing has its roots in this vain attempt, in both senses of the word.

She will also see that her attempt to replicate God has been defensive, keeping her from having to face her disconnection from Being. Her endless activity has really been an escape from the huge empty place that feels to her like the entirety of her soul, which has resulted from her estrangement from her depths. She will see that she has taken this emptiness where she has lost contact with her Essence to be who she is, and so she felt little choice but to flee from it and do everything she could to replicate what she had lost. Compassion for herself will gradually arise as she understands this, and her heart will begin to become part of the picture for her. As her heart opens to herself, the emptiness will cease to feel as hopeless and frightening. Facing the truth of it and allowing herself to experience it fully, it will transform into a spaciousness that is profoundly still and peaceful. In time, all of the radiant colors and qualities of her essential nature will arise out of this inner space and display themselves in all their glory, like a cosmic peacock that her personality has been so busy imitating.

In the process, as she makes repeated forays into her inner reality, she will progressively feel more real, and less like a fake person. Rather than being only conscious of and living from the surface of the soul and feeling that there is nothing more to her, she will gradually feel more and more substantial and authentic. She will gradually stop living through images projected and experienced of herself; and veracity will become more and more of her lived experience. She will differentiate progressively from familial, societal, and cultural images and ideals, knowing where they stop and she begins.

The inner sense of being a phony, a fabrication, an imitation of a person, gives way to a sense of simplicity, naturalness, and genuineness. Her soul will become more and more transparent to the depths within herself, and her actions will bit by bit express and be informed by objective reality—her essential nature. She will find in time that she is not a someone who experiences Essence but that she *is* Essence. And little by little she will find herself feeling part of the fabric of the universe, a beautiful form within it, and will finally feel in harmony with the truth. She will become more and more of a real person, a conscious manifestation and embodiment of Being, and at long last she will really walk her talk—indeed becoming a Pearl Beyond Price.

ENNEA-TYPE ONE:
EGO-RESENTMENT

Ones are the perfectionists of the enneagram. They often look bright and shiny, with a clean and scrubbed quality, as well as a sense of righteousness and piety about them. Ones experience themselves as good people, trying to do what is correct, just, and moral, while often unconsciously, they see themselves as flawed or not fundamentally right. Taking the moral high ground, their antenna is out for what they perceive as imperfection or wrongness, which triggers their resentment and anger, since in their minds it should not be that way. Tolerating something that they see as not right feels almost impossible for them, and so they want to fix it and correct it. In particular, the behavior of others is often the target of their attempts to set things right. They are aligned with their superego, and tend to be judgmental and critical, both of themselves and of others.

Ones often feel burdened by their criticality and intolerance of imperfection but feel at a loss to do anything about it. The solution is for others to behave correctly and for things to go in ways that are optimal as they see it. They can be quite controlling, trying to make others do things the "right" way, although in their own minds they are simply trying to do the right thing. They are also self-controlling, restraining and holding themselves back from behaving, thinking, or feeling in ways that they consider wrong, immoral, or sinful. This self-constraint limits their spontaneity and vitality, which sometimes leak out in various forms of acting out, whether sexually, in terms of substance abuse, or in rages.

The Holy Idea that Ones have lost touch with is Holy Perfection. When we see reality from this angle, we perceive that it has an inherent rightness about it that is fundamental. The moment we step beyond the blinders of the personality, we see that implicit in all that exists are dimensions of increasing depth, of which the physical is the outermost and the Absolute, a state beyond manifestation, presence, even consciousness, the most fundamental—this is essentially the recognition of the existence of spiritual dimensions in all that exists. Or to put it differently, we see that everything is made up of and is therefore inseparable from True Nature. Beyond this perception of the multidimensionality of the universe, from the angle of Holy Perfection we see its perfection. We see that all that exists has a fundamental rightness to it and that everything that occurs is correct and perfect.

This Holy Idea is one of the more difficult to understand because even the sense in which the word *perfection* is used is so much at variance with egoic reality. When we say that something is perfect, what we are typically doing is measuring that thing against our inner yardstick of what we believe is ideal, and determining that it approximates that model. It is difficult to conceive of a sense of perfection that is not based on comparing one thing to another and judging which most closely resembles our inner standard of excellence and thus which seems better. Such a sense of perfection determined by comparative judgment is based on subjective standards that have been shaped by our culture, family values, and personal preferences and history, and is the only perfection known to the realm of the personality.

Without the filter of the subjective self, we see that all of existence has a quality of completeness, wholeness, and faultlessness just because it *is*. This sense of perfection that we experience when reality is seen through the lens of Holy Perfection is perhaps most closely conveyed by formulations borrowed from the traditions of the East: "isness" and "suchness." In Zen Buddhism, this view of things is called *kono-mama,* which translates as the "as-it-is-ness of this," or *sono-mama,* the "as-it-isness of that"; in Sanskrit the term is *tathata,* or "suchness"; and in Chinese it is *chih-mo* or *shih-mo.*[1] Perceiving this "as-it-is-ness" of things is perceiving the fundamental nature of them. In other words, if we see things as they are, what we see is the inner nature as well as the outer form of them. Each manifestation in the universe, be it planet, tree, or person, is seen here to be continuous with and inseparable from the fundamental nature common to all forms, and that fundamental nature is seen to be just right. The outer shape of one flower may be more graceful than the one next to it, but that has nothing to do with each flower's inherent rightness as it is, since both are manifestations of Being. From this perspective, to say that one flower is more perfect than another makes no sense.

It is difficult to understand how we can say that reality is perfect when there is so much suffering on the planet stemming from natural disasters, disease, and human foibles. Perhaps an analogy, borrowed from Almaas, will help to explain the perspective from which reality looks this way: We know from physics that atoms are the building blocks of all matter, and they in turn are made up of subatomic particles like electrons and photons, and smaller still, quarks and gluons. All atoms are complete, whole, and perfect unless they are altered, which is what happens when we create a nuclear explosion. At this atomic level, whether the atoms make up an emerald or excrement, the reality of each atom is still perfect.

Holy Perfection is only possible to glimpse when we are not living on the surface of our experience and of our lives. I think this is a very difficult Holy Idea to understand because this is the level most people live from. Perhaps the following quote from Almaas will make it clearer:

> *The way we ordinarily see the world is not the way it really is because we see it from the perspective of our judgments and preferences, our likes and dislikes, our fears and our ideas of how things should be. So to see things as they really are, which is to see things objectively, we have to put these aside—in other words, we have to let go of our minds. Seeing things objectively means that it doesn't matter whether we think what we're looking at*

is good or bad—it means just seeing it as it is. If a scientist is conducting an experiment, he doesn't say, "I don't like this so I'll ignore it." He may not personally care for the results because they don't confirm his theory, but pure science means seeing things the way they really are. If he says he is not going to pay attention to the experiment because he doesn't like it, that is not science. Yet, this is the way most of us deal with reality, inwardly and outwardly.[2]

It does not make sense to think of improving or of adding anything to atoms, and in the same way, the ultimate nature of reality is not improvable and cannot be made better than it is. When we are in touch with all of the dimensions of reality—when we are in touch with the fundamental nature of things, in other words—it becomes difficult to say that what transpires, even if physical or emotional pain results, should be different or that it is wrong.

Much of human suffering is the result of people experiencing and living their lives out of synch with their inner depths in which Holy Perfection is obvious. For those firmly entrenched in egoic reality, the surface of their lives and experience is a distortion of the fundamental perfection of their depths. On this level, people behave in ways that are hurtful and inconsiderate of others, to say the least, but this does not mean that who they fundamentally are is imperfect or wrong. Even if a person's consciousness is filled with hatred and greed, that person's soul is nonetheless made up of and inseparable from its depths and so it is inherently perfect. When the depth dimension is part of a person's conscious experience, it is not possible intentionally to hurt another person or cause harm without instantly suffering. From this perspective, we can see that no one is fundamentally bad, and that what we call evil is only based on judgments we make on the egoic level.

It is important to understand that I am not condoning humanity's mistreatment of each other, nor am I suggesting that those who treat others in harmful ways should go unpunished. I am simply saying that such behavior is only possible when we live our lives out of synch and out of touch with the totality that we are, and that such actions do not reflect our fundamental nature. I am also suggesting that our interpretations and judgments about what transpires both within and outside of ourselves are clouded by our subjective positions and beliefs, which often limit our perception of the larger picture.

When our view becomes deep enough, we can see the perfection even in things that seem tragic on the surface, such as a massive forest fire—which clears the ground for new growth; or a crippling accident, like that of Christopher Reeve—who has inspired millions with his courage and will to live. Even the terrible suffering of the Tibetan people at the hands of the Chinese may have served the deeper purpose of bringing the wisdom of Tibetan Buddhism to the rest of the world. Rather than deciding that something is bad, our response becomes one of compassion for the suffering that we see, which supports life, rather than rejecting what seems wrong to us, which doesn't help at all.

In terms of our experience of ourselves, Holy Perfection translates as meaning that who we are is inherently and implicitly perfect, that we are just right as we are, that we do not need anything added to us or subtracted from us. Integrating this understanding may totally change our approach to inner work, since from this angle we see that we do not need to become better, that we do not need to be different, and that there is nothing fundamentally wrong with us. All we really need to do is to connect with and realize our inherent perfection. From the enlightened perspective of Point One, that is all working on oneself is for and all that it is about.

As we integrate the view of reality seen from the angle of Holy Perfection and become conscious of the inherent perfection of everything, our inner experience and, as a result, our lives, align and express that level of reality. In other words, to the extent that we are in touch with Holy Perfection, our lives take on a quality of extraordinariness and sublimity, and we feel that what occurs in our lives is on the mark—just what is needed and what is appropriate both for ourselves and others. This is real change—far more radical and basic than self-improvement. We will discuss a bit about how this comes about for Ones when we explore the virtue of this point at the end of this chapter.

—⁓— For an Ennea-type One, losing contact with his essential nature feels like losing touch with the inherent perfection of all that exists and with his own intrinsic perfection. To the young soul of a One, contact with Essence was experienced as the ultimate perfection, a sense of bliss, of heaven on earth, a condition where his soul was totally relaxed and fulfilled, in which nothing needed to be done and he could rest and settle into his depths. When direct contact with that profound sense of perfection is lost, the result is a deep sense of anguish that he is no longer abiding in that perfection and cannot get in touch with it. He loses the sense that he and reality are fundamentally just right, whole, and complete; and this absense is felt as a not-rightness—a wrongness. He comes to feel that he is imperfect, and it may seem to him as if the very substance of his soul had a fundamental flaw, a basic badness or wrongness about it. There arises a mental fixation or underlying and all-pervasive belief that he and the reality he perceives are essentially imperfect, not good enough. We find this fixation encapsulated by the word resentment on Diagram 2. What is really amiss is that he has lost contact with his depths, but this loss appears as or is interpreted as being basically damaged goods. In other words, the inner felt experience that results from nonperception of Essence for a One feels like a wrongness. This becomes an inner conviction that he is tainted and bad, the sense that he has a fatal flaw and is not made of the right substance. This is the cognitive distortion underlying all of the other characteristics of this ennea-type, and it is what is termed his deficiency in rightness on the Enneagram of Avoidances, Diagram 10 in Appendix B—his painful core sense of deficiency, which feels too intolerable to experience fully.

This sense of basic imperfection may arise in concert with an early childhood in which the message was communicated directly or interpreted internally that he just wasn't good enough or wasn't the right thing. This may have resulted from his biological needs being subtly or overtly judged and rejected, leading to the sense that they were wrong, or from having an overcritical and emotionally withholding parent who imposed very high standards that seemed to the young One impossible to live up to. One or both parents may have had very One-ish tendencies such as strong moral judgmentalness and fundamental religious beliefs. Sometimes the whole early situation was a setup, in which he was looked to by the parents to fulfill unfillable needs, such as replacing a lost loved one, resulting in a profound sense of not being good enough or having what it takes for the task.

Regardless of the source, the One is left with the sense of not being what was needed or wanted in the environment and of being somehow wrong. In order to return to his prior state of bliss, it becomes critical for him to deduce, form, and create an idea of what perfection is. He tries to figure out what mom wants, what will restore the sense of harmony and once again allow his soul to relax and reconnect him with the lost perfection. So his instinctual drive to reestablish homeostasis is turned toward trying to be good, achieve perfection, and make mommy happy. Eventually his drive energy gets fully coopted into this striving for perfection, and in time this quest turns him against his own instinctual energy. Ultimately the perfection he seeks is his depths—the realm of Being—with which he has lost touch, and the memory of contact with this realm takes on the distorted outlines of ideals that the One uses as his subjective yardstick. Reality, inner and outer, is gauged against these pictures and beliefs of how things ought to be, and the relative distance to "perfect" is calculated. Inevitably reality always falls short of his standards, and he seems unable to perceive anything as perfect, particularly himself. This is the source of his intense self-criticism, in which he is constantly judging and rebuking himself for his imperfections.

This assessment of proximity to the ideal is definitely not neutral. A further step is then taken, which turns the Ennea-type One into a perfectionist: what is not perfect is deemed bad. To tolerate what he determines to be bad would mean tolerating his estrangement from Being, which in the depths of his soul is intolerable, and so what is bad becomes unacceptable. In this way, he creates distance and defends himself against the experience of loss of Being.

A One's judgments about what is good and what is bad are relative, determined by his own orientation. So being sexually liberated might be seen by a feminist One as good, while to a born-again Christian, it would probably seem bad. Whether conservative or liberal, however, Ones tend toward orthodoxy in whatever views they hold. It is important to them to be politically correct—or in spiritual circles, spiritually so—and to hold tenaciously what they consider to be the right "line."

With his determinations of good and bad in place, it becomes obvious then what needs to be done: he sets about trying to improve himself and others to make them good and therefore acceptable. This becomes an inner orientation and way of relating to life both inwardly and outwardly: trying to make things better. Driven by this deep feeling of wrongness, Ones are constantly striving to correct things, and are restless and anxious about the way things are, which to them is not as they should be. The quest for perfection, then, is his trap, as we see on Diagram 9.

This orientation toward perfection is apparent in the extreme need of Ones to be seen as good and, conversely, in the extreme difficulty that they have when what they consider a flaw or imperfection is pointed out to them. Feedback becomes instantly translated internally into criticism, which they may fend off by becoming defensive, obviously trying to resurrect an inner evaluation of being good. When they confront a psychological issue or an undeveloped capacity, they believe that they should already have mastered the difficulty, they judge themselves harshly, and then assume that since they have not resolved it yet that they never will. Then they feel hopeless about themselves, assuming that something is wrong with them, confirming their underlying sense of wrongness. When they relate to themselves in this way, as though they should already be enlightened, it is clear that there is little room for growth and little tolerance for development in the inner world of a One. On the other hand, Ones sometimes look for criticism from others as a way of orienting themselves in terms of knowing what is wrong and therefore what needs fixing and how to do it.

Another manifestation of this need for things to be good is an intolerance of negative emotions. It is very difficult for a One to tolerate complaints, sadness, or hostility both in themselves and in others. They tend to try to keep things positive, and will offer counsel such as, "Cheer up— think of all you have to be grateful for," "How can you be unhappy—you have so much going for you," and "Look on the sunny side of things," even to the point of telling the other person that they are not *really* feeling sad or ill. Or, trying to make things better, a One might give advice such as "Just do this and everything will be fine." Allowing the negative threatens to bring up his unbearable sense of wrongness.

They try hard—and pride themselves on trying harder than others—to correct and make things better. They have a sense of moral superiority, driven by an inner gyroscope of what is right and good. They preach, advise, crusade, and try to help others become more the way Ones believe they should be, feeling a sense of mission to achieve perfection even if it means wringing it out of the world around them. This was exemplified in the turn of the century "white man's burden" of bringing civilization to the "less developed" races, believing Christianity and Western culture would save the souls of those they regarded as heathens. They are grammarians, moralists, and experts about what is proper and how to do things correctly. Miss Manners comes to mind, as well as Martha Stewart, who tells us how to do things perfectly around our homes, and in her magazine *Martha Stewart: Living* devotes a section to "good things."

Dedicated to what appears to a One as right, it is inconceivable to him that there might be more than one correct way things could be, and so there is little room in his mind for divergence from his opinion. He has little regard or respect for the boundaries or the wishes of others in his quest to make things perfect, since what is right supersedes all personal preferences in his opinion. Making the world perfect is for Ones a just and noble cause in which they are the champions. They are the good cops, policing the world. Proud of their own self-control, they are often very controlling of others. What you do is their business, and they let you know when you are stepping out of line.

While these perfectionistic traits may be difficult for others and are also often painful for Ones themselves, they feel obligated to do what they perceive as right; this is an obligation rooted in their love and loyalty for the lost sense of perfection. This continual effort to perfect themselves and the surrounding world becomes in itself idealized, and it is part of what they believe makes them good. The way this works is that even though they feel they are fundamentally bad, because they know this and are trying to be better, they have some chance at redemption. In fact, to stop trying to improve things often means to Ones losing the only shred of goodness that they feel they have and losing their only hope of finding the lost sense of precious perfection. To stop this trying would be tantamount to succumbing to their estrangement from True Nature and really being without any possibility of salvation. Trying to change things becomes viewed as noble, and so they become evangelical, zealots for the "good." The focus gets shifted in the process from their inner sense of imperfection—which often gets buried in the unconscious—to all the flaws they see in others and in the world. The effort to make reality conform to their ideals becomes a kind of holy crusade, which sometimes feels uplifting and at other times a cause they resent feeling compelled to participate in. We will return to this resentment that gives this ennea-type its name when discussing the passion.

The Crusades of the Middle Ages exemplify on a mass scale what it is like to be a One. Christian Europeans believed they had a moral obligation to save the Holy Land from the infidels and that they would be ennobled by making this effort, even if they failed. From a psychological point of view, every One becomes identified with his superego, fighting a campaign against the inner infidel, which to him resides in the seething cauldron of instinctual drives that is the id. Inner pictures of how he should be stand in stark and anxiety-provoking contrast to the dark and forbidden impulses of the instinctual self. To a One, this instinctual self is seen as the enemy, as what is wrong with himself and others. This is because the instinctual self is essentially self-centered and pleasure driven, oblivious to others except as sources of gratification, uninterested in anything beyond corporeal enjoyment, and is greedy, amoral, and unrefined. It feels animalistic, although animals are never as base and gross as this part of human beings is.

There is a grain of truth buried in the belief that this instinctual self is the problem. We have seen that it is the reactivity to impingements and unmet physical needs in early infancy that gradually severs the soul's connection to Being, as discussed in Chapter 1. We become identified with the body and its instinctual drives, and the paradise of oneness with Being becomes a distant dream. The Ennea-type One deals with this animal part—which, it is important to remember, all of us have—by identifying with what he considers to be the "good" parts of himself: those that are virtuous, selfless, compassionate, and benevolent. Through his superego, he tries to control and reform the "bad" instinctual parts and so becomes identified with being on the side of the good. In his righteousness about fighting the good inner fight, he neglects to see that his rejection of the primitive within does not transform it but instead only gives it more power in the unconscious and causes it to leak out behaviorally in one way or another. We have seen this exemplified often enough in the religious zealots who preach about morality and decry sinfulness, only to be caught in seedy and scandalous sexual peccadilloes or revealed to have embezzled vast sums of money from their faithful flocks.

He also ignores the fact that a great deal of aggression, which itself is fueled by the rejected and buried instinctual self, goes into his quest to make things good and right. Because this aggression is unacceptable in its raw form and so blocked, it is no longer pure instinctual drive but rather a distortion of it. This distortion takes the form of anger, the passion of this ennea-type, as we see on the Enneagram of Passions in Diagram 2. He is angry at the bad, to put it succinctly, and his anger is an attempt to change it while at the same time distancing himself from it.

Ichazo, according to Naranjo, defines anger as a "standing against reality,"[3] and perhaps this sense of being at odds with what is, most purely describes this passion. Ones meet reality with preconceptions/false affirmation, the phrase that appears at Point One on the Enneagram of Lies, Diagram 12. With their sense of how things ought to be acting as a compass, Ones pit themselves against and try to change what they encounter both inwardly and outwardly. Nothing is ever quite right, and so they are never satisfied. Feeling responsible for fixing what they perceive as bad, they end up feeling frustrated and resentful.

This perpetual hostility toward reality, which is the passion of anger, is at root a malice toward himself: he is self-resenting, dissatisfied with and indignant toward his own soul, as we see on the Enneagram of Anti-self Actions, Diagram 11. His anger has many nuances. It covers the spectrum from an underlying resentfulness thinly concealed beneath a veneer of politeness to violent outbursts of pure rage. Along with his sense of being wrong, directly experiencing his anger is a One's most avoided experience, and this is why anger also appears on the Enneagram of Avoidances, Diagram 10. Most Ones repress their anger unless they are convinced that it is objective, and then they feel justified in giving vent to it. Some Ones simply seem perpetually annoyed, peeved, and irritated by everything and everyone, while others have flashes of righteous indignation which feel fully warranted because of the "obvious" badness, meanness, or unworthiness of another. Some Ones are like pressure cookers who keep a lid on their rage until it reaches critical mass and they blow the gasket. They may appear calm and serene most of the time, but in the privacy of their own homes with those they feel comfortable with, they explode in critical tirades or violent rages complete with thrown dishes, slamming of doors, if not physical violence.

The anger may manifest as a general attitude of faultfinding, criticality, nit-picking, and fussiness in which the One emanates the message that things are just not up to snuff; or a One may point out all of your flaws and offer supposedly helpful "constructive criticism," given for the best of reasons—your own good—which cuts nonetheless to the quick. They may be constantly correcting your grammar or making it painfully clear to you which unspoken rule you are breaking. They tend to be preachy and take the role of teacher or exemplar. They may give you unsolicited advice—which they really feel is for your own good—in which they communicate the obvious fact, in their eyes, that they know what is right and you clearly do not and are screwing up in one way or another. Ones may not recognize their criticalness and advice giving as adversarial and belligerent, but the hurt and anger triggered in those on the receiving end leave no doubt about the One's underlying and often unconscious aggression.

It is easy for a One to recognize and align himself with his anger if he feels justified, i.e., that he is right and correct, or if his anger can be made into a cause in which God or goodness appears to be on his side. And it is relatively easy for him to feel that his anger is warranted when the wrongness appears to reside firmly outside of himself, as it seems to a One who has done little introspection and inner work. Internally the "bad" parts of himself are pushed away, and so they also appear to be outside of the good self he takes himself to be, and his aggression is directed just as mercilessly against these bad parts as it is toward the badness he sees in others. The more conscious a One becomes, however, the more he will see that his underlying critical and angry attitude is itself an issue. The compulsive assessing, carping, and fits of pique themselves become an enormous source of anguish to a One. His internal self-criticism and relentless self-blame, which become obvious once he turns his attention from outside himself to what is going on inside, in time come to be felt as brutal and hurtful, and perhaps not serving what is good after all.

Just as the aggressive drive of the instinctual self becomes distorted into the various shades of anger, the libidinal drive also undergoes a twist: sexuality becomes a highly conflictual area for Ones. It is viewed as naughty, if not downright bad and immoral, since there is so much un-bridled instinctual energy involved and so little control. If sex can be jus-tified as fulfilling some higher purpose than pure mutual pleasure, such as doing one's duty to procreate for the good of one's nation or religion, then it is tolerable—if it is not enjoyed too much.

Physical pleasure is itself subversive and suspect to most Ones, cer-tainly those of previous generations. Contemporary Ones tend to be more liberal sexually but nonetheless still have difficulty and often guilt about fully allowing themselves pleasure. Enjoying himself, being carefree, and—God forbid!—hedonistic smack of amorality to many a One, and so are forbidden territory. Fully allowing himself to feel saturated in pleasure seems sinful. Underlying this judgment is fear—of his superego ruth-lessly judging him, of enormous guilt, and of losing control—and so is not allowed. It is as though allowing pleasure would be opening Pandora's box and would lead to becoming a slave of his animal instincts and there-fore perpetually running amok. There is a self-denying, self-punishing, or self-castigating and penitent quality about a One's sexual inhibition and restraint. As a result, a One's sexuality remains largely unintegrated, re-maining raw, crude, juvenile, and often quite awkward. It often retains the feel of a schoolboy or schoolgirl doing something very lewd and nasty that they seem not too familiar with but are nonetheless tantalized by.

The disparaged and thus suppressed instinctual drives sometimes break through in Ones in episodes of uncontrolled and uncontrollable act-ing out alluded to earlier. In the extreme, this is what happens in the fiery bouts of rage mentioned above, and in the scandals that surface from time to time in which some prominent member of Congress or the British Parliament, for example, turns out to have a propensity for kinky sex with prostitutes or transvestites; or when a priest is revealed to have had ongoing affairs with his female parishioners, particularly the married ones, or to have molested his choirboys; when the proselytizing twelve-stepper disappears for days at a time on drunken binges about which he remembers nothing later; and when the antiwar activist turns out to have a long history of spousal abuse. Less extreme ways that a One's suppressed drives leak out might be in dreams of debauchery, fantasies of lewd orgies, reading steamy romance novels, or watching X-rated videos or television while professing to deplore licentiousness.

Ones have what is clinically called an obsessional character. They are methodical, organized, collected, productive, and hardworking. They tend to be compulsively neat and tidy, wanting everything to be both clean and in its proper place. This can reach the extreme of being truly obsessive, in which the person is driven by an inordinate need for order, is miserly and totally inflexible—as was the character Melvin Udall in the film *As Good As It Gets.* Some Ones are so obsessed with doing things perfectly and thoroughly that it takes them forever to get anything accomplished, while others rush through things out of anxiousness about their capacity to do the job well and also out of a desire to unburden themselves of the responsibility. This same insecurity may arise around decision making: fearing that they will make the wrong choice, they often procrastinate. All of these characteristics are, from a clinical point of view, of the obsessive-compulsive variety, and are the manifestations of deep superego and id conflicts, which we have discussed earlier. Seen from this angle, the obsessive tendencies in a One are attempts to clean himself up and make himself pure, as well as a means of expiating the profound inner guilt for his "imperfections."

The preoccupation with cleanliness belies an attempt to eradicate an inner sense of uncleanness, just as the preoccupation with orderliness bespeaks a fending off of internal chaos resulting from unintegrated instinctual energies. This attempt to keep an anxiety-provoking state or emotion firmly locked away in the unconscious by overemphasizing its opposite brings us to and describes the defense mechanism of this ennea-type, which is called reaction formation. In reaction formation, whatever emotion or behavior we believe to be dangerous to feel or act upon gets pushed out of consciousness, and an opposite and acceptable emotion or behavior replaces it. If feeling hatred is taboo, for example, we might defend against the inner threat of feeling it by experiencing love instead. On the other hand, if we are afraid of love, we might substitute rejection, indifference, or hatred in its stead. Reaction formation lies behind the mechanism central to Ones in which the sense of being bad is warded off by identifying with their superego and seeing themselves as good and others as bad. It also underlies the One's continual staving off of instinctual temptations through morally pitting themselves against them. As Charles Brenner says about reaction formation:

> One consequence of our knowledge of the operation of this defense mechanism is that whenever we observe an attitude of this sort which is unrealistic or excessive, we wonder whether it may not be so overemphasized as a defense against its opposite. Thus we should expect that a devoted pacifist or antivivisectionist, for instance, has unconscious fantasies of cruelty and hatred which appear to his ego to be particularly dangerous.[4]

Ultimately Ones are defending against a deep inner sense of wrongness though imitating purity and goodness.

Keeping at bay forbidden urges and the perception of forbidden flaws requires of Ones a great deal of inner discipline and self-control. The attempts to control others and the environment are a mirror of this internal checking, curbing, and restraining of themselves. The result is a characteristic stiffness and lack of spontaneity. This may make them appear stilted in their movements, manner, or speech as they carefully and deliberately rein themselves in and hold themselves back. Their thinking may reflect this tendency, making them stick to known and accepted ideas, and not venturing into anything more creative. Their ideas tend to become rigid and fixed, with little room for innovation or experimentation. What does not clearly fall within their concept of rightness is threatening, and so playing with ideas that have not found their way into categories of right or wrong, good or bad tends to be anxiety provoking. When a new idea or insight does arise, it becomes a new standard, reflecting their tendency to make rules out of truth. They are sticklers for following the rules and the law dogmatically, disregarding the uniqueness of a particular situation. There is for them a certain security in methodically following preestablished guidelines, and a corresponding insecurity that arises in questioning underlying principles.

Energetically and emotionally the self-control of Ones leads to a particular kind of rigidity and contraction. While some Ones do not experience or express negative emotions like pain and fear, even in those who do, there is a characteristic lack of ease, relaxation, flexibility, vulnerability, and softness about them, a sense that their guard is always up. They tend to have a tight-jawed and tight-lipped quality, related to curbing their wants and stopping the expression of their anger, which, along with their propensity for advice giving and preaching, accounts for the mouth being the part of the body associated with this type. At the extreme, they seem to others pinched, severe, austere, straitlaced, formal, humorless, prosaic, and stiff-necked. To his detriment during his presidency, the persona of Jimmy Carter exemplifies this One-ish quality; and Hillary Rodham Clinton is sometimes perceived in this way. Other exemplars displaying less of this stiffness who were or are probably Ones include Jimmy Stewart and Katharine Hepburn and, more currently, Anthony Edwards, Barbra Streisand, Nicole Kidman, and Cybill Shepherd. Dana Carvey's Church Lady is a great caricature of a One.

Ones tend to be inflexible and uncompromising when they believe they are correct. There is little room for discussion and disagreement with a One once they have made up their minds about something, and they are tenacious once fixed on something. It is perhaps for this reason that the animal associated with this type is the dog, who can chew on a bone that cannot be wrested from him. Dogs are also unswervingly loyal, as Ones are, to what they consider right.

Ones, then, come across as good, clean, nice people—with a lot of latent hostility and frustration. They are compulsively honest, the George Washingtons who cannot tell a lie—even if the truth hurts another. They are dependable, trustworthy, and hardworking—righteously so. They are earnest and clean-faced—to the point of plainness, as exemplified in the farming couple in the famous painting *American Gothic.* They are people driven by good intentions—even if you don't want their charity—and high moral standards—to the point of becoming puritanical.

Puritanism itself is a One-ish phenomenon. The American Puritans of the seventeenth century broke away from the Anglican Church, which was far too liberal for them, and brought their religious fervor to the New World. They believed that God is absolutely sovereign, that man is totally depraved and completely dependent on God's grace for redemption. Believing themselves to be God's elect with a mission to enforce His Will in the nascent commonwealth, they dictated colonial politics until their influence declined in the eighteenth century. These Pilgrims, the Founding Fathers of the United States, are the source of the very One-ish current in American culture: our strong sense of morality, of doing what is good, right, and just, as well as our tendency to act as the world's moral enforcer. The current hyperinterest in and scrutiny of presidential sexuality, which is inconceivable and incongruous to Europeans, for instance, who do not have such a history of moral aspiration, reflects this One-ish cultural strain. American idealism and emphasis on being good coexist uneasily with the other dominant cultural current, our Three-ish drive for personal success and gain with its self-serving amorality, as mentioned in the previous chapter.

One-ish behavior is also associated with Victorianism, named for Queen Victoria, although Prince Albert is really responsible for the prudishness and austerity associated with the era. He imposed strict decorum at the English court and infused propriety and primness into British cultural mores. The English culture seems to be a mix of One and Four tendencies—its emphasis on social form and decorum, and its aesthetic inclinations resulting from the latter—with its current queen, Elizabeth, and perhaps Elizabeth I as well, seeming to be Ennea-type Ones.

More currently, we see One-ish phenomena in the right-to-life movement, whose defense of life paradoxically does not prevent extremists from killing doctors who perform abortions or blowing up Planned Parenthood centers. A more widespread example would be advocates for social reform who have very little consideration for actual people. We see it whenever there is a group who believes that they are right and have God on their side and pit themselves against another group whom they see as

bad or wrong. Bertolt Brecht may have been summarizing One-ish philosophy when he wrote, "We who wanted a world based on kindness could
not ourselves be kind."

⎯∿⎯ We have seen that the personality traits of each of the ennea-
types mimic and attempt to replicate a particular spiritual state, as
though the soul were attempting to reconnect with the lost Holy Idea by
shaping itself into a copy of a state that seems to embody this missing
Idea. In the case of Ennea-type One, this state—the idealized Aspect—is
called Brilliancy in the terminology of the Diamond Approach. Brilliancy
is the intelligence of Being. It is a particular presence that is like a flash of
lightning or the sparkling of sunlight on the ocean. It has a brightness
to it, an illuminating quality, a radiance, a clarity, an acuity. It is Being
penetrating with its intelligence, and discerning, understanding, and
synthesizing what it encounters. We ordinarily think of intelligence or
brightness as being purely mental qualities, but here we see that true intelligence is something more than that. It is the intelligence of our souls
when we are truly being, when we are fully present. Being fully present
means that we are embodied and open emotionally to what our consciousness comes in contact with, and when our intelligence penetrates
what we encounter, we experience this bright presence.

The state of Brilliancy also has the qualities of purity, timelessness,
and refinement about it. Like the pure radiance in a flash of insight, Brilliancy illumines the soul with understanding in a way that is clean, clear,
and right to the point. One of its central characteristics is its synthetic capacity, in which all of the elements of a situation form a unity in the
mind, all the various threads merge into one understanding. Brilliancy is
the source of the human ability to synthesize—it is what we experience in
the moment that all the elements of a situation come together and form a
whole within us. It is also the source of true wisdom. The purity of Brilliancy opens the heart of a One. His heart's desire is to see purely and completely and to experience himself as pure and complete. Brilliancy holds
for him the promise of connecting him with his lost sense of perfection. It
is the Essential Aspect or state of consciousness that feels like the embodiment of the lost Holy Perfection.

Imitation Brilliancy takes the form of having to have the correct answers and needing to be right, and of being a know-it-all who thinks in a way that is divorced from experiential contact. Such knowing is intellectual, of the mind only, and has little to do with the situation at hand. When we are being falsely brilliant, we are convinced that our view is the correct one, that how we see things is how they are. We are taking a position of asserting our identity as someone who has the correct knowledge. Such preconceived ideas can only be based on opinion and on the past, and this "someone" we take ourselves to be is inevitably a mental construct, and so not immediate.

Seen from this angle, Ennea-type One looks uncannily like a facsimile of Brilliancy. The overriding concern about being right and being good, which assumes that there is only one right answer or way to be and that they need to figure it out and live it, as well as the overarching characteristic of meeting life with preconceived standards, illustrates this. These central traits of Ones are distortions of the direct knowing that arises when we contact the moment in a direct and experiential way, with a freshness devoid of preconceptions. The One's drive to be pure is an emulation of the purity inherent in the experience of Brilliancy. Their proclivity to impose their values and standards upon others is an emulation of the quality of our true intelligence, which knows no boundaries and can penetrate into anything we wish to understand. Their sharpness, whether in manner or in criticality, emulates the acuity and precision of Brilliancy. Ironically, many Ones, such as Hillary Rodham Clinton, have a shiny, scrubbed, and clean appearance, reflecting the luminosity of this essential quality that they are attempting to embody.

⸺ To transform their consciousness, Ennea-type Ones need to approach their inner process as well as their outer lives with an attitude of serenity, the virtue of this point, as we see on the Enneagram of Virtues in Diagram 1. What does serenity mean in this context? Primarily it means not going along with the personality's characteristic tendency to react against what we are experiencing. When we are identified with our personality, instead of simply allowing and being with our experience, we try to do something about, to, or with it. We cannot just leave it alone and be open to touching it directly with our consciousness so that understanding can arise. This is the pitting of oneself against reality which, as we have seen, is Ichazo's definition of anger, the passion of this ennea-type. When we oppose our experience, we are simply reinforcing the "I" that is reacting. We are, in other words, strengthening our personality and our identification with it.

While all personality types share this kind of reactivity, it is most central to Ones and is the biggest stumbling block in their inner work. It is very difficult for Ones to relate to inner experiences or perceptions about themselves without immediately evaluating them, i.e., attempting to ascertain whether they are good or bad, on the basis of judgments and evaluations rooted in the past. This is a reflexive reaction for Ones, a central and compulsive inner movement, and it is hard for them to imagine responding to their experience in any other way. If a One decides that what he is experiencing is bad, he tries to change it so that it is good. If he decides that a perception about himself is bad, he becomes defensive about it. In either case, he does not leave the experience alone, meeting it as it is, without an attitude toward it. Although the focus remains primarily on what is not right about his experience, sometimes what he encounters he decides is good—at least momentarily. If so, he tries to hold on to the experience, and that clutching disengages him from it. Any reaction to our experience—whether moving toward it, away from it, or trying to alter it—creates a contraction in the soul and blocks our capacity to learn from it. Our Brilliancy cannot function and we cannot understand ourselves more deeply, which is what is necessary for our consciousness to grow and change.

Anger blinds us to the truth. When we are in its grip, we are defending ourselves against what we are reacting to. We are trying to push it away or push at it to change it, and we are caught in the grip of our subjective reality. We are supporting who we take ourselves to be, and we are siding with and defending our identifications. Rather than trying to understand what button inside of our own psyches has been triggered, we are set against the object of our wrath.

If we are serious about discovering the truth of who we are, an orientation of serenity toward our experience is necessary. Serenity means meeting the moment with openness of heart and mind—accepting whatever arises within or without—and not contracting against it. Rather than habitually judging or evaluating our experience, we simply open, allowing ourselves to be touched by what is there. This necessitates allowing ourselves not to know, which in turn means defending against our superego's demands for certainty. It also means letting go of our beliefs about what should or shouldn't be happening, and about what is good or bad. It means not protecting ourselves from what we consider bad, unpleasant, or uncomfortable. It means letting our consciousness fully meet our experience so that we can know directly what it is that we are in touch with. As we do this, we open to the truth of the moment, and so our consciousness can be impacted by it. Rather than attempting to preserve a positive sense of self, we see ourselves as we really are. Without our judgments, what we find is just what is, unobscured with veils from our past.

So for a One, a serene attitude toward himself initiates specific stages of inner transformation. These stages begin with perceiving his identification with the superego—seeing in bold relief the pattern of judgments and standards, seeing their arbitrariness, and the suffering, pain, and torment within that they cause. He needs to understand why this need for standards is so strong, which will mean understanding it as a defense against experiencing himself as bad as well as against deeper layers of his personality, and as his hope for return to the lost bliss of perfection. The psychodynamics—the influences of his history in creating this pattern— also need to be seen and digested. His habitual defensive attitude toward what he experiences as criticism and toward what he considers not good about himself will also need to be perceived and understood. This will eventually lead to a relaxing of the need to evaluate his experience and set himself in opposition to it. Gradually as he becomes more open and non-reactive—i.e., more serene—the parts of himself that he has been judging and defending against will begin to reveal themselves. Emotional states that he has viewed as negative will arise that he increasingly learns to tolerate and feel fully, and these in turn begin to be transformed. The more that he embraces and accepts these aspects of himself, the more his soul relaxes, and his ego activity stills with the sense that there is nothing to do and nothing to fix inside.

Ichazo's definition of the virtue of serenity might be useful here: "It is emotional calm, expressed by a body at ease with itself and receptive to the energy of the Kath [the belly center]. Serenity is not a mental attitude but the natural expression of wholeness in a human being secure in his capacities and totally self-contained." So rather than attempting to be perfect, he experiences his completeness, and so is serene. Access to the belly center comes through integrating his instinctual layer. The source of many of his drives and feelings, this layer will come to the surface of consciousness and needs to be digested through awareness and understanding of it. As he does this, these deep drives that he has been so busily defending against become more and more refined and less and less compulsive.

Beneath his object relations and the animal-like parts of the soul, he encounters empty places that he initially interprets as meaning that he is bad and not good enough. To the extent that he does not react to these holes, his consciousness can investigate and penetrate them. A profound inner spaciousness arises to which the labels "good" and "bad" have no relevance. Beyond the obscuring structures that clouded his consciousness, the vibrancy and aliveness of Being gradually shine through. Integrating these aspects of himself makes him and his life increasingly feel more rich, three-dimensional, real, full, spontaneous, unpredictable, and wondrous.

This process is neither linear nor rapid, and while each individual One's traveling of this territory will have individual variations, these are the rough outlines. The receptivity and openness to inner experience, which are the attitude of serenity, are necessary at each juncture. At the same time, serenity becomes more and more of an inner state as a One's inner work progresses. The Latin root of the word *serene* means "clear, unclouded, and untroubled." This is how a One becomes as he progressively ceases reacting to his experience. Who he is beyond the clouds of the personality—the veils of his historical self—becomes clearer and clearer and he sees reality increasingly more objectively, as it is. In the process, his consciousness calms down and he becomes less easily ruffled. His heart opens, his mind relaxes, and his perception becomes more transparent—truly brilliant. Perceiving with love and enjoyment instead of judgment, he can settle into the moment and just be. More and more consistently, he abides in a deep inner quietude and is at peace with himself and the world. He can at last know his inherent and unalterable perfection.

CHAPTER 6

ENNEA-TYPE FOUR: EGO-MELANCHOLY

Fours are dramatic, emotive, romantic, and seem to suffer more than the other types. There is often a tragic quality about Fours, arising from an inner hopelessness about ever being truly content. It is as though they are eternally pining for a lost connection that has been missing as long as they have been alive, and the inner grief seems inconsolable and forever unchangeable. In some Fours, this melancholy is obvious, while other Fours appear very upbeat and exuberant. The zeal behind such a Four's efforts to present herself as buoyant and optimistic, however, belies the despair underneath this façade.

Fours want to be seen as unique, original, aesthetic, and creative; and being one of the image types—those on either side of and including Ennea-type Three—present themselves in this way. They value their refined taste and sensitivity, which they usually feel is deeper and more profound than that of others. While they often seem superior and standoffish, inwardly they feel socially insecure, afraid of not being loved and included. They tend to feel alone and abandoned, estranged and not really reachable by others. Their primary focus is usually on relationship, which more often than not is fraught with problems and frustrations. They long for connection with others, but satisfying relationships always seem to elude them. Others appear to have more fulfilling lives and relationships than they do, and so they experience a great deal of envy. How they are and how others are is never quite right, and they yearn for things to be different.

The lost vantage point on reality—the Holy Idea—underlying this ennea-type is Holy Origin. Depending upon our degree of consciousness, we can understand this Holy Idea in different ways. If we take who we are to be our bodies and so are primarily identified with physical reality, Holy Origin tells us that all of life originates from a common source and obeys shared natural laws. In terms of a common source on the physical level, the big bang theory postulates that the entire universe was generated in one giant cosmic explosion, and so all that exists has its roots in this moment of creation. Universal principles that govern all of life are recognized in astro- and subatomic physics, in biology, as well as in the sciences that specifically deal with human beings: sociology, anthropology, psychology, and so on. Celestial phenomena in distant galaxies obey the same laws of physics as phenomena in our own solar system and on our own planet. Life on earth is currently understood as originating from a common spark igniting in the primordial soup, so on a physical level, all of nature appears to have a collective source. All human beings are born and develop physically in the same way regardless of ethnicity or culture, and all are subject to the same genetic and biological laws. While each of our faces and bodies is slightly different and therefore unique, the overarching physical blueprint is nonetheless the same. So from the most universal physical phenomena right down to our own bodies, all of matter is united by collective principles.

At another level of consciousness, when we know ourselves to be more than our physical form and recognize that it is our soul that inhabits and animates our body, we understand Holy Origin as saying that all human beings share this characteristic. To know ourselves to be something beyond the physical is to recognize the realm of Spirit as part of our existence. The recognition of soul as our nature, then, leads us to the Spirit of which each soul is a part. We see here, then, on this level of understanding Holy Origin, that Being is the Source out of which all individual souls arise. So while each of us is a unique soul, we all have as our fundamental ground the realm of True Nature. On this level, not only is Being or True Nature seen as the wellspring of the human soul but it is also seen as the source of all of manifestation. Everything, then, is seen here to originate out of Being, and to return to it when that manifestation ends. Our orientation at this level is with ourselves as separate entities whose inner nature arises from a Source common to all that exists.

Beyond this comprehension of Holy Origin is another level grounded in the realization that all of manifestation not only arises out of Being but is in fact inseparable from It. At this stage of perception and understanding, everything that exists is experienced as differentiations of Being Itself, and so the form and the Source are indistinguishable. Another way of saying this is that all manifestation is seen as ripples arising on the surface of one thing, and we know ourselves to be inseparable from it. Here we do not experience ourselves as rooted in Being and arising out of It, but rather as Being Itself. Here we are not connected to Being—we *are* Being. We are the Origin. At this level then, our identification is with Being Itself, rather than with our separate embodiment or manifestation of It.

Just as our understanding of Holy Origin reaches more and more inclusive levels, so our understanding of Being also becomes progressively deeper. Our experience of Being begins with experiencing it as Essence, the inner nature of ourselves, and culminates with experiencing it as the Absolute, a state beyond conceptualization and even consciousness. When we experience everything as Being at the level of the Absolute, we are experiencing a huge paradox unsolvable by the mind: arising and nonarising are indistinguishable. It becomes impossible to talk about an Origin out of which forms arise, since manifestation and nonmanifestation are the same thing at this level. To perceive things from this depth is to be in touch with a profound mystery.

As we have discussed, the Holy Ideas are not states of consciousness or specific experiences but rather different angles or dimensions of understanding derived from direct experience. Specific types of experiences, however, give rise to these nine different ways of understanding reality. These types of experiences are those of the idealized Aspect. This may sound complicated, but if we understand this in relation to Point Four, it will become clear. Experientially, contact with the perception of reality that is signified by Holy Origin arises from being centered within oneself. When we feel centered in ourselves, we feel connected to and in contact with what we consider to be our source. Just as our understanding of Holy Origin reaches increasing levels of depth, our sense of what that source is will vary as our sense of who we take this "I" to be deepens.

Initially we may feel united with ourselves when we are strongly in touch with our bodies, feeling ourselves to be fully "in" our bodies—deeply in touch with our physical sensations and immersed in them. This sense of contact with ourselves, which is grounded in the body, is for many people the impetus for physical activity ranging from participating in vigorous sports to working out at a gym, and many people do not "feel like themselves" without it. In addition to physiological reasons such as the release of endorphins, exercise also gets us out of our thoughts and more in contact with our immediate experience, and so we feel more in touch with ourselves. However, this level of access to ourselves is time restricted and health determined: illness or physical disability and the inevitability of aging will severely limit this physically dependent way of coming into contact with ourselves.

Others feel in touch with themselves when they are fully feeling their emotions. Emotional catharsis can lead to a sense of inner connection, especially for those who have difficulty accessing and/or expressing their emotions. Such emotional release is very useful and necessary at the particular stage of inner work when we are dealing with our emotional repression and inhibition, but once we have access to our feelings and ease in expressing them, continual catharsis can be unproductive. Many people become addicted to venting emotionally because it provides a quick high and makes them feel connected with themselves. Since emotions are the feelings of the personality—when in Being we do not experience emotional states as we normally think of them—in time this dependency on emotional expression and discharge only serves to support our identification with the personality. Because emotions appear to be the key to making contact with ourselves at this level, we also take them as definitive and do not question our reactions, and so stay attached to them. On the other hand, moving into and through our emotions without holding on to them can lead us beyond the personality and into the realm of Being, and this is part of the reason that emotional access is necessary for our spiritual unfoldment. It is also necessary if we are to do the hard work of fully digesting and transforming the personality rather than merely rising above it.

As our development progresses, to feel truly in contact with ourselves means to be in touch with Being. At this stage in our unfoldment, when we feel engulfed in physical sensation because of pain or illness and cannot get beyond it, we do not feel in contact with ourselves. When we are in the midst of an emotional upheaval, we also do not feel in contact with ourselves. Only when we are profoundly in the moment and our consciousness is anchored in its depths do we feel that we have arrived at our center. At this stage, we know ourselves to be Being.

This experience of ourselves as Being is called the Point or the Essential Self in the language of the Diamond Approach, and it is the idealized Aspect of Point Four. It is the level of contacting ourselves described above, in which we know ourselves to be Being. Rather than identifying ourselves with our body or our personality and its emotions and reactions, we know that who we really are is True Nature. This experience is that which is referred to in spiritual literature as self-realization, awakening, or enlightenment—which are all different ways of describing the experience of coming to consciousness about who we really are.[1] The personality style of Ennea-type Four is an attempt to replicate the point; it is the personality's facsimile of it. We shall return to this after exploring the psychodynamics of this type.

——∿—— For an Ennea-type Four, loss of contact with Being in early childhood is synonymous with the loss of perceiving and experiencing herself as inseparable from and arising out of Being. What results is a profound inner sense of disconnection from the Divine, which is the underlying all-pervasive belief or fixation of this type, described as melancholy on Diagram 2. In order to experience ourselves as disconnected from anything, we must take ourselves to be a separate something that has lost its connection to a separate something else. The apparently inevitable identification with the body, which is the deepest identification a human being rooted in the personality has, leads to the conviction of our fundamental separateness for those of all ennea-types. In other words, because each of our bodies is distinct from everything else, we come to believe that we are all ultimately discrete entities. While fundamental to all personality types, this belief is the foundation upon which all of the resulting assumptions and characteristics rest for Ennea-type Fours due to their particular sensitivity to Holy Origin.

Like a boat loosed from its moorings, the inner experience of a Four is of being a separate someone who is cut off from Being and set adrift. There is a poignant inner sense of disconnection and estrangement from others but, more important, from the depths within. This loss of contact with Being is experienced by a Four as having been abandoned, as though Being has withdrawn or withheld Itself. Initially this is experienced as though her mother or family has pulled away from her, but at root is loss of contact with Being. What is left is a sense of lack and of lostness, which feels as though the very substance of herself were missing. There is a great longing to reconnect, to become anchored again in the connection that has been lost.

This sense of abandonment and of longing to reestablish the link with Being, however unconscious, is central to the psychology of a Four. It is so central that a Four's whole sense of self is constructed around it, to the point that longing becomes more important than getting, and people or situations that offer constancy and relatedness are often unconsciously undermined and rejected by Fours. Fours unconsciously cling to the experience of themselves as forsaken, perpetuating this deep inner sense.

Since one of the propensities of human psychology is to experience the mothering person of infancy as the embodiment of Being, the inevitable disruptions of contact with her become synonymous to a Four with disconnection from that source, Being. Filtered through the Four's sensitivity to Holy Origin, mother, who is the source of nourishment and survival to an infant, is experienced as detached, disengaged, or absent altogether. There may indeed have been actual abandonment, neglect, desertion, not having been properly cared for, and subtle or overt rejection by mother. Such experiences are not limited to Fours, of course, but because of their sensitivity to being cut off from the Source, such experiences become focal and lead to their predisposition to view others as inevitably abandoning.

The main inner mood of Fours is a sad and heavy sense of lack, a feeling of being cast away, and an inconsolable and insatiable longing, as though they are in perpetual mourning for the connection that has been lost. Hence Ichazo gave this type the name Ego-Melancholy. This sense of lack may be experienced as a feeling of scarcity, a sense of deprivation, of meagerness, of an inner poverty or destitution, of a crying inner neediness. A Four may not know or be able to put her finger on exactly what it is that she lacks, but she is convinced that something is definitely missing. At the core is a profound despair that she will ever be reconnected or included in God's love. She will always be on the outside and will never know how to get in. Everyone else has the secret, but it has been denied to her. Her grief about this lostness is dangerous to feel: it might throw her into the despair or make her feel ordinary. We will return to the latter momentarily. So, on the Enneagram of Avoidances, Diagram 10, despair (lost)/simple sadness appears at Point Four.

Compounding this feeling of privation is the assumption, conscious or unconscious, that it is her fault that the connection to the lost paradise—however that is conceived—was severed. She may feel that her very needs and longing for connection were the problem, or the sense of deficiency may take on an assumption of badness, of insufficiency, of inadequacy, and of being fatally flawed, which for some Fours reaches the point of feeling that there is something inherently evil or poisonous about them. There is a tragic and absolute quality of finality about this sense, as though it were irreparable and in the end nothing can be said or done to take this badness away.

The sense of lostness may feel like a disorientation, a sense of not really knowing where she is or how she got there, the sense of not really being connected to anyone or anything, but especially a sense of being disconnected from herself. There is a sense of living on the periphery of life compared to others, with no sense of orientation or direction. Some Fours seem perpetually spaced out, a bit dazed, glazed, and not fully in the present moment. Some Fours have no physical sense of direction and get lost even if they have been somewhere repeatedly. Some Fours constantly bump into things or people, lacking a physical perception of space that includes all of the objects within it.

Reconnection, the longed-for resolution to the inner scarcity, is sought externally. To a Four, it is as though all that is positive resides outside of herself. This longing to be filled by others and by what the external world offers is not a passive and quiet desire—it is a demand, no matter how unexpressed. It is as though the Four were saying, "I feel that I must have it and so I *should* have it." While this sense of entitlement is not restricted to this ennea-type, all Fours have it relative to some aspect of their lives. It appears that they believe that unless they insist upon what they want, they will not receive. Also conveyed in the entitlement is the sense that since they have been so deprived and have suffered so much, the world owes it to them to meet their desires. Deeper still, the entitlement is a way of not experiencing the intolerable inner sense of lack.

Once her desires have been fulfilled, however, the sought-after object begins to lose its appeal and her longing shifts elsewhere. Looking outside of herself for satisfaction inherently offers only limited gratification, since only reconnection with her depths will resolve the Four's sense of lack. Nothing and no one can ever fill the inner deficit completely, and so the Four is left in a perpetual state of discontent. However to a Four the fault often appears to lie in the sought-after object. It is not that "This longing cannot be filled externally so no wonder I am not satisfied" but rather "There is something wrong with the person or the thing I desire, or maybe he or it wasn't what I really wanted anyway."

The Four blames the object of her desire, finding flaws and imperfections that justify the lack of fulfillment, and the object is pushed away. Or once a desired object has been obtained, the Four's focus moves on to what else is not right in her life or what else needs to be acquired. Unsatisfied, ungratified, and displeased, nothing is ever quite right to a Four. What she has or procures always loses its shine, and the longing shifts to what is just out of reach. Things could always be a little different, a little better, more of this or of that, and then perhaps, just perhaps, she could be happy at last. But happiness for a Four is ephemeral, something inevitably spoils it, and the longing for fulfillment begins again. This pattern belies the professed desire for happiness, and we see that beneath the surface what the Four really wants is to maintain her identity as someone who longs and does not get.

The perpetual faultfinding and longing of Fours keeps their gaze focused externally and so protects them from their inner sense of deficiency. If nothing fulfills, they must keep searching for the perfect thing that will bring them contentment, and then they never have to face the truth that anything external *cannot* provide the satisfaction they desire. If this truth were faced, the inner attitude of longing and desiring would have to be given up, and some pretty painful inner feelings would have to be felt.

Longing connects them with the lost Beloved of childhood—Being filtered through mother. In the deep recesses of the soul, to let go of longing would mean letting go of this Beloved, and this would mean being truly lost, adrift, and without hope of redemption. So the addiction to desiring and yearning for what is just beyond her grasp keeps the Four in contact with this Beloved. It also makes Fours incurable romantics, raising them above ordinary life through the idealism and nobility of their quest—at least in their own psyches. They thus remain loyal to the lost Beloved and in this convoluted way attempt to stay connected with Being.

Just as Fours experience themselves as abandoned by others, so they in turn abandon themselves through this frustrating yet relentless external longing for fulfillment. With the inner conviction of their own inherent badness or, at best, paucity, they long for intimacy and closeness with others and yet it is difficult to allow. To really open up and be vulnerable would mean revealing the inner sense of lack and of badness, and then they believe they would *surely* be abandoned, repeating the initial intolerable wounding. So although Fours profess to long for closeness, they tend to keep themselves and others at arm's length. It is far safer to long from a distance and to feel the sweet sadness of unrequited love than actually to risk exposure. Relationships consequently are difficult for a Four; a source of bruised feelings and the inescapable feeling that love is being withheld. Nonetheless, or perhaps therefore, relationship is a central focus for Fours, and the stormier the relationship, the more appealing. The typical pattern of a Four's relationships is attraction to someone unavailable emotionally or otherwise, intense encounters, sudden breaks, longing, reconciliations, only to repeat the cycle again and again.

What they don't have looks better to Fours than what they do have. What others have looks better to them than what they have. What others are seems better to them then how they are. Others appear to have what they do not—whether actual possessions or personal attributes. The grass, as the saying goes, is always greener on the other side of the fence. The passion, then, is envy, as we see on the Enneagram of Passions in Diagram 2. The passion of envy runs the gamut from simply wanting something that someone else has to a malicious hatred toward the object of desire. "If I see another blonde, I'm going to kill her," is the way a Four friend of mine, a dark-haired beauty, once characterized the hatred in her envy. On the subtlest level, the envy manifests as a wish to be experiencing something different internally, something that seems better and more desirable than what is happening at the moment.

Through her theoretical formulations, the psychoanalyst Melanie Klein, probably herself a Four, gave envy a position of central importance in understanding psychopathology and in working with the most intractable psychoanalytic patients—those who seemed not to benefit from the experience. In typical Four fashion, her work created a schism in the British Psychoanalytic Society, which to date has not been resolved; in the words of Jay Greenberg and Stephen Mitchell, "Amid the swirl of controversies and antipathies surrounding Klein's contributions, there is understandably little consensus either as to the precise nature of her views or to her place within the history of psychoanalytic ideas."[2] It is difficult to tell whether her phantasmagoric descriptions of the destructive and vindictive inner world of the infant are accurate, or whether they are the overlays of an adult consciousness with a distinctly Four-ish skew. Regardless of how accurate her perceptions are in a generic sense in the realm of developmental psychology, her understanding gives us great insight into the psychology of this ennea-type.

Again, to quote Greenberg and Mitchell, Klein "suggests that early, primitive envy represents a particularly malignant and disastrous form of innate aggression. All other forms of hatred in the child are directed toward the *bad* objects. . . . Envy, by contrast, is hatred directed toward *good* objects. The child experiences the goodness and nurturance which the mother provides but feels it to be insufficient and resents the mother's control over it. The breast releases the milk in limited amounts and then goes away. In the child's phantasy, Klein suggests, the breast is felt to be hoarding the milk for its own purposes. . . . As a consequence of envy the infant destroys the good objects, splitting is undone, and there is a subsequent increase in persecutory anxiety and terror. Envy destroys the possibility for hope."[3] We will return to the subject of hope and hopelessness later, as it is particularly relevant to understanding the psychology of Fours. Missing in Klein's understanding of infant envy is the interpersonal element—that the child, whose identity is still merged with her mother, is responding as the Four experiences her mother—as hateful and vindictive. A Four's experience of her childhood is often that her mother would not let her shine or occupy a place of central importance, and was competitive and envious of her.

Implicit in the envy is a pushing away and a rejection of what the Four has or is experiencing. This has its roots in the particular flavor of superego characteristic of Fours. They have a vicious superego that is constantly measuring them up against an idealized picture of how and what they ought to be, and tearing them apart for not making the grade. Naranjo has observed that as an image type, belonging to the corner of the enneagram whose hallmark is excessive concern about one's presentation, "the ennea-type IV individual identifies with that part of the psyche that *fails* to fit the idealized image, and is always striving to achieve the unattainable."[4] Identified as they are with the part of themselves that doesn't fit their inner picture of how and what they ought to be, they are continually at the mercy of the barbs and taunts of their inner accuser. Unlike the superego of Ones, the issue here is, as Naranjo says, "more aesthetic than ethical"[5] in the sense that it is the presentation that counts: the superego of a Four does not berate her for being fundamentally a bad person but rather for being somehow wrong and therefore not displaying an ideal image. Nothing that they do or feel seems good enough or even right to their inner judge who is cutting, disparaging, reproachful, and inevitably hypercritical. The degree of maliciousness and venom that Fours can display toward others is minimal compared to what they heap on themselves.

This pattern is rooted in holding themselves responsible for and savagely attacking themselves for their inner sense of disconnection. Their aggression, then, is usurped by their superegos and directed against themselves. In the extreme, this can lead to a profound and ongoing self-hatred arising from the unshakable conviction that she is a failure as a person.

This rather brutal self-rejection and self-hatred is part of the picture contributing to the depressive tendency that typifies Fours. While Fours are not by any means the only ennea-type who experiences depression, the pull in that direction is inexorable because of the inner forces at work. The quality of depression characteristic of Fours is of a profound inner blackness in which life appears unbearable and unendurable, and in which the self appears, in Freud's terms, "poor and empty."[6] Everything—particularly themselves—seems completely hopeless. Aggression is turned in upon themselves.

In psychoanalytic theory, a number of factors are involved in depression—all of which are relevant to this ennea-type. The first is some kind of loss or failure of relationship with the mothering person of early childhood, a period in which the sense of self is developing and is fragile at best. The second is an overzealous superego. Turning to the first factor, because mother and self are not fully discriminated in the child's consciousness, loss of relatedness with mother is experienced as both the loss of her and the loss of self. Margaret Mahler believed that the particular developmental phase involved at the root of depression is that of rapprochement, at around fifteen months to the age of two, in which the child is developing a separate sense of self and of his capacities but still needs merger and contact with mother. She attributed failure on the mother's part to accept and understand the child's alternating drive during this period toward expansion and freedom from her and his sudden needs for "refueling" contact with her. She believed that this leads to ambivalence and aggression toward mother, loss of self-esteem, and eventually to depression. It also leads to a perpetual looking to others to shore up one's self-esteem.

Gertrude Blanck and Rubin Blanck explain Freud's theory on depression thus: "The essential difference between normal mourning (grief) and melancholia (depression) is that, in the first instance the object has been loved and lost, and in the second, love is overridden by aggression."[7] Grief at the loss of an object does not usually involve self-recriminations and loss of a sense of one's own value. In depression, however,

> loss of such an object is tantamount to loss of part of the self-image; the depressed person may identify with the lost object in an attempt to recapture what has been lost. In that case his or her self-criticisms are derived from criticisms originally directed toward the emotionally significant person, either the one lost or one connected with the loss. The self-criticism is therefore an expression of anger that was part of the original ambivalent attitude toward the object when it was present.[8]

In depression, then, aggression that was originally felt relative to the lost object becomes directed toward oneself in the form of the superego.

Other factors involved in depression are failure to live up to ego ideals and a sense of powerlessness and hopelessness about something in particular or life in general. Here we see again the Four's pitting of herself against impossible inner pictures of how she ought to be, as well as an often-concomitant sense of inability to achieve what she believes she ought to be able to. The attitude of envy is implicit in this—desiring what one does not have and trying to be what one is not. For this reason, simulation, posturing and projecting the desired appearance, is at Point Four on the Enneagram of Lies, Diagram 12. The hopelessness inherent in depression is not a giving up of hope but rather it is a sense of failing to attain or get what one desires. If you truly let go of hoping for something, a sense of neutrality and of peacefulness arises. Seeking and striving cease. On the other hand, when you feel hopeless about something, you are clinging tenaciously to what you want, and feeling despair about not getting it.

The heart of a Four's hopelessness is about not measuring up to the idealized inner picture of how or what she ought to be. Inherent in it is the firm conviction that she is not okay as she is and that she should match this ideal. Fueling this is the unconscious hope that if she did match the idealized inner image, perhaps the lost object would return. There is no giving up or letting go of this image of perfection but rather a tenacious holding on to it and a resulting sense of despair for not at-taining it. What results is a despondency that feels dark, melancholic, and tortured. It is this dismal and smarting hopelessness that colors a Four's emotional state.

Also implicit in the holding on to the Four's ego ideal of perfection is the defense mechanism associated with this type by Naranjo, that of in-trojection. Introjection refers to the incorporation of some of the qualities, attitudes, or characteristics of the loved object into one's own psyche. In the case of Fours, what is incorporated is the ego ideal and the resulting superego demands, punishments, and rewards of the parents, particularly mother. While it may at first glance seem far-fetched to consider a Four holding on to her sniping and hateful superego as a defense mechanism, if we see this as a way of avoiding complete inner loss of the object and con-sequently of the sense of self, it becomes more understandable. It is for this reason that Blanck and Blanck criticize the therapeutic technique they call "the reversible raincoat method" of treating depression in which the patient is encouraged to externalize his or her inner aggression: The whole inner economy of the depressive person in which aggression is di-rected toward oneself is a way of preserving contact with the object, and so externalizing one's anger and hatred is tantamount to the psyche to los-ing the beloved object. It is also for this reason, as we have discussed, that while Fours may feel miserable and profess to long for happiness, it is really their suffering that they cling to, since through it they maintain connection with the lost object. Only through understanding this dy-namic and getting in touch with the love for the object underlying it can this painful pattern begin to dissolve.

Introjection also manifests in other ways in Fours: they incorporate parts of those they love and admire. They take on and mimic their speech patterns and turns of phrase, their style of dress, ways of eating, thinking, and behaving; they adopt their forms of exercise—or lack thereof—and their attitudes and mannerisms.

Some Fours are more depressive, while others seem perpetually cheer-ful with a kind of manic ferocity, as mentioned at the beginning of this chapter. Others alternate between these two extremes of behavior. On the manic side, Fours stay very busy trying to find and fill themselves with things that will obviate the internal melancholy and provide some emotional stimulation, in the form of tempestuous relationships, interpersonal dramas, entertainment, work, acquisitions, and so on. This type of Four appears happy, but there is a forcedness to their vibrancy, a sense that they *have* to appear positive, vivacious, and energetic. Whether high or low or moving back and forth between these emotional extremes, common to all styles of Fours is emotional intensity. The mundane and ordinary are spurned in favor of excitement and emotional amplification. We will go into this more later.

Because of the inner dynamics that we have been exploring, shame figures largely in the psychology of Fours. Shame "refers to a broad spectrum of painful affects—embarrassment, humiliation, mortification, and disgrace—that accompany the feeling of being rejected, ridiculed, exposed, or of losing the respect of others."[9] Fully being, expressing, and exposing oneself is the source of shame for Fours, since who they are does not match how they think they should be. This makes it extremely difficult for Fours to reveal something they feel, think, or believe that doesn't fit their image of perfection. They anticipate that the external world will shame them, which is a projection of the shame that they experience internally at the hands of their superego. For many Fours, the fear of being seen as improper, inappropriate, flawed, and defective forms a constant preoccupation in relation to others.

To avoid the disgrace and resulting loss of self-respect that they fear will result from exposing themselves, many Fours withdraw, becoming aloof and distant, and holding themselves apart from others. Their movement away is usually blamed on those they are isolating themselves from, and perpetuates their sense of estrangement. They also become reserved, revealing little about themselves and coming across to others as very composed, private, and constrained. They become, in a word, self-controlling, as we see on the Enneagram of Antiself Actions, Diagram 11. They are careful about what they express and how they behave. Every move is filtered through an inner censor, and the result is a studied, restrained, and often stilted manner. A sense of formality, decorousness, even primness as well as an affectedness and a sense of posturing is often the result. Like the horse, the animal associated with this type, they present an image of controlled elegance, restrained power. There is, obviously, little room for spontaneity in the behavior and, more important, in the inner life of a Four.

On a social level, the world of protocols, codes of behavior, rules of conduct, formalities, and correct form are the Four's province. Diplomatically getting a message across without voicing it directly, indirectly communicating anything that might be conflictual or regarded as improper are realms in which the Four excels. Japanese culture, in which strict protocols govern all aspects of interaction, exemplifies this Four-ish characteristic. For the Japanese, bringing shame upon oneself, one's family, clan, or the country itself is one of the most grievous offenses, which has led to the ritualization of suicide as a way of saving face. Even the choice of a gift, where it is purchased, and how it is wrapped are determined by strict protocols governed by the occasion. While Japan, like the rest of the world, is rapidly taking on more and more Three-ish tendencies, speeding up the pace of life, with a focus on personal attainment and the packaging rather than the content, its fundamental orientation is Four-ish. The spiritual path of Zen Buddhism, with its stress upon spontaneity and bringing a fresh beginner's mind to each moment, appears to have arisen as an antidote to the overly ritualized and formalized Japanese culture. Its forms and practices, however, now follow centuries-old proscriptions and for many are empty rituals.

Although not the norm, occasionally one comes upon someone of this type whose behavioral style looks quite the opposite of the more typical reserved and refined Four-ish style. This type of Four places a premium upon behaving spontaneously with no self-inhibition, even if she behaves audaciously and outrageously, or even rudely and brashly with seemingly no regard for propriety, convention, or for her effect upon others. Rather than expressing an absence of shame, this style is in defiance of it, which is simply a defense against experiencing it. And, as with her more obviously controlled sister, she is not necessarily making any more direct contact with her experience, appearances to the contrary.

Whether of the more controlled or more flamboyant style of Four, this ennea-type and Ennea-type Two—Ego-Flattery—which we will turn to momentarily, are the two "wettest" ones on the enneagram—the most

emotionally labile. Extreme emotionality filtered through control manifests as a flair for the dramatic, and rather than spontaneously expressing
what they feel, Fours dramatize their emotions. There is a distinct theatricality about them, the sense that what they are expressing is part real
and part performance piece. The posturing of Oscar Wilde comes to
mind, as does the great dancer Isadora Duncan, who in true Four fashion
was strangled by her flowing scarf, which caught in the wheels of her open
car. They make great actresses—Uma Thurman and Gwyneth Paltrow are
current examples. Connected with this theatrical tendency is the body
part associated with Point Four, the lungs. Grand gestures of moaning
and bemoaning, sighing, fainting, and bewailing come to mind, and the
lungs are associated with grief in some of the wholistic medical traditions.
What is avoided, as we see in the Enneagram of Avoidances, Diagram 10,
is simple sadness.

Fours can be venomous, spiteful, and bitter toward others, often expressed in indirect ways through humor, slights, and underhanded attacks
cloaked in a show of politeness and civility. The usually unconscious intent
is to inflict upon others the shame that they want to avoid experiencing, as
well as preserving or establishing a sense of their own faultlessness. On the
surface, Fours tend to blame others for their problems, and it is very difficult for them to acknowledge their side of a conflict with another, since to
avoid the onslaught of inner scorn they need to see the other as wrong.

As a further defense against experiencing shame about and within
themselves, Fours take a superior stance relative to others. Feeling and
suffering intensely—more intensely than others from their point of view,
and perhaps in fact, since their attention is oriented toward it—confer
upon them a specialness and a nobility that raise them above others,
whom they see as less sensitive, less refined, and less attuned to the nuances of the soul than they are. It is as though through their nostalgia,
melancholy, and extreme investment in emotional subtleties, they are remaining loyal to the lost Source, and even if they don't feel in touch with
it, they are retaining some kind of contact with It. Because of this, they
seem perpetually stuck in mourning and grieving for the contact and love
that has been lost, and tend to cling to their pain and emotional reactions.
They may, for example, suffer over a marriage or relationship that ended

twenty years ago, seemingly unable to move beyond it. They sometimes seem to be bearing up against the unbearable—the grossness and insensitivity of the rest of humanity—and bearing their burden with a stiff upper lip if they are of the less flamboyant type, or with loud demonstrations of grief if otherwise.

They often feel that no one can truly understand the emotional depths and heights that they experience, and so out of their pain of disconnection from others, they derive this sense of being better than them. Holding themselves back becomes transformed into a haughtiness and a snobbishness in which others are looked down upon. This may reach the extreme of perceiving others in general, or particular people, as contemptible and the butt of their derision and ridicule. Some Fours simply ignore those whom they don't feel are worthy of their attention. They tend to be elitist, behaving as though they believe themselves to be the crème de la crème, obviously a reaction formation to feeling quite the reverse deep down.

This tendency may also be a form of entitlement in reaction to the inner sense of having been neglected and abused, such that the Four feels due special treatment and privileges. As Naranjo says,

> Though the individual may seethe in self-deprecation and self-hate, the attitude to the outer world is in this case that of a "prima-donna" or at least a very special person. When this claim of specialness is frustrated it may be complicated by a victimized role of "misunderstood genius." In line with the development, individuals also develop traits of wit, interesting conversation, and others in which a natural disposition towards imaginativeness, analysis, or emotional depth (for instance) are secondarily put to the service of the contact need and the desire to summon admiration.[10]

The inner sense of disconnection implicit in the loss of Holy Origin leads to a craving for what makes one feel connected—for what is original, authentic, creative, and direct. For this reason, Fours are drawn to the arts and other aesthetic pursuits as either creator or appreciator. Suffering and the artist have been perennially linked, and part of a Four's clinging to her emotional states is because of this linkage. Intense emotional states lead to a particular sense of contacting oneself, as discussed at the beginning of this chapter. The depths of emotion take us to the edge of our holes, those places in our souls where contact with Essence has been lost. We experience a sense of depth and of meaning; and out of our suffering, creativity many manifest. There's nothing like a tragic romance to stir the creative juices, as evidenced in the great love songs throughout time and exemplified in the sixties by the tragic love songs of Joni Mitchell and Leonard Cohen, surely two Fours.

Things and people who are truly original and creative connect the Four to those qualities, and through proximity she partakes in them. Her valuing of the refined and beautiful, however, may reach the point of preciousness, an exaggerated fawning over such things, or, to use that great British expression, they become bijou, treated like jewels. She may, for example, treat a work of art or piece of music with a reverence usually reserved for the religious. But, as Naranjo says,

> An inclination to refinement . . . may be understood as efforts on the part of the person to compensate for a poor self-image (so that an ugly self-image and the refined self-ideal may be seen as reciprocally supporting each other); also, they convey the attempt on the part of the person to be something different from what he or she is. . . . The lack of originality entailed by such imitativeness in turn perpetuates an envy of originality—just as the attempt to imitate original individuals and the wish to emulate spontaneity are doomed to fail.[11]

The importance of originality, authenticity, and spontaneity to Fours leads us back to the idealized Aspect of this type that we began discussing at the beginning of this chapter. Having explored the behavioral, emotional, and belief patterns of a Four, we can now fully understand how this type is an emulation of the Essential quality called the Point in the language of the Diamond Approach. Experiencing the Point is experiencing ourselves as someone completely undetermined by our circumstances or our personal history and so free and liberated. It is recognizing our true identity—unique and individual expressions of the Divine, inseparable from it. It is the experience of being a shining center of illumination. Try-

ing to appear like someone who is original, creative, authentic, spontaneous, and special—taking on an image that embodies the qualities of the
Point—is the Four's attempt to replicate this experien . Although impossible, this desired authenticity is the trap for Fours, as we see on Diagram 9.

The theatricality and drama of Fours can be seen as an attempt to lend
weight to the feelings of this self-representation or false self, as well as imitating the experience of the Point, that of being a star, full of significance,
depth, and meaning. It is this self-image that a Four looks toward to provide a sense of realness, and so to a Four, the emotions emanating from
this self-concept are to greater and lesser extents sacrosanct and "real." For
this reason they are often convinced of the validity of their reactions and
are defensive about them, as we have seen. From this angle, we can see
that the characteristic resistance of Fours to how things are, both outwardly and inwardly, is an attempt to shore up the false sense of self of the
personality, the self-representation. This pattern originated in saying no
to help us discriminate between ourselves and the mother of early childhood, and so as an adult supports the sense of being distinct.

The key to the development of a Four is the virtue associated with this
point, equanimity, as we see on the Enneagram of Virtues in Diagram 1.
Ichazo's definition of equanimity is as follows: "It is balance. A whole
being lives in complete harmony with his environment. His moves are
economical and always appropriate to his circumstances. He is not emotionally affected by external stimuli, but responds to them exactly as
much as is necessary."

As we have discussed, the virtue is both what is needed for one's spiritual evolution as well as a by-product of it. To live the balanced life Ichazo
is pointing toward, emotional and mental evenness, and an imperturba-
bility, are necessary, as well as an acceptance of what is and a capacity not
to be inflamed by external events. Fundamentally a Four needs to approach her experience without reacting to it, without clinging to it, and
without needing it to be right, dramatic, or out of the ordinary. Only then
is it possible to respond to life with equilibrium.

This implies a number of things in terms of inner process. First of all,
it means fully landing within herself and her experience and not resisting

it. Not fully entering into their experience is what keeps Fours on the surface of themselves, disconnected from anything deeper. Longing for something different to be happening and comparing themselves to others only perpetuates this disconnection, as we have seen. Equanimity, then, means that the controlled and controlling Four behavior needs to be replaced with an attitude of surrender and openness to what is occurring, internally or externally, rather than fighting it. This necessitates not wishing to be different or to be experiencing anything other than what is happening in the moment. This in turn means not comparing herself to others and not measuring herself against her inner picture of how one ought to be.

For this change in orientation to come about, Fours must recognize how they continuously judge, censor, and control themselves in order to approximate their inner picture of how they believe they should be, and further, how they shame themselves for not measuring up to it. They need to see how this nonallowing distances them from their direct experience and thus perpetuates the sense of being disconnected and is therefore how they abandon themselves. They also need to understand how this pattern makes them feel hopeless about themselves, and they need to give up the hope of matching some ideal and accept themselves as they are. It also means getting in touch with the aggression and self-hatred embedded in this resistance to themselves, and really feeling and understanding that they inflict suffering upon themselves in this way.

Fours need to see that their resistance to negative affects and states only perpetuates them. They need to understand that working through our emotional reactions and mental beliefs is only possible when we fully allow them, because otherwise our understanding cannot penetrate them. True disidentification, then, which is not a distancing from our experience, is only possible through diving fully into our experience. Paradoxically, at least to the mind, the more we immerse ourselves in our experience, the more we become disidentified with it. In terms of process, this means that a Four needs to not dramatize what she is experiencing, as well as not distance from it out of shame. Meeting inner experience with equanimity involves allowing it yet not being swept away by it, which means experiencing it completely.

To the extent that a Four fully feels her inner contents, her consciousness can penetrate them and reveal their underpinnings, which in turn reveals depths beyond them. This process leads a Four to becoming more and more centered within, and less externally focused. Striving for the exceptional, the exciting, and the extreme gradually becomes replaced with an appreciation of calm and of simplicity. The need to be special becomes replaced by a recognition of her humanness—how alike she is to others—which in time she sees is in itself extraordinary.

As a Four gets out from under her superego and begins to disidentify from her attitude of envy and from her reactivity, the deficiency state of lostness and of lack that these cover will begin to surface. Rather than trying to fill this emptiness, like everything else it needs to be fully experienced. She may feel as though she were lost in deep space that feels vacuous and empty, but as she opens to it, it begins to change into a presence that feels spacious, free, and peaceful. As she allows it further, she begins to find and recognize herself, to experience her original face before she was born, to paraphrase the Zen koan. A sense of connection arises, a sense of recognition of herself when all has been stripped away. She gradually begins to experience herself as a shining star in the firmament—a real star, rather than the imitation one she has tried to be. She experiences balance within, center within, and no longer needs to long for the Source she has felt separated from: she is and knows herself at last to be that Source. This experience will arise again and again with different nuances until in time her identification shifts from the false personality to her real self, the Point of existence.[12]

E N N E A - T Y P E   T W O :
E G O - F L A T T E R Y

Twos, like their Four sisters, are emotive and dramatic, and are preoccupied with their relationships with others. Their need for love and approval is extreme—they feel dependent upon it—and in order to get it, they try to please and play to the object of their affection, fawning over and excessively praising them. Hence the name of this type, Ego-Flattery. The disproportionate value they place on those they admire and want to be loved by is their deepest form of flattery. An image type, Twos want to be seen as loving, generous, kind, empathic, and above all, "there" for others. Their image, then, is of being a lovable person, and they will go to great lengths to convince others that they really are. Because of this, they have difficulty saying no to another's request, and will override their own feelings and pragmatic constraints in order not to disappoint others. The extremes that Twos go to in an effort to impress others about what wonderful people they are belies their inner sense of not being worthy of love.

Ingratiating themselves and being helpful, they try to make themselves indispensable. Rather than ask directly for what they want from others—especially affection—

they give it and tokens of it with the expectation that the other will reciprocate. Hidden strings are thus attached to all of a Two's giving—and
Twos can be extremely generous with their time, resources, and even their
bodies. If the other does not fulfill his end of the unexpressed bargain,
Twos can become masters of guilt tripping. Presenting themselves with a
veneer of false humility, beneath the surface Twos suffer from a prideful
self-inflation, feeling themselves to be special and, like Fours, entitled to
singular treatment. While pride infuses much of a Two's behavior, it is
nonetheless compensatory for low self-esteem.

Turning to the Holy Idea associated with this type, there are two
names for it: Holy Will and Holy Freedom. We explored in Chapter 4
when discussing the Holy Idea of Point Three how the universe is a conscious living presence in a constant state of movement, change, and unfoldment. We also saw that its functioning is not random; its dynamism
follows organic and natural laws and principles. All that occurs is part of
this continuous unfoldment, like the changing patterns in one endlessly
vast fabric. We saw that each of us is one part of this immense fabric, each
of our lives forming a changing design within it. Or, to use the analogy
we used in discussing Holy Law, we are each like a drop of water in a great
ocean, our own movements inseparable from the continual undulations of
that enormous and endless sea. Holy Will takes this understanding of the
dynamism of the universe one step further, and focuses on the force behind its movements, which has a directionality and an intelligence implicit in its momentum. There is a unified will, in other words, in the
functioning of the universe.

Everything that happens is an expression of Holy Will, from the birth
of a star in a distant corner of the Milky Way to your hand turning a page
of this book. In theistic terms, everything that occurs is God's Will. God's
Will is not something mysterious or removed from us—it is expressed in
what is occurring right now and what will occur in the next moment, in
every corner of the universe. Even though human actions may be out of
synch with Being, from a nondualistic perspective even those events are
part of God's Will. Everything that happens, then, is what God wants to
have happen.

Whatever thoughts are going through your mind in response to what

I am saying, whatever feelings you might be having, the impetus to go get a glass of water and look out the window are all God's Will manifesting through you right now. If everything is a part of Being, then everything that transpires everywhere—including within ourselves—must be part of Its unfoldment and therefore inspired by Its momentum and intelligence. We may not experience ourselves as an indivisible part of Being, and so may not perceive that everything that occurs within our psyches and within our lives is part of the will of Being, but that does not change this fundamental truth. All it means is that our perception is filtered through the separatist lens of the personality, and so our vision is cloudy and we are not seeing reality clearly.

You might argue that wars and murders and all of the other destructive things that happen cannot possibly be God's Will, but if you perceive reality from its most fundamental level, the picture cannot be otherwise: if the ultimate nature of everything and everyone in the universe is Being, and everyone and everything is made up of It and so inseparable from It, then it is impossible for anything that happens to be other than part of the momentum of Being—part of the manifestation of God's Will, in other words. Cataclysms and natural disasters only seem not to be part of God's Will if we take a subjective position about them and decide that they are not good things. Human behavior that is hurtful, insensitive, and negative may seem bad to us, but it is nonetheless emanating out of souls whose ultimate nature is Being, even if they are not functioning in harmony with It. So their actions, too, can only be part of God's Will. Additionally, it is a huge presumption to decide that an event is bad and should not be occurring, since if we could see the bigger picture that encompasses the future we might see that the event actually has a beneficial function in the long run—and that long run might be well beyond our lifetimes. That presumption derives from the pride of the personality, a key feature of this type, as we shall see.

As in our discussion of Holy Perfection, the Holy Idea of Point One, I want to clarify that I am not condoning or excusing all of the hurtful and malicious ways that humanity treats its fellow members, nor am I saying that such behavior should not be mitigated and punished. When our view is informed by seeing life without the veil of the personality—when we see things objectively, in other words—we see that since most of humanity lives on the surface of themselves, out of touch with their inner depths, such behavior is inevitable and needs to be curtailed and controlled. To say, however, that such things should not happen does not make sense— they are a natural consequence of humanity's estrangement from its depths. Also, what we consider evil behavior is simply behavior rooted in ignorance of how things really are. Rather than destructiveness estranging us from the Divine, it is an expression of our estrangement, which has nothing to do with the underlying presence of that dimension of existence. The solution to human destructiveness does not lie in trying to regulate or eradicate it but rather with connecting to a dimension within ourselves in which such behavior does not make any sense.

Just as it is an immense presumption to assume that what is happening externally should not be happening, so it is also an immense presumption to assume that what we are experiencing is not what we are supposed to be experiencing: that we should not be angry at our partner or unsympathetic toward our best friend, for instance, or that we should be more open and enlightened and not caught in some emotional state or other. Out of this kind of evaluation of our experience we then set about trying to manipulate ourselves so that our experience is otherwise. This propensity to be constantly tinkering with what is going on with us is one of the characteristics of the personality. From the perspective of Holy Will, everything that we experience and that happens in our lives is what is supposed to happen. As Almaas says,

> *You try to relax, you try to quiet your mind, you try to make yourself feel better or make yourself feel worse. You are always interfering, trying to make something happen other than what is actually happening. You can only do this if you believe you have your own separate world and you can make things in it happen the way you want, while really, it is not your choice at all. You are alive today not because you want to be, but because the universe wants you to be. If you experience anger today, it's because the universe chooses to. If you experience love today, it's because the universe decides to.*
>
> *This "choosing" on the part of the universe is not the same as predesti-*

nation. Predestination implies that there is a plan spelled out somewhere in which everything that is going to happen has already been determined. Here, we are talking about a universe that is intelligent and creative, where what is going to happen in the next moment cannot have been planned because it's going to come out of this moment, rather than out of some plan written at the time of creation. So from this perspective there is no predestination, but there is also no free will.[1]

When we perceive reality from this perspective, we know ourselves to be participants in the Holy Will of the universe. We know that each of our lives is an expression of God's Will. When we are in alignment with this reality, we know that we are being moved rather than being the mover. Moving with the current of what is happening both inside of ourselves and outside of ourselves is what the other name for this Holy Idea, Holy Freedom, means. Holy Freedom is the understanding that we're only free when we do not resist the flow of what is—when we do not resist God's Will. What we call free will is choosing to align with what is or to resist it, and in time we see that only by surrendering to what is are we truly free.

Holy Freedom, then, is Holy Will perceived from within our human experience. Holy Freedom means seeing that your personal will and the will of the universe are inseparable. Rather than needing to assert what you want or manipulating reality to conform to how you think it ought to be, which is the will of the personality and a central characteristic of Ennea-type Two, when you perceive through the lens of Holy Freedom you understand that real freedom is being able to surrender to the flow of what is happening, both inwardly and outwardly. Ultimately the more you perceive reality objectively, the more clearly you see that even the notion of having your own personal will is a delusion of the personality. If each of us is a cell in the body of the universe, and that body is moving and changing organically, it only makes sense that each of us must be part of that unfoldment and the momentum—the will—behind it. Our personal momentum and direction and that of the larger body of which we are a part can only be inseparable—it cannot be otherwise. Freedom is not one cell trying to do its own thing and pushing to have things go the way it wants—again a characteristic of Twos—but rather every cell knowing that it is participating in the momentum of the Whole and going along with that movement.

Even the terms *surrender* and *go along with* are inaccurate if we are to understand Holy Freedom completely, since they imply a separate someone who gives up her will and acquiesces to the flow of the universe. While it feels that way from within the veils of the personality, this is not how things really are: the notion of a separate will is an illusion, since none of us is inherently separate from the oneness of Being and, hence, of the direction in which it is unfolding. As Almaas says regarding Holy Freedom,

> *The issue of getting one's own way is a big one for the personality, and the thought of surrendering to God's will may seem to involve giving up your own will. However, if you are sincere and truthful with yourself, and you stay with your experience without trying to change it in any way, you find out that having your own way is really a matter of surrendering to your inner truth. Your way is following the thread of your own experience. It is not a matter of choosing or not choosing it; your way is something that is given to you. It is the road you are walking on, the landscape you are traveling through. You discover that it is a huge relief not to feel that the territory you are crossing should be different than exactly how it is for you.[2]*

Within our personal perspective, Holy Will points to the fact that, if unhampered, our souls have an inherent gravitational pull toward contacting the depths within. This is to say that the human soul longs to reconnect with and understand the deepest levels of reality. The need to know, to make conscious everything from the laws of nature to the functioning of our bodies to our inmost Spirit, is an irrepressible drive within us. Mankind has struggled from the beginning with trying to understand what we are about and what life is about, and has always had a concept of the transcendent, the Divine, of what we call God. Within each of us, then, is a drive to know who we really are. Our souls have a drive to connect with, know, and live the innermost nature of what we are. We have an innate drive to actualize ourselves, to live our human potential fully, which if allowed takes us to deeper and deeper levels of reality beyond the subjective, beyond the personality, beyond the separate self.

——— For someone who is an Ennea-type Two, losing touch with Being in early childhood also means losing the awareness that she is part of the ongoing flow of the whole universe. There develops a sense of being cut off from the unfoldment of reality, and the sense that she is not an inseparable part of it, which she might feel initially in relation to her mother or family, and later more globally. Rather than experiencing herself as a cell in the larger body of the universe whose functioning is intrinsic and important to the functioning of the whole, she feels herself to be peripheral and unimportant. Lost is the sense that she has a place and a purpose in life in her own right, and so lost is the sense of inner momentum and direction. Personal development and unfoldment as her natural human potential and driving force become replaced with the sense of being cast out by the universe, left without direction in some backwater. This is her fixation, her fixed cognitive belief about how things are. (On Diagram 2, we see that the phrase for Ennea-type Two's fixation given by Ichazo is flattery. This refers to a Two's solution to her sense of disconnection from God's Will: playing to others.)

Lost is the perception of the intelligence and directionality behind what occurs, and so she feels that she cannot trust that the way things are going is okay, and must make things happen the way she thinks they ought to be. Not only does she lose a sense of personal purpose and of direction but she also loses the sense that the universe is inherently supportive of her. She develops the conviction that she is a separate person, unloved and rejected by Being; and lacking an inner sense of inherent purpose and connection with the cosmic Will, she must take things into her own hands and make things happen. Lacking a perception of being part of God's Will, in other words, she takes on that function and imitates it through becoming willful. She imposes her individual will on reality within and without and tries to make it conform to how she thinks it ought to be through manipulating it. Fundamentally she is trying to create a sense of direction, momentum, purpose, and support which she has lost contact with in the process of losing contact with her essential nature.

Lost is her trust and perception of her own essential Will, the momentum of her soul, and so she feels she must manipulate reality and herself to survive.

Her inner sense is one of flatness, a lack of dimensionality and of depth. Hence the nickname of this type, Ego-Flat. It is as though there were an inner glass ceiling, a limit to the depths she can contact within herself. Without perception of the support of Being and convinced that her soul does not have an inherent gravitational momentum toward this realm that she has become estranged from, salvation must therefore come through others. She turns her gaze to them for that missing sense of a foundation, an underpinning, a mainstay. The door to her depths seems to lie in making intimate contact with others, and in this crucial assumption we can see the overlay of her early relationship with mother, which we will look at shortly. Her inner orientation is focused outward on others whom she tries to please since she feels dependent on them to connect with herself, and her inner states ascend and plummet depending on the quality of her contact with them. This dependency is the central psychological orientation of Twos.

This dependent orientation rests on the Two's loss of contact with and loss of value for her inner process. She rejects her inner world and her own experience, mimicking her unconscious sense of having been rejected by the universe. What she is experiencing is not what is supposed to be happening, and seems much less important, valid, and interesting than what some valued other is experiencing. There is no sense that she is being propelled to any place of significance—or indeed any place at all—by anything within herself, and so she must attach herself to the momentum of someone else. Rather than being moved to actualize her potential, then, she is driven to connect with some special other.

The vicissitudes in her early interactions with her mother are filtered through her sensitivity to Holy Will, and the result is the sense that who she really is was not attended to and her real needs were not met. Her needs and wants seem subordinate to mother's will—who gives and withholds nourishment according to her own timetable, and the inevitable lack of complete attunement translates in the preconceptual language of the soul into the sense that mother does not love her and rejects who she is. The Two is acutely sensitive to rifts in attunement, and the impression left on her soul is that mother's needs are more important than hers. What develops is the sense of not being centrally important as a person and of her needs being secondary to those of mother and later to those of all significant people in her life. Her function becomes satisfying their needs, and she loses touch with the potential for her own unfoldment as a person.

Whether a Two's mother was in actuality more self-centered than the mothers of other types or not, the imprint left on a Two's soul is that mother is self-absorbed and so not fully there for her, not fully available or loving. The Two comes to believe that since she could not capture mother's love and attention, she is not inherently lovable and must therefore manipulate to get love, and her soul becomes oriented toward that pursuit. From one angle, all of the Two's subsequent personality traits can be seen as efforts to catch mother's attention and as seductions to win her love in an attempt to heal this wound in her soul. Her focus becomes, then, to make herself lovable and loved.

Often in the history of a Two is the sense of growing up in the shadow of an idealized parent who imposed his or her will on the Two—a parent who was the focus of attention and to whom the Two had to subordinate herself and had to please. This may have been the mother, but often is the father, and this pattern repeats in later life as the Two attempts to become connected with a prestigious and prominent partner. There is often in the history of Twos the sense of having been rejected by the mother and of being the father's favorite, but in many cases there is the sense of being both parents' most beloved child. In this lies one of the paradoxes of Twos: while often being the preferred child of one or both parents, Twos nonetheless feel rejected. This is probably because in the Two's soul, her value in the family seemed to have come through the role she played, the image she presented, the things she accomplished, rather than from her real self.

Regardless of the details of her history, more than anything a Two wants to be loved. Reconnecting with the flow of the universe is sought through merger with another. In this, we see the idealized Aspect of this point, the quality of love called Merging Gold in the Diamond Approach. This is the kind of love we feel when we are in love with someone—that orgasmic sense of melting in ecstatic union with our beloved, of being enveloped in a blissful cocoon of oneness. The feeling is the stuff of romantic legends: a rapture of oneness, complete fulfillment in which all separateness is gone, and we feel dissolved in a golden puddle of bliss. There are no boundaries between us and our beloved, no sense of where we begin and the other ends. We are completely caught up in this ecstatic love, galvanized and electrified by it, enthralled in the elation of this sense of profoundly intimate connection. This Essential Aspect is central to the devotional religious and spiritual paths in which the goal is letting go of the sense of separate self, the ego, through merging with the Divine in blissful union.[3]

This state of being in love evokes our inner state when we were approximately one to six or eight months old, when our sense of self was fused with our mother, a developmental phase Margaret Mahler has called symbiosis. During this period, the infant's predominant experience seems to be that of being one with mother, and the feeling state is of a sweet, adoring, blissful kind of in-loveness. Mothers during this period usually feel inseparable from their child and enraptured by him or her. The sense for both is of being deeply intimate with each other in a merging that feels like ecstatic union. Being and mother are indistinguishable during those early months, and so this earliest relationship with another feels inextricably linked in the soul of a Two to union with her depths. The imprint of this symbiotic relationship, then, leaves the Two with the conviction that union with Being happens through union with another person.

The psychoanalyst Karen Horney, probably herself a Two, has written eloquently about three types who she has at different points called those who move toward, against, and away from others; or self-effacing, expansive, and resigned types—which correspond very closely to Ennea-types Two, Eight, and Five respectively. About the type that moves toward others, which corresponds to Ennea-type Two, she says:

> *Erotic love lures this type as the supreme fulfillment. Love must and does appear as the ticket to paradise, where all woe ends: no more loneliness; no more feeling lost, guilty, and unworthy; no more responsibility for self; no more struggle with a harsh world for which he feels hopelessly unequipped.*

Instead love seems to promise protection, support, affection, encouragement, sympathy, understanding. It will give him a feeling of worth. It will give meaning to his life. It will be salvation and redemption. No wonder then that for him people often are divided into the haves and have-nots, not in terms of money and social status but of being (or not being) married or having an equivalent relationship. . . . To love, for him, means to lose, to submerge himself in more or less ecstatic feelings, to merge with another being, to become one heart and one flesh, and in this merger to find a unity which he cannot find in himself. His longing for love is thus fed by deep and powerful sources: the longing for surrender and the longing for unity.[4]

Awakening out of the sleep of ego, then, is sought by Twos through transcendent romantic love. Like Sleeping Beauty, the Two's life feels suspended until she is rescued by the love of that special Someone. Wealth, power, and success are all fine, but what she really wants—and feels that she can't fully be alive without—is passionate love. The Two's fairy tale is that if she receives enough support through being loved, she will be able to be fully herself. Love will set her soul free, and in this we see one aspect of the personality's distortion of Holy Freedom. Her will is projected onto others, who can give or withhold from her the support of love and thus freedom. True freedom is being yourself—fully being your real self, which is who you are beyond your personality, your historical self. For a Two, freedom is lost in projecting her will and support onto others, rather than realizing them within herself. From being centered in herself, the Two becomes centered in and thus dependent upon others, which is a far cry from real liberation. Freedom that depends on the quality of relationship with another is not freedom at all, since it is completely conditional. Somewhere deep in the soul of a Two, she knows this, and this is probably what is behind her inevitable resentment toward those she feels dependent upon, claiming that they are limiting her freedom. Feeling limited by others upon whom she feels dependent, and attempting to become free of them rather than of her dependency, describes her trap of freedom, as we see on Diagram 9.

Twos are not global in their dependency. In addition to evaluating others based upon their relationship status, as Horney describes, Twos like

Fours divide people into those they consider superior and those they consider inferior, the elite and the peons, the special ones and the hoi polloi. This is her lie, false valuation, as we see on Diagram 12. The special ones are those at the pinnacle of the Two's culture, subculture, or social group, and it is these who matter to her. She can detect them with her inner Geiger counter and is drawn to them like a moth to a flame. The archetypal groupie and camp follower, she plays to those she considers important and attempts to seduce them into caring about her. Her idealization of those she considers special is her highest form of flattery, and hence the name of this type, Ego-Flattery, as mentioned at the beginning of this chapter. Those she considers unimportant are expendable to her.

Some Twos do not appear dependent, and in fact go out of their way to demonstrate how little they care about the affection and opinion of others and how autonomous they are. Rather than being truly independent, they are counterdependent. Instead of playing to some prominent other, they woo others into paying court to them. Self-important and regal in their demeanor, such Twos tend to treat others as subservient and inferior. There will, however, be someone in a counterdependent Two's life who she feels dependent upon, whether she can admit it consciously or not. And whether overtly dependent or counterdependent, the referent is nonetheless the other.

Her central preoccupation, then—indeed her obsession—is the quest for romantic love, and the emphasis here is clearly on the word *quest*. While her professed wish is having the object of her desire reciprocate her love, what actually happens in the life of a Two contradicts this: it never quite works out the way she envisions it, and she always feels rejected to greater or lesser extents. It is difficult, if not impossible, to idealize and be obsessed with someone you are in day-to-day relationship with, and this is one of the reasons Twos unconsciously seek out those who will always be a bit out of reach. Horney describes and explains the object of desire in the type of obsessive relationships Twos are prone to, which she descriptively calls "morbidly dependent":

Morbidly dependent relations are initiated by the unfortunate choice of a partner. To be more accurate, we should not speak of choice. The self-

effacing person actually does not choose but instead is "spellbound" by certain types. He is naturally attracted by a person of the same or opposite sex who impresses him as stronger and superior. Leaving out of consideration here the healthy partner, he may easily fall in love with a detached person, provided the latter has some glamour through wealth, position, reputation, or particular gifts; with an out-going narcissistic type possessing a buoyant self-assurance similar to his own; with an arrogant-vindictive type who dares to make open claims and is unconcerned about being haughty and offensive. Several reasons combine for his being easily infatuated with these personalities. He is inclined to overrate them because they all seem to possess attributes which he not only bitterly misses in himself but ones for the lack of which he despises himself. It may be a question of independence, of self-sufficiency, of an invincible assurance of superiority, a boldness in flaunting arrogance or aggressiveness. Only these strong, superior people—as he sees them—can fulfill all his needs and take him over.[5]

Graphic depictions of such morbidly dependent relationships appear in Somerset Maugham's novel *Of Human Bondage* and in the movie about Victor Hugo's daughter, *The Story of Adele H.* In the latter, Adele Hugo became obsessed with a man who had barely exchanged two words with her, and unbeknownst to him she followed him doggedly from seaport to seaport. Such relationships—or infatuations, more accurately—can only be frustrating, and protestations to the contrary, it is frustration rather than gratification that Twos unconsciously seek out. Again like Fours, once the conquest has been achieved, the object's value drops precipitously, as though saying, "Anyone who loves me must not be worth being in relationship with." This is also known as the Groucho Marx syndrome: "I wouldn't want to be a member of any club that would have me." Part of what is behind this frustrating pattern is that truly being intimate with another brings the risk of being exposed as unlovable and of being rejected. Another part is that truly being loved, and letting the love in, would mean having to give up the sense of self ravenous for the love of an elusive and thus endlessly enticing other that is basic to a Two's identity. Over and above these two explanations, the inner hunger and inner neediness can never be satisfied by another since what is missing is contact with Being, and so trying to fill that need through relationship is doomed to failure.

It may sound as though Twos never marry or form committed relationships, which is not the case. Some famous Twos, such as Meg Ryan and Alan Alda, seem from the outside to have good marriages, while others like Shirley Maclaine, Melanie Griffith, Barbara Walters, and Liz Taylor have had a rocky time in this arena. The point is that regardless of whether a Two's relationship is really simply an infatuation or a long-term marriage, some degree of frustration is usually felt by the Two. Even from the "healthy partner" who Horney "leaves out of consideration" in the quote above, the Two will always feel some distance. A female Two's husband may be somewhat aloof, preoccupied with work or another woman, or just a bit insensitive to her needs. It seems that a Two needs some degree of frustration for a relationship to remain compelling.

A Two's primary focus is on getting love as we have seen, and so she tries to get it by presenting herself as a lovable person, someone who deserves to be loved. An image type, she attempts to present herself and act in ways that imitate the qualities of Merging Gold, qualities Horney unwittingly describes in the following quote:

> *The need to satisfy this urge {for love} is so compelling that everything he does is oriented toward its fulfillment. In the process he develops certain qualities and attitudes that mold his character. Some of these could be called endearing: he becomes sensitive to the needs of others—within the frame of what he is able to understand emotionally. For example, though he is likely to be quite oblivious to a detached person's wish to be aloof, he will be alert to another's need for sympathy, help, approval, and so on. He tries automatically to live up to the expectations of others, or to what he believes to be their expectations, often to the extent of losing sight of his own feelings. He becomes "unselfish," self-sacrificing, undemanding—except for his unbounded desire for affection. He becomes compliant, overconsiderate— within the limits possible for him—overappreciative, overgrateful, generous. He blinds himself to the fact that in his heart of hearts he does not care much for others and tends to regard them as hypocritical and self-seeking.*[6]

While the last sentence quoted is a bit extreme for most normal neurotic Twos, the Two's image, then, becomes one of selflessness, giving without limits, sacrificing herself for another, being self-effacing, compliant, empathic, sensitive, and attuned to the needs of others. She demands of herself that she be, or at least present herself as being, totally compassionate, loving, considerate, understanding, in touch with and doing something about the suffering of others, and like a Bodhisattva, putting her fulfillment second to saving everyone on the planet. On top of all that, she must above all be humble. Naranjo used to characterize the Two "package" as "seductive false humility."

Only these lovable attributes are allowed by the Two's superego, which relentlessly requires that this saintlike image be attained. The punishment is guilt, and Twos are experts at guilt tripping both themselves and others. Guilt for not living up to this image forms part of a Two's emotional atmosphere, consciously or unconsciously. The inner demand to fulfill the image is impossible because it *is* an image, and so not their reality. On the one hand, they feel guilty for not fulfilling this angelic image, and on the other hand, they feel guilty when they have succeeded in making someone believe that's how they really are since they know it is not the truth.

The Two's superego also demands that in addition to being a saint she also be loved, and if a relationship does not work out, it is inevitably her fault. If she had tried harder to be a more loving and desirable person, the inner litany goes, things would have worked out. Jealousy and envy are highly verboten, but the worst offense for a Two is being selfish. Thinking of herself first, rather than her partner, family, ethnic group, et cetera, is *the* capital crime, and so self-sacrifice to the point of martyrdom are part of the demands of her superego. Because of this, simply setting limits or saying no to someone is next to impossible for a Two, prior to doing a lot of inner work. She harbors a secret pride and sense of specialness about her lovable qualities and about what a good person she is being, but because pride does not fit the humble image she is trying to live up to, it also becomes pushed to the recesses of her consciousness. We will return to the subject of pride, the passion of this type, shortly.

She manipulates herself in order to fit the all-loving image. She is constantly fiddling with her inner experience, measuring it against how she thinks she ought to be and pushing herself to experience something a little closer to it. The body parts associated with Twos are the hands and arms, fitting for one who moves things about, pulls strings, and tries to make what she wants happen in imitation of Holy Will. Internally she does this primarily through repression, the defense mechanism of this type, in which she simply pushes out of consciousness anything that doesn't fit the image. Critical perceptions and negative feelings about esteemed others, self-centered thoughts and impulses, as well as neediness and her secret sense of specialness are pushed out of awareness. It is not that these contents disappear, much as a Two would wish it were so; if they don't arise to consciousness, they appear in dreams, psychosomatic conditions, and neurotic symptoms such as anxiety, sleeplessness, and so on. Although it takes tremendous psychic energy to keep the forbidden contents out of consciousness, the alternative is worse: it often brings up acute anxiety for a Two to expose to herself and others thoughts and feelings that do not fit with her idea of being a loving and lovable person.

Naranjo initially saw Twos as the classic Freudian hysterics, but that psychological term has now fallen out of favor and *histrionic* has taken its place. Freud's observation about hysterics is that their sexuality is deeply repressed because of oedipal conflicts, and the result is psychosomatic symptoms, what he called fugue states, and other dissociative mental states. Subsequent psychologists have defined the hysterical character as a person who is "histrionically exhibitionistic, seductive, labile in mood, and prone to act out oedipal fantasies, yet fearful of sexuality and inhibited in action,"[7] an accurate description of a Two.

Twos repress what they feel and anesthetize themselves to their own impulses, particularly sexual ones, and the result is a kind of psychic pressure cooker: their emotions are dramatic and their sexuality leaks out in seductive behavior and appearance. Female Twos tend to dress provocatively although they are not usually conscious of it. Despite the nonverbal come-on, Twos are uneasy and nervous about the sexual act itself. They cry easily and copiously—more often with others than when alone, unlike Fours—and have fits of temper, pique, and impatience when things aren't going the way they want them to. Despite the appearance of a lot of affect, Twos are hysterical in that they discharge emotion rather than fully experiencing it—they tend to be emotionally expressive, demonstrative, and effusive, yet are not deeply in touch with what they are feeling.

As hysterics, most Twos are nonintellectual, as Naranjo has said, but there is a whole category of Twos who have highly developed minds and fit Wilhelm Reich's description of the "big brain" hysteric. This type of hysteric uses her mind defensively—or, as Elsworth Baker, psychiatrist and Reichian therapist, says, "uses her intellect as a tall phallus to defend herself against all men."[8] While Reich thought such hysterics were only female, I have known male Twos who also use their minds in this defensive way, seducing with their intellect while at the same time preventing real contact.

Neediness, touched on above, deserves a special place in the disallowed emotional experiences for a Two. Busy intuiting and filling the needs of others, two functions get served. First, a Two fulfills the image of being a kind of human cornucopia, brimming over with help and resources for others; but more important, she gets to keep out of consciousness her own gnawing inner sense of neediness and helplessness. Her dependency on others is difficult to tolerate; she berates herself for feeling weak and needy. Experiencing her needs, especially for love and attention, blows the bountiful image that she relies on to get the affection she feels her survival requires, and it also reawakens the early deficits in attunement that are unbearable memories to her. It is one of the experiences she most avoids, and so we find neediness at Point Two on the Enneagram of Avoidances, Diagram 10.

She cannot tolerate feeling deprived since this would bring her within dangerous proximity to her inner sense of neediness. Because of this, Twos generally have poor impulse control and tend to develop all sorts of addictive patterns such as overeating, alcoholism, shopping addictions, and obsessive love relationships. In the personality's imitation of Holy Freedom, Twos have little tolerance for any sort of limitations, restrictions, regimens, et cetera, far preferring to throw all practicality, reason, and caution to the wind in the quest to lead a glamorous and exciting life. A Two usually appears falsely abundant, as Naranjo notes, even though she may be knee-deep in credit card debt; and a life of excess seems to be her only acceptable standard of living. License, then, takes the place of real freedom in the life of a Two and obscures the underlying neediness. This is another aspect of her trap of freedom. As Naranjo says, "The affectionate and tender type II individual can become a fury when not indulged and made to feel loved through pampering such as is characteristic of a spoiled child."[9]

She has difficulty tolerating delayed gratification, like buying that great dress or that classy pair of shoes next month when she will actually have the money to pay for them, or not eating those pieces of chocolate every night since she is trying to lose a few pounds. Obviously because of her self-indulgent tendency, her relationship to her body is affected: Twos often have weight problems. They crave pleasure and tend to equate food with love, and have little endurance for the deprivation they feel when limiting their food intake, and that's much too sensible, anyway. Some Twos are a little or a lot overweight; some—again, like Liz Taylor—have wild weight swings. For most, regardless of size, food and intake of all sorts is an issue.

How others see her—particularly others whom she idealizes and looks up to—matters more to her than anything else. To say that their opinion matters more than her own would be missing the point, since she often does not have her own opinion because her sense of herself is so dependent on how others see her. Her self-worth is fragile, resting to a great extent on whether that special other pays attention to her or not. Quoting Horney:

> A third typical feature is part of his general dependence upon others. This is his unconscious tendency to rate himself by what others think of him. His self-esteem rises and falls with their approval or disapproval, their affection or lack of it. Hence any rejection is actually catastrophic for him. If someone fails to return an invitation he may be reasonable about it consciously, but in accordance with the logic of the particular inner world in which he lives, the barometer of his self-esteem drops to zero. In other words any criticism, rejection, or desertion is a terrifying danger, and he may make the most abject effort to win back the regard of the person who has thus

threatened him. His offering of the other cheek is not occasioned by some mysterious "masochistic" drive but is the only logical thing he can do on the basis of his inner premises.[10]

This need to be liked, desired, and not rejected makes it very difficult for a Two to tolerate others being upset or angry at her, and also makes her repress her own negative feelings toward others. Conflicts mean loss of love, and that would be intolerable. Rather than risk such a loss, she is understanding and amenable, seeing the other person's point of view and forgiving him, at least on the surface, while inwardly noting and holding on to the offense. A Two may offer you her other cheek, but eventually there will be a price to pay.

With her self-esteem dependent on how others feel about her and her central belief that she is not lovable, she needs constant reassurances that she is indeed loved. With her perpetual sense of inadequacy, she needs constant praise. Like a cat, the animal associated with this type, she wants her back scratched and demands lots of stroking and enormous amounts of attention. Twos are attention getters who often wear tinkling jewelry or noisy shoes and loudly sigh or weep in groups to draw attention to themselves. They will often do whatever it takes to get noticed, even if the attention they get is negative or brings notoriety. Monica Lewinsky, probably a Two, is a current case in point.

Also like a cat, she will walk all over you to get the attention she wants, although you would have a difficult time getting a Two to acknowledge her self-referent behavior. Rather than asking directly for attention and pats on the back, Twos give it in order to get it back. The credo of a Two could easily be Jesus' precept to "Do unto others as you would have them do unto you." Twos lavish attention, love, and flattery onto those they want to be loved by, in the hope that what is given will be returned in kind. There is nothing selfless about what a Two gives. This becomes very obvious if you don't fulfill your end of the unspoken bargain: she will try to make you feel guilty and will accuse you of exploiting her generosity and of using her, and will turn on you with venom and hatred.

Like the proverbial Jewish mother, Twos feed you chicken soup laden with plenty of adoring schmaltz whether you are hungry or not. But it comes with strings of obligation and guilt attached, which run something like, "Look at all I do for you, and even though you never call me or think about me, here I am, sacrificing for you out of the goodness of my heart. Don't worry about me, I'll be fine," accompanied by a loud sigh and mopping of the brow. Or, as the joke goes, how many Jewish grandmothers (you can substitute Twos here) does it take to change a lightbulb? "None . . . I'll just sit here in the dark." You don't have to be Jewish, of course, to give in order to get, or to feel like a martyred victim: there are versions of the same game in all ethnicities and religious groups.

Twos, then, manipulate through giving to get what they want. They feed you, flatter you, play to you, cajole you, and as Naranjo used to say, unlike Sixes, who lick boots, Twos—to use a vulgar but apt phrase—kiss ass. Their biggest manipulation, however, is being helpful. They will help you out with whatever you need—whether you were aware of the need or not—whether it's financial help, doing something for you, listening to your troubles, matchmaking, counseling, cajoling, supporting you, and so on. They try to insinuate themselves and make themselves indispensable to someone they need in this way so that they will be needed in return.

Sexuality is the currency Twos often trade in, exchanging sexual favors for love. Twos frequently equate their lovability and desirability with the number of sexual conquests they have made, and female Twos often "collect famous cocks," to use a sixties expression. Sex is used by Twos to fulfill their need for attention rather than enjoyed as an expression of affection. As discussed earlier, while Twos often project a very sexy image, they are rarely relaxed and open sexually, appearances to the contrary.

Giving to get is inherently a frustrating way of operating since a Two's real needs go unacknowledged internally and so are unexpressed and ungratified externally. Using their image and role to elicit love and admiration, Twos rarely feel loved for themselves. Using sexuality as a way of making contact and gaining acceptance is inevitably unsatisfying. We have discussed the frustration implicit in a Two's quest for love, and it's obvious that thwarting herself and remaining perpetually unfulfilled are strong threads running through the life and psyche of a Two. The root is her turning away from herself and depending on others for connection, which is an inherent frustration of her personal unfoldment. For this reason on the Enneagram of Antiself Actions, Diagram 11, which describes each type's relationship to their soul, self-frustrating appears at Point Two.

Not only do Twos frustrate themselves but they can be profoundly frustrating to others. While complaining bitterly to you about how miserable/frustrated/upset they are—and Twos do complain a lot—any attempts on your part to offer a solution will usually be met with a reason why your suggestion won't work. Eric Berne, the founder of Transactional analysis, calls this kind of interaction the "game" of "Why Don't You— Yes But."[11] Berne defines a game as a repetitive social interaction in which the outcome is predictable and fulfills a motive other than what is being explicitly discussed. The object here is to prove that no suggestion will work, and like a mild projective identification, this game makes the other person feel as helpless, hopeless, and frustrated as the Two feels internally. On a deeper level, if a Two is not taking issue at something, i.e., pitting her will against something, she would lose her sense of who she is. Some degree of negativity, oppositionality, and disgruntlement is therefore necessary for a Two to maintain her sense of self.

The passion of Ennea-type Two is pride, as mentioned earlier, as we see on the Enneagram of Passions in Diagram 2. It is not real self-esteem and an inner sense of self-worth but rather what Horney calls "neurotic pride." It is not based on real abilities or achievements but is an inflated sense of self that is compensatory for the inner feeling of being unlovable and not valuable in herself. Twos believe they are special—both especially gifted, talented, loving, giving, and so on—but also especially complicated, neurotic, troubled, put-upon, and so forth. So the prideful self-inflation is both about their positive as well as their negative qualities. They are larger than life, different from ordinary people. They are capable of more. They can do more, accomplish more, feel more deeply, care more, and so on. The other side is their belief that they are especially bad human beings, bigger failures, more rejectable, more unlovable, and more unworthy than others. They are filled with their own self-importance and often behave as though they were royalty, currying the admiration and praise of others. Their pride lies in their puffed-up inner image of themselves—not for being who they are.

They are proud when they are indispensable to that prestigious other; they are proud when they are sexually desired; they are proud when someone they value gives them special attention; they are proud when they have given to others in superhuman ways and have behaved like a veritable Saint Teresa. When their self-sacrifice is not acknowledged or when it is taken for granted, and when they are not given the special treatment to which they feel entitled, or when they are not the center of attention, Twos feel deeply hurt and humiliated.

A Two's pride is not always visible. This is because there are two styles of Twos: those who manifest the pride more overtly in a grandiose, exhibitionistic, pompous, and entitled manner; and the more self-effacing type who present themselves in a more humble manner but whose pride is nonetheless just below the surface.

The virtue associated with Point Two is humility, as we see on the Enneagram of Virtues in Diagram 1. Ichazo defines humility as the "acceptance of the limits of the body, its capacities. The intellect holds unreal beliefs about its own powers. The body knows precisely what it can and cannot do. Humility in its largest sense is the knowledge of the true human position on the cosmic scale." So key to the working-through process for a Two is arriving at an objective sense of herself.

Developing humility means for a Two settling into herself first of all. Rather than orienting herself outward—trying to please, reacting to and responding to others—she needs to turn her attention inward. Since Twos seem so demanding and so self-referential, it may sound ironic that what she really needs to do is to focus on herself and give herself the attention she craves from others, but it is the only way she will ever truly get the contact she craves. Focusing on herself entails getting in touch with what is truly going on inside under the blather of hysterical emotions and the exciting events and crises in her life. So she must slow down her frenzy of activity and her flurry of emotion and sense deeply into herself, getting in touch with what she is actually experiencing. Although the emotions of a

Two can be quite dramatic, she is not really deeply feeling them, as discussed earlier, and fully experiencing them is necessary for her to develop an authentic sense of self. In the same vein, actually sensing her body and feeling where its edges are is extremely important for a Two to develop a real sense of where she leaves off and where her inflated self-image begins.

As she settles into herself, she will see that she is constantly comparing herself to her all-loving and all-giving idealized self-image and either rejecting herself when she doesn't measure up or puffing herself up with pride when she does. She will need to acknowledge her pride and sense of specialness—not an easy thing for a Two to do. She will get in touch with how her superego continuously rejects how she is, both inwardly and outwardly, if she does not conform to the grand image it demands she live up to—and how it usually doesn't. She needs to see how much her self-assessment shifts depending upon whether she feels loved or rejected by that significant person in her life, and that fundamentally she has little self-love and self-acceptance. She will see that she is so sensitive to rejection from others because it supports her own self-rejection, and she needs to understand psychodynamically how this way of relating to herself resulted from her early childhood conditioning. She will see that this internal dynamic is pitting herself against her reality, and rather than this willfulness changing her or freeing her, it only makes her suffer terribly. Part of the key to being willing to defend against her superego and beginning to accept herself lies in experiencing directly how painful and hurtful this dynamic is.

The more she gets out from under her superego and opens to her inner reality, the more she will see that she is human and that both her capacities and her limits do not determine her value or her lack thereof. She will be able to accept what she is truly capable of and what she isn't, what she is really experiencing and what she would like to be experiencing, and will cease feeling subhuman and having to compensate for it by acting in superhuman ways. She needs to understand that she is lovable simply for who she is, not for what she can do for others. This will lead to an honest sense of what she truly wishes and doesn't wish to do for others, rather than feeling obligated and guilt ridden if she is not being there for everyone. It will also lead to knowing and accepting what her limits are physically, energetically, psychically, and in honoring them, learning to feel comfortable with saying no to others.

It also entails seeing that her lack of inner limits, which she has called freedom, is simply license and in fact imprisons her. She needs to see how much she is a slave to her desires, her likes and dislikes, how difficult it is to say no to gratifying them even if it puts her in financial, physical, or emotional jeopardy. She needs to see that being realistic about how much money she has or when her belly is actually full or whether she really needs another new outfit does not make life dull, boring, and unromantic but in fact provides the ground for her to do things that are truly liberating and meaningful in her life.

Humility means taking care of herself and giving attention to herself in a pragmatic way, and instead of seeing this result in her becoming selfish, which she often fears, she will find that she becomes more and more centered within herself. The more seated in herself she becomes, the more she can accept, surrender to, and flow with her inner reality, and the freer she becomes of her historical self and of her dependency on others. The more she opens to herself, the more she will accept others and truly be able to receive and give the love she has been so desperate for. She will be able to let go of herself, truly surrendering to what is, and in this, becoming one with her deepest nature. She will know herself to be one with Being, a drop of sweet honey, melted in ecstatic union with the Divine.

CHAPTER 8

ENNEA-TYPE
EIGHT:
EGO-REVENGE

Eights tend to be self-confident, domineering, control-ling, and no-nonsense kinds of people. These are the bad boys of the enneagram, eager to get down and get dirty, and mix things up. They prefer to be in charge and run-ning the show, giving orders rather than taking them. Often they are big and blustery—energetically if not physically—making their presence felt and determined to get their way. With a fundamental orientation that life has treated them wrong, they are out for justice and to set things right by exacting vengeance—hence the name of this ennea-type, Ego-Revenge. Their method is the bib-lical one: an eye for an eye, doing to others as they feel they have been done to. They are confrontational, always on the lookout for a challenge and a fight, something to pit themselves against.

Inwardly it is weakness and need that seem to be the causes of their problems, so they push these feelings away, often denying that they might have them even un-consciously. They have little tolerance for "soft" emotions like fear, sadness, and especially weakness, or any other feelings that smack of inferiority, indecisiveness, needi-ness, or deficiency. They value being tough and strong, able to take the knocks that life dishes out and come back swinging. They are straight shooters, speaking their truth plainly and bluntly, regardless of the impact on others or the consequences for themselves. Often earthy and passionate, sometimes even crude, they have a lust for life, seeming to devour as much of it as they can. They can be thick-skinned and insensitive to the feelings of others, but occasionally a sentimental side shows itself, and instead of coming across like a grizzly bear, they seem more like harmless teddy bears.

These personality traits stem from the loss of the particular view of reality—the Holy Idea—associated with Point Eight, which is Holy Truth. We have discussed some of the characteristics and qualities of reality when perceived objectively—without the filter of the personality—in discussing the other Holy Ideas. For instance, Holy Perfection elucidates the ultimate "suchness" of reality, Holy Love articulates that it is made out of love and is an expression of love, Holy Origin tells us that we arise out of and are made up of Being, Holy Faith tells us that Being is what supports and sustains us and all of life, Holy Law and Holy Will describe various nuances of the functioning of Being. Holy Truth points directly to the existence of Being and its coemergence with all of reality. It is the perception of reality in all of its multidimensionality, from the physical world to the deepest spiritual dimension of the Absolute. Here we see that all of these dimensions are real—they are the truth about how things are—and we also see that they exist inseparably from each other. This perception is in stark contrast to that of the personality, in which we base our sense of reality on the assumption that the realm of matter is all that exists. Even if we entertain the notion that there might be deeper dimensions to reality, when push comes to shove, the physical is fundamental for most of humanity. Since each of our physical bodies is separate from all other objects, believing we are inherently discrete entities is implicit in the personality's materialistic perspective.

From the enlightened view of Point Eight, we see that material form is the outermost layer of a multidimensional reality. This reality is a oneness, an indivisible unity such that all of its dimensions make up and are inseparable from its wholeness. This is a nondual perspective in which reality is experienced as one thing. This sense of oneness is often difficult to grasp, since we usually think of one in contrast to two. Here oneness means everything or, to put it a little differently, everything that exists on all dimensions forms our one reality. Matter and Spirit are one thing; the physical world and the divine world are the same. So from this non-dualistic or coemergent perspective, if we use our analogy and liken reality to an ocean, our focus may be on the waves or on the ocean itself, but they are nevertheless inseparable one from the other. Just as we can experience the ocean by seeing its waves, matter is one way of experiencing Spirit. Matter, then, is like the waves, making up the surface of the Ocean that is everything.

So the various levels of increasing depth from the physical through the essential dimension through the Boundless Dimensions to the Absolute are all present at the same time and are inseverable from each other. They are different depths of the same thing, each one of increasing proximity to the Absolute, and we could call this perspective seeing reality in its verticality, although in actuality such spatial terminology isn't really accurate. Horizontally, on the most superficial level, none of the forms of the material world are discrete or separate from the oneness of which they are a part.

From the perspective of Point Eight, enlightenment is a matter of seeing beyond the delusion of duality, the sense that there is this and that, self and other, matter and Spirit, ego and Essence, and awakening to the reality of the oneness of all things. This is the basis of all coemergent teachings such as Dzogchen, the Tibetan Buddhist practice that cultivates abiding in our "nondual state of pristine awareness," using its terminology.[1] It is also implicit in the philosophy of Advaita Vedanta, a branch of Hinduism, in which reality is "defined as 'one-without-a-second' (*a-dvitiya*)" and the human situation is that

> the life-monad is in error about its own true character. It regards itself as bound. But this error vanishes with the dawn of realization. The life-monad (jiva) then discovers that it is itself the Self (atman). Bondage thereupon is nonexistent. Indeed, with reference to that which is always free such terms as bondage and liberation are inappropriate. They seem to have meaning only during the preliminary stages of spiritual apprenticeship, when the pupil has still to make the critical discovery. The term "libera-

tion" is used by the guru only in a preliminary sense, as addressed to one in a state of bondage that exists only in his own imagination.[2]

From within our own experience, Holy Truth is the recognition of our basic nature as Being and of Its inseparability from our bodies and our souls. In other words, your body and your ultimate nature make up a oneness that cannot be broken down into parts. Just as you normally perceive your body as a solid mass or, when viewed with subatomic magnification, as mostly made up of space, both realities coexist and are different perceptions of the same phenomena. To say that one is more real or more true does not make any sense. Likewise, from one angle we are animals with highly developed brains, and from another we are windows on the universe. Both are true.

Even conceiving of your personality as distinct from your essential nature does not make sense when reality is seen through the lens of Holy Truth. Your personality is simply a more or less fixed shape that your soul is taking, which is the cumulative result of your personal history; it is a pattern of beliefs, emotions, and behaviors that you define as yourself. Regardless of how rigid your consciousness is, your soul is nevertheless inseparable from Being. It is like a wave that conceives of itself as static and separate from the rest of the ocean, while clearly this cannot be the case. Peak experiences and moments of contact with Being are simply glimpses into our true state of affairs.

So whether perceived from a more universal perspective or from within our personal experience, Holy Truth is the experiential understanding that the reality we are part of is an indivisible and multidimensional unity. The loss of this understanding gives birth to a sense of duality, that one thing can be ultimately separate from something else. This in turn gives rise to various dualistic notions: that we are made up of Spirit and matter which are fundamentally separate or of different natures; that the universe contains two opposite forces of good and evil; and that the manifest and the unmanifest are different things.

While this sense of duality is implicit in all of the personality types and is one of the cornerstones of egoic reality, it is predominant for an Ennea-type Eight and forms the underpinning of all of the psychological characteristics of this type. The fundamental duality that arises for an Eight in concert with his loss of contact with Being in early childhood is that of believing himself to be and feeling like someone who is separated or cut off from Being. In other words, the loss of contact with Being creates the sense that he is devoid of It and so to all intents and purposes, It does not exist for him. As we have seen, this cannot be the case since he is made of Being and inseparable from It, but upon this delusion rests the Eight personality's orientation toward life.

While not the norm, some Eights with a spiritual bent don't feel that they ever lost contact with Being, and to them it is others and the world that seems devoid of It. Nonetheless his personality crystallizes around this take on reality, and while contact with his depths may be maintained, he develops a personality with which he identifies and which forms a rigid shell armoring his soul to protect his inner depths. To the extent that an Eight has developed a viable personality structure, he has reified a sense of self and of other in which one side has Spirit or God and the other side is devoid of It.

Most Eights, however, feel that they have been more or less completely stripped of Being at a very young age. An Eight's innermost feeling is that something terrible has happened, although on this preverbal and preconceptual level, he does not even have the concept of loss of contact with his depths. There is just the sense that something not right has occurred, that something bad has been done to him, and that his soul has been corrupted or tainted in some way. There is a vague sense of having lost his primordial and natural state, a dim sense that he has fallen from grace. What is most real, the deepest and paramount truth about himself, has been wiped out of his consciousness. His soul knows that a sense of unity with what is most precious about him has been lost, and his ego crystallizes around this sense.

Out of the eradication of his inner sense of oneness with Being which results in a sense of self and other—duality—arises the conviction that someone must be responsible for this terrible state of affairs. Blame is a word that figures largely in the psychology of an Eight—ascertaining who is at fault and avenging the wrong is a central preoccupation. This is why this type is called Ego-Revenge as mentioned at the beginning of this chapter, and why Ichazo named the Eight fixation vengeance, as we see on Diagram 2. Most deeply, although it takes a great deal of inner work to make this conscious, he holds himself as culpable. He believes that he should have been strong enough—yes, as an infant and very young child—to withstand the force of conditioning and not lose touch with Being. Or, if he does not experience having lost that contact, he believes he should have been able to make those in his early environment conscious of Being, both in themselves and within him. A tall order indeed for a baby, but one that sounds plausible and even reasonable to an Eight.

In either case, he believes he is a bad person for having let this happen. This sense of being an ultimately separate entity who is responsible for having lost contact with Being is probably the source of the Christian doctrine of original sin. Like Adam and Eve, he has been thrown out of the Garden of Eden because of his badness. He blames himself, but this is very difficult to tolerate, so in a decisive psychological move, he projects the blame outward: it is the fault of others. His parents and the rest of his early holding environment become responsible for this profound loss in his mind, and this wrong must be righted. He must be vindicated and restitution must be extracted. Blaming his early milieu and staying stuck in his anger about his childhood not only keeps him from hating himself but also protects the memory of that preciousness that he once experienced as himself. He protects the goodness of his True Nature in this way. This is his own personal *jihad*,[3] and restores to him a sense of virtue.

While it may seem that he is being excessively hard on himself (if his self-blame is conscious) and unforgiving toward his early caretakers, this stance actually protects him from something that is to him far worse: experiencing his powerlessness. To do so would mean capitulation to him, a surrender to the forces of egoic reality, both within and without. Continuing to hold others accountable and trying to set things right keeps an inner fight going with reality, which keeps him from having to accept it, and for an Eight this was a necessary psychological survival strategy of early childhood. To have fully experienced his helplessness and defenselessness would have meant psychically giving up, and he indeed might not have survived if he had done so. This is especially true if he experienced severe trauma or abuse in his childhood. His inner powerlessness, helplessness, and vulnerability to the forces of conditioning are what he considers the core of his weakness, and this is his most avoided experience, as we see on the Enneagram of Avoidances, Diagram 10, where weakness appears at Point Eight.

As we have seen, he fundamentally holds himself responsible for his fall into egoic reality, and from one angle the rest of his life can be seen as an attempt to grapple with this basic sense of culpability and the resulting feeling of guilt. All of his self-chastisement and self-castigation—which far exceed any that he lays on others—has its roots in this way that his soul interprets his loss of contact with Being. For this reason, on the Enneagram of Antiself Actions, Diagram 11, which describes each type's relationship with his soul, the term at Point Eight is self-punishing.

If only he had been stronger and more powerful, he tells himself, this would not have happened. If he had been more forceful and assertive enough, he could have made mommy perceive his depths and he would have retained contact with Being. If only he had been stauncher, he could have resisted the force of egoic reality. If only he had been tougher, he could have stopped all the abuses, large and small, of which he was the recipient—and many Eights had childhoods in which they either were abused physically or sexually, or felt as though they were. His take on his childhood is that he was humiliated, exploited, and punished for reasons that had little to do with him or his behavior. Many Eights have the impression that mother withheld her love and did not protect him from his dominating and brutal father. A sense of profound injustice is left in his soul, and the world appears more or less malevolent to him.

What is wrong with him, in his mind, is his weakness and vulnerability, his openness and receptivity, since these qualities are responsible for his impressionable infant soul losing contact with his inner truth. Strength, then, looks to him like the quality he needs, and this leads him to develop a personality style that replicates it more than any other trait. He imitates essential strength—called the Red in the language of the Diamond Approach—and this is the idealized Aspect for this type. He becomes hard, tough, forceful, inflexible, and immovable so that he can never be "fucked with" again, using the language an Eight would use to describe what he has been through. He fortifies himself, making himself impregnable and impenetrable. He develops a tough skin, a leathery protective layer in an attempt to preserve and protect the sensitivity of his soul.

Unlike the true strength of Essence, the false strength that characterizes the Eight personality type is static, rigid, and inflexible. He is always strong and tough, using the same amount of force for everything he does, as though he needed a blow torch to toast a piece of bread, or a bonfire to create a little heat. He is continuously making himself hard, as if that rigidity were the same thing as strength. In fact, from a purely physical point of view, a strong muscle is one that is toned, relaxed, resilient, and able to respond with power when needed. Real strength is like that: flexible and responsive to the situation at hand. We see it in bears, the animal associated with this point, who are able to act with enormous force when in search of prey or defending their cubs, yet who also relax completely and lick their cubs undefendedly when such strength isn't needed. For us humans, real fortitude is not measured in the number of pounds of weight we can lift or in how powerfully we can harangue someone else. It takes far more real strength—the might of our souls—to speak our truth regardless of the reception, to open our hearts fully and tell someone we love them or to let down our defenses and admit that we have made a mistake or have hurt another.

The toughness that an Eight develops as compensation for his lack of contact with real strength is like tough armor blanketing his soul. He tries to protect his heart by rejecting all emotions that he considers weak: fear, sadness, shame, remorse, neediness, helplessness, vulnerability, longing, and so on. Unfortunately you cannot close your heart to one set of emotions and not to all others, so he also shuts out his capacity to experience innocent joy, the tenderness of love, affection, appreciation, and compassion, to name a few other feelings he seals himself off from. He may even toughen his heart so much that he is unable to experience the blissful state of falling in love, and has unconsciously made the decision that such protection is worth the price. As Horney says of the neurotic corresponding to Ennea-type Eight, which she classifies as moving against others and variously calls the aggressive, vindictive, and expansive type:

The choking off of tender feelings, starting in childhood and described as the hardening process, is necessitated by the actions and attitudes of other people and is meant to protect him against others. The need to make himself insensitive to suffering is greatly reinforced by the vulnerability of his pride and climaxed by his pride in invulnerability. His wish for human warmth and affection (both giving and receiving it), originally thwarted by the environment and then sacrificed to the need for triumph, is finally frozen by the verdict of his self-hate branding him as unlovable. Thus in turning against others he has nothing precious to lose. . . . "It is out of the question that they should love me; they hate me anyhow, so they should at least be afraid of me." Moreover healthy self-interest, which otherwise would check vindictive impulses, is kept at a minimum through his utter disregard for his personal welfare. And even the fear of others, though operating to some extent, is held down by his pride in invulnerability and immunity.[4]

This very act of trying to protect himself ends up cutting him off from himself, and in this lies the irony of an Eight's defenses. Toughening himself and rejecting his "soft" emotions make him lose the very sensitivity that gives him access and makes him transparent to his soul's interior nature, Essence. What began as an attempt to protect his soul ends up sealing him off from its inner truth. He loses touch with what gives his soul vitality and aliveness, and is left with a feeling of deadness within.

Because he has numbed his heart, he has little empathy, sensitivity, or compassion for others, just as he has little for himself. At the extreme, he cares little about what others feel or how they feel about him, since he has come to the conclusion that he is unlovable anyway, as we have seen. With his lack of empathy, he is often unaware of the suffering and hurt feelings of others and is inconsiderate, not noticing the effect of his often brusque, blunt, and callous manner upon them. If he does notice, rather than feeling remorse, he is contemptuous of the vulnerability the other person is allowing him to see.

Closely related is his characteristic lack of tolerance for subtlety. He likes things to be straightforward with no beating around the bush. He does not want to look beneath the surface of things, any more than he wants to look beneath the surface of himself for fear of experiencing the lack of aliveness that has resulted from his toughening of his soul and the guilt that surrounds his emptiness. What he can contact with his physical senses is real to him, and what he cannot is airy-fairy and a lot of bullshit (an important and frequently used word for an Eight) to him. Obviously this includes the emotional realm and the spiritual realm. He is very skeptical of religious and spiritual experience and for the most part believes that organized religion is simply a shrewd way of exploiting the gullible.

He approaches reality with a fixedness and closed-mindedness rather than an openness. The personality's replication of strength leads his mind to become unreceptive, unbending, inflexible, and profoundly opinionated. What he sees is prejudiced by his negative opinion about what might be there, and this to him is only being realistic. He views reality from the perspective of someone who might be conned, exploited, humiliated, or otherwise threatened, and so his prejudice is to look for the potentially hurtful, the more powerful, the darker and more animalistic side of things. People are bastards and bums until proven otherwise in his inner world. His eyes—the body part associated with this type—are not open to things as they are, but rather see life through a veil of prejudice. The character Archie Bunker from the seventies television show *All in the Family* exemplifies this bigoted quality of Eights. We see in his brand of "realism" a distortion of Holy Truth, as well as in his unswerving conviction that what he sees through his jaundiced eyes is indisputably accurate.

So while Ones are predisposed to give everything a positive spin, Eights are predisposed to give everything a more sinister one. For this reason, on the Enneagram of Lies, Diagram 12, which describes the veils through which each type sees reality, the phrase prejudice/false denial occupies Point Eight. His biggest denial is of the optimistic, the upbeat, the hopeful side of things, and it is his primary defense mechanism. He is driven by a profound distrust of others and of life itself, convinced that he must fight to wrest anything good out of the world. It is as though he were afraid of being duped by believing anything positive, and so better to see everything from its darkest side than risk being disappointed and let down by reality again. Like Sixes, he lives in an animalistic Darwinian world in which only the fittest survive, but unlike Sixes he identifies with the strong.

Many Eights' deepest denial is of the source of all goodness: the realm of Being. Rather than feeling the unbearably painful sense that he has been cut off from the Divine, he denies that Being exists. God is dead to him. It is not that God once existed and now is no more but rather that the whole notion is bullshit in the first place. He becomes a pragmatist, pugnaciously engaging with the shell of the world—what is left when Being is excluded from the picture.

His negation of the multidimensionality of existence may be his deepest denial, but the mechanism of denial functions in large and small ways constantly within his personality. It wards off from his consciousness anything that would be painful to him, i.e., anything that might compromise his internal ideal of being strong and powerful. So anything that might make him appear wrong, weak, lacking capacity, or needy is simply disavowed. This runs the gamut from denying actual events to negating inner thoughts and emotions.

Denial also makes it appear to him that the problem is always outside of himself. The enemy is the other, who seems out to get him, wants to humiliate him, is treating him unjustly, and so on. He always seems to be the innocent victim who is being picked on for reasons he does not understand. He rebuffs responsibility for how he is treated or related to when it is not to his liking, and accuses the other person of having it in for him. He does not see that blaming others for his difficulties and believing that the decks are stacked against him is his own distortion of reality which influences what manifests in his life. The anger and venom he frequently, if not continually, experiences is an inevitable emotional reactivity to holding reality in this way.

So while an Eight may pride himself on being down-to-earth, matter-of-fact, and facing life squarely without the blinders of sentimentality and idealism, his realism leaves out all goodness and allows for only the material world as fundamental reality. Even though his behavioral style is an imitation of Holy Truth in his exaggerated forthrightness and plain-spokenness, his version of truth is only partial and prejudiced. In the following description by Horney, we see clearly the Eight's attempt to replicate the lost Holy Truth:

> His feeling about himself is that he is strong, honest, and realistic, all of which is true if you look at things his way. According to his premises his estimate of himself is strictly logical, since to him ruthlessness is strength, lack of consideration for others, honesty, and a callous pursuit of one's own ends, realism. His attitude on the score of his honesty comes partly from a shrewd debunking of current hypocrisies. Enthusiasm for a cause, philanthropic sentiments, and the like he sees as sheer pretense, and it is not hard for him to expose gestures of social consciousness or Christian virtue for what they so often are. His set of values is built around the philosophy of the jungle. Might makes right. Away with humaneness and mercy. Homo homini lupus.[5]

Her Latin phrase brings to mind the memorable recent role of an Eight actor, Jack Nicholson, in the movie *Wolf*, in which he transforms from being a subservient schlemiel into an aggressive—and unmetaphorical—wolf. Apropos of this, rather than ever being at the mercy of another, Eights strive to dominate, control, and overpower others. As the saying goes, "There's no defense like a good offense": he aggressively fights his way to be on top—the strongest and most powerful—so that he can't be exploited or subordinated. Because of his fear of being controlled, he needs to be in charge of things. He wants to be the boss, calling the shots and giving the orders rather than taking them, pushing others around so that he doesn't have to submit to another's will. He has little tolerance for taking orders and puts up with that only as long as it serves his ends. He never wants to be in a position in which he feels weak, less than another, or under another's control, and he will go to great lengths to be sure that this doesn't happen. To this end, he will browbeat and bully others into submitting to him and respecting his authority.

He is hard on others, driving them and demanding more from them. But as hard as he pushes others, he pushes himself more. His punitive superego drives and castigates him, goading him on to be stronger and tougher. The ideal he is trying to live up to—his ego ideal—is of being indomitable, strong, and powerful, and when he does not conform, his superego punishes him with brutal attacks. It is relentless and demanding, putting him down for being a weakling and a wimp when he feels hurt or tired. He allows no limits for himself, physical, emotional, or otherwise. Just as he bluntly puts others down and attempts to decimate them with his invalidating sarcasm, his superego berates and batters him at least as harshly. And just as he bludgeons others into submission, his superego beats him into conforming to his ego ideal of strength.

He is gutsy, aggressive, intimidating, loud, and boisterous, like his animal, the bear. Some Eights have a teddy bear quality, as mentioned at the beginning of this chapter, an innocent cuteness that sneaks through the gruffness, and in it we glimpse the part of an Eight's soul that was encapsulated very early, sealed off from the rest of his personality. This is beautifully portrayed by Dennis Franz in the character Andy Sipowitz on the television series *NYPD Blue*. We see it also in the actress Roseanne Arnold. An Eight takes up a lot of room, commanding attention and running the show. Eights are often physically large, robust-looking, and frequently overweight. They tend to be barrel-chested, reflecting their defendedness in the heart area and corresponding difficulties with softening and surrendering. Softness to him is weakness; surrender is capitulation.

He is often openly arrogant, dismissive, and disparaging of others in his assumption and assertion of his own superiority. He is not held back by his own feelings, those of others, social conventions of modesty, courteousness, politeness, or other niceties. He does not seem to be constrained by guilt or conscience as other types are, and acts out things that others only imagine doing. Because of this, more inhibited types often admire him and wish they were more like him. He is not as free as he appears, however, as Horney tells us:

> *The aggressive type looks like an exquisitely uninhibited person. He can assert his wishes, he can give orders, express anger, defend himself. But actually he has no fewer inhibitions than the compliant type. It is not greatly to the credit of our civilization that his particular inhibitions do not, offhand, strike us as such. They lie in the emotional area and concern his*

capacity for friendship, love, affection, sympathetic understanding, disinterested enjoyment. The last he would set down as a waste of time.[6]

He is subject to bursts of rage and violent behavior, which are for him as compulsive as repressing them is for other types. Anger comes to him more easily than other emotions. He is compelled to lash out and fight back and, unless he has done a great deal of work on himself, has little freedom *not* to respond in this way. Anger is a reaction to something we experience as constraining and limiting us, and when we let it move through us, we feel strong, vital, and alive. Because these are the very qualities that an Eight wants very much to feel, anger is his emotion of choice. When he feels hurt, he gets angry. When he is afraid, he gets angry. When he is needy, he gets angry. Usually blaming someone else for these "soft" emotions that he is being "forced" to feel accompanies his blasts of rage.

He is practical and blunt. He is willful and tough minded. He is the ruthless and despotic CEO, the vicious mob boss, the rancorous defense lawyer à la F. Lee Bailey. He is the corrupt despot—the Idi Amins, the Saddam Husseins, the Duvaliers, and the Augusto Pinochets of the world. He is the no-bullshit political animal—Nikita Khrushchev pounding his shoe on the table at the United Nations, Lyndon Johnson dropping the bombs on Vietnam. He is Henry VIII, breaking from the Catholic Church and creating his own so that he could divorce and remarry in the hope of producing a male heir, and dissolving the abbeys and annexing their vast wealth to seal the split.

While it may not appear so, given some of the exemplars above, justice is an important word to Eights. Just as Ones have their antennae out for imperfection, Eights have theirs out for injustice. The quest for justice, then, is an Eight's trap, as we see on the Enneagram of Traps, Diagram 9. The world appears to him as an unjust place—especially regarding himself—and he wants to even the score. He is a great champion of the underdog, often becoming the spokesman for others weaker and less powerful than himself in opposition to some monolithic force. He is a rebel against established authority and openly opposes it. So he is also the political activist and revolutionary—the Fidel Castros and the Lech Walesas of the world.

His form of justice is definitely of the biblical sort: an eye for an eye, and a tooth for a tooth. He wants retribution. He wants to inflict upon others what has been inflicted upon him. He delights in planning and fantasizing about how he will avenge himself. His form of justice is really a personal vendetta in which the other suffers in the same way that he feels he has. He is Sean Penn, who *Newsweek* quotes regarding his punching of photographers, beating up of those who ticked him off, and his assault-and-battery conviction as displaying "a lack of discretion relative to witnesses present" and "entirely justified behavior."[7]

Obviously fairness does not enter into his notion of justice. While he sees the world as inequitable, biased, and partisan, he is not interested in changing that. He is not interested in making the world a better and less corrupt place. He only wants his side to win, and once it has, he will subject the losers to humiliation.

The Mafia exemplifies this Eight-ish tendency. Formed originally in Sicily during the Middle Ages as private armies fighting against various invaders, the Mafia in the eighteenth and nineteenth centuries turned upon the landowners who had hired them and became the de facto rule of the land. In America, the immigrating mafiosi began by protecting Italian families who were being exploited by bosses and landlords, and evolved into notorious organized crime families. Revenge and retaliation, a strict code of loyalty, and a refusal to cooperate with any legal authority became the modus operandi. Marlon Brando's movie portrayal of a Mafia godfather is an excellent example by an Eight actor of an Eight character in an Eight subculture.

Another aspect of his quest for justice or vengeance (depending on the spin you wish to give it) is his particular sense of entitlement. The following quote from Horney describes this well:

> *The most important expression of his vindictiveness toward others is in the kind of claims he makes and the way he asserts them. He may not be openly demanding and not at all aware of having or making any claims,*

but in fact he feels entitled both to having his neurotic needs implicitly respected and to being permitted his utter disregard of others' needs or wishes. He feels entitled for instance to the unabridged expression of his unfavorable observations and criticisms but feels equally entitled never to be criticized himself. He is entitled to decide how often or how seldom to see a friend and what to do with the time spent together. Conversely he also is entitled not to have others express any expectations or objections on this score.[8]

As we are seeing, the primary orientation of an Eight is outside of himself. For this reason, there are proportionally fewer Eights in spiritual work than other types. There are, however, a few Eight spiritual teachers who have left indelible marks. One is Madame Helena Blavatsky, cofounder of the Theosophical Society, a spiritualist sect of the turn of the century. She claimed, despite two marriages and a child, to be still a virgin, swore in numerous languages, and was variously received as a true teacher and a fraud. Another was G. I. Gurdjieff, mentioned in the Introduction, whose teaching style involved pushing his students beyond what they considered their limits and who was famous for enormous meals washed down by huge quantities of Armagnac. A more recent Eight spiritual teacher is Swami Muktananda, deceased leader of Siddha Yoga, a form of Hinduism. Very much against forgiveness and turning the other cheek, he believed that violence could be beaten out of people; and although his order was supposed to be celibate, rumors of sexual scandals crop up from time to time.

In view of the obvious appetites of our spiritual exemplars, it is time to turn to the passion of this type, lust, as we see on the Enneagram of the Passions in Diagram 2. Lust as the passion of Eights is not restricted to the sexual arena although it decidedly includes it. Lust is an attitude, an emotional orientation toward all of life. It is a passionate voraciousness, desire magnified to the level of a driven ravenousness. It is animalistic, raw, and crude; straightforward with no pretenses. Mae West, Sharon Stone, and Bette Midler, movie sirens past and present, demonstrate on the screen this unabashed, explicit, and bad-girl quality of Eights in the arena of sexuality.

Lust colors the whole feel of an Eight. It is reflected in his gusto, his

gutsiness, his bravado, his passionate engagement in life, and most con-
spicuously in his appetites for all that gives pleasure. It is a zealous drive
for sensory and sensual gratification and physical pleasure with, of course,
a vengeance to it. Janis Joplin's wholehearted and whole-souled singing
and engagement in life and love come to mind, as does her tough veneer
covering her neediness. Forget the hors d'oeuvres and the foreplay—he
wants to get to the beef right away and gorge himself on it. Enough is definitely not enough to an Eight; he demands not just gratification of his
desires but excess. Smothering, devouring, burying, and enveloping himself completely and rolling around in the objects of his lust is what he
wants. This is exemplified in Von Stroheim's great silent film *Greed,* in
which the character played by ZaSu Pitts pours a sack of gold coins onto
her bed and lies down on them and literally writhes.

Fritz Perls, the founder of Gestalt therapy and a consummate Eight,
begins his book *Gestalt Therapy Verbatim* with the following: "It took us a
long time to debunk the whole Freudian crap. . . ."[9] While Perls would
probably object to my using Freudian notions in a chapter on his type, an
Eight's lust is nonetheless the venting of pure and unrefined biological
drive energy, as defined by Freud. Freud's concept of *Trieb* is that human
beings are innately endowed with two biologically and instinctually
based drives or urges. While his drive theory evolved and was modified
over the years, in essence he says that we humans have a libidinal drive
that impels us toward union with and acquisition of what we love and desire, and an aggressive drive that impels us to conquer and prevail over
others. The extent of the aggressive drive's orientation toward destruction
has been a matter of debate among psychoanalytic thinkers, as has the ex-
act interrelation of the two drives. Regardless, in the lust of an Eight we
see libido fused with aggression, with all of the latter drive's implications
of assertiveness, domination, and destructiveness. Part of the pleasure in
lust is wrestling it away from someone else or from life in general. As
Naranjo says, "We must consider that lust is more than hedonism. There
is in lust not only pleasure, but pleasure in asserting the satisfaction of
impulses, pleasure in the forbidden and particularly, pleasure in *fighting
for pleasure.*"[10]

There is a grabbiness and a pushiness to an Eight's lust, as though he

were going to wring out of life all of the enjoyment, satisfaction, aliveness, and vitality that he lacks inwardly. There is an insatiability about his
drive for more, as though filling an endless and bottomless inner chasm.
In keeping with his whole perceptual skew on reality, it is as though he
were grabbing for things that the other means to deprive him of, as
though he were still trying to snatch his mother's withheld breast and
force the milk out of it.

Naranjo points out that in contrast to other ennea-types who defend
against pure recognition and expression of their passion, Eights appear
very up-front about their lust, but, "though the lust type is passionately
in favor of his lust and of lust in general as a way of life, the very passion-
ateness with which he embraces this outlook betrays a defensiveness—as
if he needed to prove to himself and the rest of the world that what
everybody calls bad is not such."[11] Rather than defending against the perceived badness of his objects of desire, I think he is defending against his
fundamental belief that he is himself bad, devoid of spirit and of the
goodness of life, and so not entitled to receive and enjoy it.

Looking at the Eight's passion of lust from a different angle, we can
understand more about the function it fulfills in the economy of his soul.
We saw earlier that in the wake of losing contact with his inner depths, an
Eight loses the recognition that matter and Spirit are one and the same,
and turns his attention outward, away from his inner reality as he denies
the world of the Spirit. As a result, we also saw that his characteristic deficiency state is an inner sense of a dead kind of emptiness. From this perspective, we can see that the passion of lust is an attempt to take in and
devour as much as possible from the physical world so as to abate the inner deadness he feels. His efforts to toughen his soul have left him with an
inner dullness and numbness, which require more and more tastes and
sensations to penetrate so that something touches him. With his denial of
the spiritual dimension of reality, he is an empty soul trying to fill himself with an empty world. This is inevitable when we take the physical as
absolute: We become empty shells and the world also becomes an empty
shell to us.

Having explored the main characteristics of the Eight's personality
structure, we can now see more of the ways that his style imitates the es-

sential quality of the Red. As a state, the Red infuses the soul with a sense of strength, as we have mentioned earlier, but also has many other characteristics. It gives us a sense of aliveness, vitality, and vibrancy, of passionate engagement in life and a sense of capacity to meet challenges inward and outward. It gives us the sense that "I can." It feels scintillating and exciting, dynamic and energetic. It fills our hearts with the courage to assert ourselves and to venture into new territory inside and outside of ourselves. At perhaps its deepest level, it is the drive in our souls to move beyond the familiar sense of self defined by our history, the urge to overcome the inertia of the personality and experience reality directly in all of its dimensionality, to adventure into, discover, and explore the endlessly vast terrain of the universe within ourselves.

The fervor, drive, and gusto with which an Eight engages life and the world mimic and embody to a certain extent (to the extent that it is not compulsive) the aliveness and vitality that characterize the Red. His lack of respect for boundaries—as in what is his and what is someone else's—reflects the quality of the Red that has to do with expansion of the soul, moving beyond the limits of the personality as self-concept. His brazenness and brashness reflect the direct engagement with life that the Red gives the soul. His rebelliousness and intolerance for being under someone else's thumb reflect the Red's function of supporting our becoming truly autonomous from the parental images within our psyches and of separating our sense of self from object relations and other constructs derived from our past.

For an Eight to be in touch with the real qualities of Red that his personality style imitates, he needs to approach his process with the virtue associated with Point Eight, innocence. We find it on the Enneagram of the Virtues in Diagram 1. The following is Ichazo's definition of the virtue of innocence: "The innocent being responds freshly to each moment, without memory, judgment, or expectation. In innocence one experiences reality and one's connection to its flow." At the deepest level, what this implies is approaching each moment without any overlays from the past. This means experiencing the moment without memories that prejudice our perception. Without our histories influencing our perception, our souls are indeed fresh and innocent. What we experience in the present touches and impacts our souls directly, free of our associations or preconceived ideas about it.

This of course necessitates a complete openness to what we are experiencing, which in turn implies that we are not protecting or defending ourselves from some imagined threat. For an Eight, this means letting go of his primary object relation: the belief and felt sense that he is someone who will be attacked or challenged and that the other—others and the world as a whole—is out to get him. As this mental construct dissolves, what goes is the orientation that the decks are stacked against him and that he must fight the world and avenge himself to survive. Ultimately what ceases is the sense that he is a separate entity for whom physical reality is fundamental and who must struggle to keep body and soul together. Then instead of protesting his innocence in the face of an inner sense of guilt, he experiences the true pristineness of his soul.

How does an Eight arrive at this point? What is necessary first of all is a willingness to lay down his sword, at least momentarily, and pay attention to his inner world. This means reorienting his focus from all the injustices and roadblocks that he experiences as being thrown in his path, to sensing into himself. In terms of personal process, this necessitates connecting with his body and experiencing it directly. For an active and physically oriented type, this may sound redundant—of course an Eight is in touch with his body! In actuality this is usually not the case: Eights have as much as if not more difficulty than other types in directly contacting their visceral experience. The body is used—and often abused—by Eights, but rarely fully inhabited with their consciousness. Their prejudicial orientation is evident in their tendency toward aversion of direct bodily experience and their reliance on their opinion about it instead. Directly contacting his experience rather than engaging in his current story line, no matter how justified or cosmic, is the beginning of developing innocence in an Eight.

In terms of content, an Eight needs to recognize that his bitter complaints and fury about how others and life are treating him is emotional reactivity and, as such, arising from his personality and so perhaps not objective truth. While he may have been through rough if not abusive situations in his past and he may be experiencing difficulties in his present life, he needs to begin to question his inner orientation toward them. He needs to see that the problem is not what others are doing to him but rather that the real issue is his response to what is occurring in his life. In other words, resolving the outer situation or avenging himself will not fundamentally change him; shifting his attention to the real cause of his difficulties—his worldview and resulting orientation to his process—on the other hand will.

Being present to his experience is often seen as an acquiescence (if not a capitulation) to an Eight—not an easy thing for him. It necessitates relinquishing his defended stance and being willing to let his soul be directly touched. Although his defenses are oriented toward keeping out what is potentially hurtful to him, he will see that letting in the positive is not easy, either. He has a great fear that he will be tricked by allowing himself to contact something that he experiences as good, that he will believe that there is benevolence and love available to him, only to have it whisked away and be punished for having wanted it, as was his experience in childhood. As he stays with this, he will see that what he is really afraid of is experiencing the reservoir of inner pain from his distant past that led him to create the leathery hardness that numbs his soul.

Experiencing this pain means also experiencing that he was helpless to do anything about it as a child, and that is a real challenge for an Eight. He would rather get angry and blame his parents, protesting that they should have been different and should have treated him differently, about how ignorant and crazy they were, and so on. Beneath this, he would rather blame and berate himself for not having been tough enough to avoid being hurt by gross lacks of attunement and even of abusive treatment. Accepting that his parents were doing the best they could as the unenlightened people that they were and that he was a dependent and malleable small child who simply was susceptible to his holding environment is actually more difficult for an Eight than believing that he is at fault and bad for becoming a conditioned soul. This is because surrendering to the truth of what happened confronts him with his childhood powerlessness, helplessness, dependency, neediness, and vulnerability—the very things he believes are wrong with him.

As he experientially understands and digests his defended stance and its causes and allows himself to open and be vulnerable to his experience in the moment, he will contact the dead-feeling emptiness that his defenses have encapsulated. He will see how this painful state is the result of trying to protect the very sensitivity of his soul, and that while this was a viable survival strategy as a child, it now perpetuates his suffering. He will experience how protecting himself is based on the concept that he is a separate someone who needs to be protected from something outside himself—a belief rooted in identification with his body. As he sees this, he will experience how this seals him off from the oneness of Being by sustaining his conviction of separateness.

Coming into direct contact with his experience and allowing his process to unfold in itself connects him with the flow of Being and undermines his conviction of separateness. Opening to the dynamism of his process, rather than fighting against it, dissolves some of his fundamental self-concepts and allows him to contact the real truth of who and what he is: an inseparable and individual manifestation of the unity that is Being. Rather than affirming his worst fears by letting go of his defensive and vindictive structures, he will see that the very substance of his soul is an aliveness and an individuating dynamism. He will know that his openness and vulnerability are his greatest strengths, and that the best defense and the ultimate revenge is the dissolution of his separatist sense of self: if you are open and transparent, even if the body is hurt, your soul remains an immaculate window of the Divine that nothing can injure.

ENNEA-TYPE FIVE: EGO-STINGINESS

Those of this ennea-type tend to be very private people who value their solitude and often resent intrusions. Fives tend to feel unseen and isolated from others, very much alone and separate, which does not seem to bother them much. Afraid of engulfment, they often seem to hide from life and seal themselves off, maintaining their own private inner world. While most of the time seeming to observe rather than actively participate in what is going on around them, they can at times be quite loquacious, although they nonetheless convey the sense that they are living in their own little world.

Valuing self-sufficiency and their own autonomy, they don't want to feel obligated to others to fulfill expectations and demands, and would rather keep to themselves. They therefore tend to be retentive and stingy with themselves and their resources, thus the name of this type, Ego-Stinginess. Driven by an inner sense of scarcity and emptiness, they behave as though afraid that the little they have might be taken from them and so needs to be safeguarded. Afraid that nothing will be forthcoming from the outside, they act as though they don't want anything and furthermore that they don't care, even convincing themselves that this is how they really feel, and so they limit expression of their wishes and their desires.

Many Fives seem emotionless, dry, and lacking in vitality. Although they may experience intense emotions and have very active and penetrating minds, they show very little of this inner world to others. Energetically they may seem wispy and sometimes even fragile, as if not fully inhabiting their bodies. It is as though they are a little removed, withholding themselves from fully entering into things. They are deeply sensitive, sometimes seeming to be all nerve endings, easily shaken and startled, with thin and delicate skins. They use their minds to scout, relying on their knowledge of the territory in front of them to make entering into it safe. Many Fives, however, live entirely in their minds, substituting mental formulations for actual experience.

Behind these personality traits lies the loss of the Holy Idea associated with Point Five. To understand it, we need to recap our understanding of that of Point Eight. In the previous chapter we discussed how Holy Truth, the Holy Idea of Point Eight, is the perception that the whole cosmos is one indivisible thing and that all of its dimensions are coemergent and inseparable from each other. This means that the entire universe, from physical manifestation to the Absolute, is a oneness, and so matter and Spirit are part and parcel of each other. From this angle, we saw that all dualities are illusory: the Divine and the mundane, good and evil, ego and Essence, and ourselves and God. They are simply different parts of the one fabric of reality. The Holy Idea of Point Five, which has two names, Holy Omniscience and Holy Transparency, shifts the focus from viewing this whole as a totality to viewing it from within its various manifestations. In other words, rather than viewing reality as one thing, from this vantage point the emphasis is on the interconnectedness of all of the parts of the cosmos and on some of the implications of this interpenetration. In a sense, we can think of Holy Truth as focusing on the wholeness of reality, and of Holy Omniscience and Holy Transparency as focusing on its constituent parts.

Almaas uses the terms *unity* and *oneness* to differentiate these two perceptions. Unity refers to perceiving the wholeness of reality, and is the perspective of Holy Truth. Oneness refers to perceiving that all of the separate manifestations in reality make up one thing, and is the perspective of Holy Omniscience and Holy Transparency. He uses the analogy of the body to make this clearer: looking at the body from the outside and see-ing it as one thing would be analogous to Holy Truth, while looking at it from the inside and seeing all of the separate cells, organs, and systems that make it up would be analogous to Holy Omniscience and Holy Transparency. Or, returning to our analogy, we could say that Holy Truth is equivalent to perceiving an ocean as a whole body of water, while Holy Omniscience is equivalent to perceiving the various waves and currents that taken together comprise it.

Exploring the Holy Idea of Point Five in more detail, we will concen-trate first on Holy Transparency since it is a little easier to grasp than Holy Omniscience. Holy Transparency refers to the human experience of being one individual part of the whole of reality. One of the central beliefs of the personality, no matter what our ennea-type happens to be, is that we are each ultimately separate from every other person. When we see re-ality objectively from the angle of Holy Transparency, we see that this is an illusion and not ultimate truth. Although our bodies are physically separate, this separateness is not fundamental to our nature. And while each of us is a distinct individual with a unique appearance, tempera-ment, and history, and possessing different qualities than anyone else, each of us is still part of the larger body of humanity and in turn of the cosmos. We are all like the various cells in the body, each having a partic-ular makeup and function and yet indisputably interconnected with one another and part of the same organism.

Beyond our interconnection as members of humanity, as individual souls we are each an expression and manifestation of Being, linked by our very nature with the rest of the universe. Again, just like the individual cells that make up our bodies, the dividing walls between each of us are porous and transparent and not inherently defining or confining. From the enlightened perspective of Holy Transparency, we know ourselves as individual manifestations or differentiations of the oneness of reality, composing it and inseparable from it. We perceive ourselves, then, to be parts of a greater Whole, and we also see here that disconnection from the rest of humanity and the rest of the cosmos is impossible.

Turning to Holy Omniscience, we might begin to penetrate its meaning by asking ourselves why the word *omniscience* is used in connection with this perception of oneness, since omniscience means the state of being all-knowing or of having complete understanding. There are a number of ways to understand the use of this term. Perhaps the simplest has to do with what spiritual development is all about: it is the process of a human being becoming progressively more conscious of and in touch with her inner nature. She literally knows more and more about who and what she is, and when this knowledge is total, she has full realization of herself as an individual expression of Being. This is what is referred to in the various traditions as total enlightenment—complete understanding of oneself and of one's nature. Because each of us is an inseparable manifestation of the Whole, an individual soul who partakes of the nature of all souls and of all of the cosmos, knowing oneself fully implies knowing the Whole fully as well. So Holy Omniscience is the perspective of the enlightened human soul: she fully knows herself and, through this knowing, fully knows the Whole of which she is a part.

Perhaps the deepest and most difficult understanding of Holy Omniscience to grasp is that each of us is a differentiation of the Universal Mind. We discussed in an earlier chapter how the universe is an alive intelligence. Looking at reality in this way, each of us is a thought expressed by that Intelligence. Or, putting it a little differently, each entity in the universe is like a separate thought in God's Mind. Each of us is an expression of God or the Absolute, then, the inner nature of the universe manifesting on its outer surface.

This might raise the question of why the Absolute expresses each of these "thoughts" that we are, which is the same question as why manifestation occurs in the first place and what is the point of human life. Many spiritual traditions say that the function of our existence is so that the Absolute can know Itself, and this is perhaps the most plausible answer to that question. As each individual soul, each expression of the Absolute, becomes conscious and aware of her True Nature, the Absolute knows Itself. So each of us is not only a differentiation of the Absolute but also a way in which It knows Itself.

Holy Omniscience, then, tells us something about the function of human existence: so that God can know Himself; about the place of humanity in the cosmos: as transparent windows of the Absolute; and about the nature of the Path: progressive understanding of one's nature. Holy Transparency tells us that as we experience ourselves as transparent windows of Being, we know ourselves to be inseparable from the rest of creation.

Simultaneous with the loss of contact with her depths, a Five also loses these perspectives on reality. So not only does she lose her sense of connection with Being but she also loses a sense of interconnectedness with others and with the rest of reality. As she inevitably identifies with her body in infancy, its boundaries become determinate to her, bounding and disconnecting her. She develops the conviction that she is separate from everyone and everything else, although obviously at this early age this conviction is only a dimly felt sense that only later becomes conceptual. Separateness as fundamental replaces interconnectedness, and as a result, she grows up without a sense of true place or function in human society and, beyond that, in the universe.

This sense of being fundamentally separate is common to all ego structures, no matter which type. It is one of the deepest beliefs of the personality and hence to the majority of humanity, and for most of us it feels like an indisputable sense of how things actually are. It is only when we have experiences that move us past the boundaries of our egoic consciousness that we experience ourselves as one with and part of all of existence.

Sealed off from others, contained within the limits of her body, the Five experiences a profound sense of isolation. She grows up feeling estranged from others, living in her own little bubble, and rarely feeling fully part of her family or community. Filtered through the loss of the sense of connectedness signified by Holy Omniscience and Holy Transparency, her experience of her primary relationship to another—her mother—is of not being fully bonded with her. A Five's memory of their early relationship is often tinged with the sense of not being fully related to, deeply loved, wanted, or fully nourished, a sense of having futilely sucked at a dry tit. A sense of deprivation, of contact or sustenance having been withheld, is left indelibly in her soul. Seemingly paradoxically, she also often has the sense of her mother being invasive, intrusive, manipulative, engulfing, and devouring, not respecting her boundaries or her space. While this may sound like the opposite of a withholding mother, the common thread is the experience of mother not relating to, connecting with, and being attuned to her reality. Rather, mother seems wrapped up in herself and so not really perceiving the Five or meeting her needs.

She ends up feeling unseen, unappreciated, and not understood, and this becomes part of her ongoing sense of self. So rather than experiencing herself as someone whose needs are apparent and whose inner process is penetrable by another's understanding as in Holy Transparency, she feels invisible. Not only do her needs and desires feel to her unseen by others but her inner world also feels to her ungraspable by them. Her inner workings do not seem to her like something others would understand, empathize with, and have compassion for. She experiences herself as different, not like other people, lacking shared human commonalities. The gulf between herself and others feels unbridgeable, and her boundaries feel impenetrable.

This sense of invisibility and isolation is both her suffering and her attempt to defend against it. In response to her mother's distance from her and mother's unattuned intrusions, she withdraws from her mother in order not to experience the devastating pain of feeling neglected. It is also an attempt to preserve herself, to seal off and hold on to a sense of self in the face of experiencing herself as unseen. This fear of loss of self arises because her not fully differentiated consciousness cannot distinguish clearly between mother and herself, and so if mother doesn't see her, she begins to lose a sense of her own substantiality. The solution her soul arrives at, then, is to separate and isolate herself to survive.

Her soul is frozen in the infant state beyond tears and rage when needs go unmet and quiet resignation and apathy take over. In her movement away, she mimics her experience of her mother's remoteness from her, and by extension the remoteness of Being, and this withdrawal becomes her dominant strategy in life. Mother becomes all others and life itself, and she pulls back physically, emotionally, and energetically from all of the forms mother takes in her psyche.

In a word, she hides from life, and so on the Enneagram of Antiself Actions, Diagram 11, we find self-hiding at Point Five, indicating that she conceals herself from others and ultimately hides from herself as well. She becomes self-enclosed and prefers to remain on the periphery of things, whether they be social gatherings, intimate relationships, or any other kind of engagement with others. She withdraws and tends to be difficult to reach on all levels, from simply being elusive regarding her whereabouts or not answering her phone for instance, to evasiveness about what is going on with her internally. She wants control over the amount and quality of interaction she has, and guards her privacy carefully. We see this exemplified in the little we know about the personal lives of Fives who become famous, as, for example, Bob Dylan and Georgia O'Keeffe. Dylan's sense of self-enclosure is evident as he refrains from making eye contact with his audience during concerts, and O'Keeffe's in the isolated life she led in the New Mexican desert.

Part of a Five's hiding is her dissembling—primarily concealing her inner thoughts, feelings, and wishes under a cloak of indifference. Because of this, dissimulation—trying to appear not as one is—is at Point Five on the Enneagram of Lies, as we see on Diagram 12. For instance, if a Five feels any danger of her response to a question being conflictual, it will be difficult to get a straight answer out of her. Rather than expressing herself and risking a challenge for which she feels unprepared or taking the chance of ruffling someone else's feathers, she hides what is going on with her. In arguments, she will readily say that she agrees with the other person, and later it becomes clear that she still holds an entirely divergent opinion. She accommodates, appearing to go along with what the other wishes, while quietly going about exactly what she secretly wanted to do in the first place. At other times, she may accommodate to the extent that she loses track of her own direction. While she secretly longs to be seen, appreciated, cared about, and loved, she is afraid to take the initiative and instead feigns indifference and waits passively to be noticed.

A Five's dissembling keeps her from making waves and helps her avoid confrontations, but it also reinforces her disconnection from others. Just as she loses a sense of connection to others, she also loses a sense of connection with life itself both externally and internally. She feels separate from the rest of reality, not part of its dynamism. Her own aliveness and vitality seem ephemeral and tenuous, and her energy, stamina, and vigor feel limited, and she may even experience herself as unreal, ghostlike. She feels small, contracted, and shrunken, with her presence delicate, wispy, and insubstantial, and her expressions of exuberance and animation appear momentary and fleeting.

In Freudian terms, her drive energy is diminished. Her investment of love and value in others and objects is blocked and held back, as is her libido, her drive toward them. Rather than going after what she wants, she talks herself out of what she wants and inwardly moves away from the wanting. With the imprint in her soul of the futility of mother truly being attuned and meeting her needs, she is resigned at the outset, convinced that she cannot get what she wants, that it will not be forthcoming, and that whatever she is given will not be what she wanted anyway. So to circumvent the pain of not getting what she desires and reactivating her early wounding, she may experience deep longing inside but blocks its expression, looking apathetic to others; or at the extreme she stops desiring altogether. She restricts her wishes and her wants, and in appearance if not in fact ceases to care about anything. As Horney elaborates on the neurotic she refers to as the detached type:

> *The resigned person believes, consciously or unconsciously, that it is* better *not to wish or to expect anything. Sometimes this goes with a conscious pessimistic outlook on life, a sense of its being futile anyhow and of nothing being sufficiently desirable to make an effort for it. More often many things appear desirable in a vague, idle way but fail to arouse a concrete, alive wish. If a wish or interest has enough zest to penetrate through the "don't care" attitude, it fades out soon after and the smooth surface of "nothing matters" or "nothing should matter" is reestablished. Such "wishlessness" may concern both professional and personal life—the wish for a different job or an advancement as well as for a marriage, a house, a car, or other possessions. The fulfillment of these wishes may loom primarily as a burden, and in fact would sabotage the one wish he does have—that of not being bothered.*[1]

Some Fives experience deep longing and caring, but, convinced that what they want will not be forthcoming, they dissemble, appearing not to care. Others, more thoroughly convinced of the futility of engagement, lose interest in anything altogether. In either case, with little inner drive toward things, a Five has difficulty initiating action, and instead she waits passively on the sidelines for attention to come her way, for her needs to be met, and for contact with others. She is held back, restrained by her reluctance to move toward anything out of fear of rebuff or loss, and so her actions are stilted and awkward, infused with self-consciousness. She often feels paralyzed, unable to move in one direction or another, and when this happens it is because she is afraid. In the same vein, she has difficulty communicating her needs, in the extreme becoming catatonic, unable to speak.

Rather than engaging life, then, and grappling with the challenges it brings, the Five retreats from it. Inwardly as well, as Horney says, such a person withdraws and looks on:

> *The direct expression of the neurotic having removed himself from the inner battlefield is his being an onlooker at himself and his life. I have described this attitude as one of the general measures to relieve inner tension. Since detachment is a ubiquitous and prominent attitude of his, he is also an onlooker at others. He lives as if he were sitting in the orchestra and observing a drama acted on the stage, and a drama which is most of the time not too exciting at that. Though he is not necessarily a good observer, he may be very astute. Even in the very first consultation he may, with the help of some pertinent questions, develop a picture of himself replete with a wealth of candid observation. But he will usually add that all his knowledge has not changed anything. Of course it has not—for none of his findings has been an experience for him. Being an onlooker at himself means just that: not actively participating in living and unconsciously refusing to do so.[2]*

The Five becomes, then, an observer of life rather than an active participator, and this is her trap, as we see on Diagram 9. Her lack of participation is based on her fear of too much engagement and involvement. As we are seeing, much of her inner dynamic is fear based; Ennea-type Five is a fear type, one of the two points neighboring Point Six where the primary focus is on existential fear itself. Like a Six, rather than identifying with the fittest in what feels like the struggle for survival, she experiences herself as one of the weaklings, and so is constantly afraid. Often ecto-morphic—thin and wiry—of body type, many Fives experience them-selves as puny compared with others, and in a physical fight, they feel sure they would lose. Many, but not all Fives, experience themselves as neb-bishy or like nerds, the guy who gets sand kicked in his face at the beach, or to use a more current term, like a geek. Many Fives feel unable to de-fend themselves physically, and this forms the basis of their fear of assert-ing themselves. Other Fives may feel physically substantial and strong, but also vulnerable and unable to defend themselves mentally or emo-tionally.

As we are seeing, a Five's attempt to preserve her inner space and the integrity of her soul through withdrawing from life ends up ironically also isolating her from herself. She withdraws from her direct experience, so rather than experiencing the vibrancy of her bodily sensations and her emotions, she observes them from a distance just as she does external things. As a result, she often feels out of touch, spaced out, and blocked, living a lot in her mind and in fantasy.

The legs are the body part associated with Ennea-type Five. Our legs are what move us toward and away from things, and a Five's capacity to run away and hide feels crucial to her safety. As Horney describes, we can readily see how fear based and survival oriented the Five's distancing is:

> As long as the detached person can keep at a distance he feels compara-tively safe; if for any reason the magic circle is penetrated, his security is threatened. This consideration brings us closer to an understanding of why the detached person becomes panicky if he can no longer safeguard his emo-tional distance from others—and we should add that the reason his panic is so great is that he has no technique for dealing with life. He can only keep aloof and avoid life, as it were. Here again it is the negative quality of de-tachment that gives the picture a special color, different from that of other neurotic trends. To be more specific, in a difficult situation the detached per-son can neither appease nor fight, neither co-operate nor dictate terms, nei-ther love nor be ruthless. He is as defenseless as an animal that has only one means of coping with danger—that is, to escape and hide.[3]

One of the key ways the Five distances internally is through the defense mechanism of isolation, which means that she separates her emotional feelings from her memories and thoughts. She can then remember painful and even traumatic situations without actually experiencing them as such, and can think about a current situation without any emotion connected with it. So, for example, she might think about a friend or partner who she is having a fight with, and feel no emotion toward that person at all. She might conclude that she doesn't care about him and never did, thus protecting herself from any emotional upset about the current difficulty. Or she might tell you about a severe childhood trauma with little or no affect connected with it, like a reporter recounting something that she witnessed, in the spirit of objectivity from her point of view.

Another form the defense of isolation takes that is more closely related to her self-enclosure is separating related thoughts from each other—compartmentalizing them—as though there were no causal relationship between them. Using our example above, she might have the thought that her friend or partner said something that hurt her feelings and another thought that she isn't sure she ever cared about that person anyway, without experiencing a connection or causal relationship between these two thoughts. So her thoughts and feelings become encapsulated, self-enclosed and out of relationship with each other, and in this way form an internal microcosm of her external relationship to others and the world.

She maintains a sense of connection with herself and the rest of life through attentively and often nervously looking on. Like a fox protecting the lair of her inner world, she peers out, sniffing the wind for danger and observing from afar. Much of her energy is centered in her eyes, and a Five's eyes are often like bright burning coals as she keenly watches what is going on, attempting to figure it out and thus protect herself. Developing a clear conceptual picture of what is occurring both within and without are her focus. Knowing what is going on and knowledge itself appear to her as the keys to her safety as well as what will bring her recognition. Rather than experiential and embodied understanding, she substitutes conceptual knowledge and information. In this we see her personality's facsimile of the lost Holy Omniscience—she is attempting to be all-knowing—as well as her idealized Aspect, which we will turn to now.

What a Five feels she lacks and believes she needs is more knowledge and understanding. This makes sense, since if you take the stance of an onlooker at life, knowing what is going on becomes central to your very sense of survival. Knowledge to her means safety, and so to feel more secure she wants foreknowledge of what she will encounter and what will ensue, as well as what is expected of her. A Five often feels that she did not understand what was going on around her in her early and later childhood, the sense of somehow being left out of the loop of life, and so she strives to make sense out of what she sees. She scouts the environment, trying to understand what is going on.

Somewhere deep in a Five's soul, knowledge feels not only her key to survival but also what can reconnect her with the lost realm of Being. She believes that if she had known what her mother wanted, she would have been seen, and she and her mother would have connected. She came to the conclusion someplace in her soul that it was this lack of knowledge that caused the disconnection. Since mother and Being are synonymous in infancy, she believes that if she had known enough, she would not have lost touch with Being, and that knowledge is the key to reconnecting. She idealizes the quality of Being that has to do with direct knowledge, which is called Diamond Consciousness or Diamond Guidance in the language of the Diamond Approach. As Almaas says:

> *This aspect of Essence is the source of true insight, intuition, knowledge and understanding. It functions through a capacity of simultaneous analysis and synthesis. . . . Unlike all other aspects of Being, it has the capacity to use knowledge from memory and synthesize it with immediate knowledge in the moment, thus utilizing both mind and Being. . . .*
>
> *The Diamond Consciousness is the prototype, on the level of Being, of the faculty of understanding. The ordinary capacity for understanding is only a reflection of this capacity. When an individual manifests an unusual or brilliant capacity for analysis and synthesis in his or her understanding, it is usually an indication of some degree of realization of the Diamond Consciousness. We can see the functioning of this capacity in the work of the*

great original synthesizers of mankind, such as Gautama Buddha or Sigmund Freud.[4]

The Buddha and Freud, by the way, may very well have been Fives, as is Almaas himself. All three abandoned prior conceptual formulations and developed bodies of knowledge that grew out of their direct experience and observations, and so embodied the idealized Aspect. The Buddha is known as the Omniscient One, and in this we see the interpenetration of the Holy Idea and the idealized Aspect. This Aspect seems to be that symbolized by the Wise Old Man archetype in Jungian psychology and by the angel Gabriel, considered the Messenger of God in Judaism and the Angel of Revelation in Islam.

In contrast to these exemplars, most Fives only imitate Diamond Guidance through disembodied and thus dry mental knowledge. To the extent that a Five is not fully experiencing herself, this facsimile is the only possibility. Of this intellectual orientation, Naranjo says:

> *Through a predominantly cognitive orientation the individual may seek substitute satisfaction—as in the replacement of living through reading. Yet the symbolic replacement of life is not the only form of expression of intense thinking activity: another aspect is the preparation for life—a preparation that is intense to the extent that the individual never feels ready enough. In the elaboration of perceptions as preparation for (inhibited) action, the activity of abstraction is particularly striking; type V individuals lean towards the activity of classification and organization, and not only display a strong attraction towards the process of ordering experience, but tend to dwell in abstractions while at the same time avoiding concreteness. This avoidance of concreteness, in turn, is linked to the type's hiddenness: only the results of one's perceptions are offered to the world, not its raw material.*[5]

Her inner world feels empty, devoid of the juice of life. This is the particular deficiency state at the core of her personality, her particular hell realm, which she will do everything she can to avoid experiencing. It has a dry, stark, depleted, sterile, and empty feel to it, filling her soul with a sense of deprivation and inner poverty. Like a vast inner desert with no oasis in sight, she feels barren, thirsty, and desiccated. In contrast to wetter—more emotional—types, she is in no danger of drowning in grief but rather is in danger of evaporating from lack of anything life-giving. She feels very much alone and unreachable here, isolated and separate from the rest of the world, and profoundly ashamed of her inner sense of scarcity. Exposure of it, both to her own awareness and to others, feels utterly humiliating since she believes she should have known what to do about it. This is the emptiness referred to at Point Five on the Enneagram of Avoidances, Diagram 10.

I mentioned earlier that her movement away, her withdrawal from life, was both her defense and her suffering, and we have seen how she uses it defensively to protect herself. Her self-enclosure also creates this desolate inner landscape and perpetuates her bone-dry sense of deficiency, forming the basis and core of her suffering. This is the inevitable consequence of her fundamental delusion—her fixation—that she is ultimately separate from every other entity, the cognitive error about reality resulting from the loss of the Holy Idea. If you create an artificial boundary in your consciousness between yourself and everything else, your soul is encapsulated and sealed off from the source of life—Being—and inner emptiness must consequently result. This is termed stinginess by Ichazo, as we see on the Enneagram of Fixations in Diagram 2 probably for the reasons that follow.

With this arid emptiness at her core, she feels that she has no inner reservoir on any level, and so must hold on to the little that she has. She is frugal to the point of stinginess with her energy, her emotions, her attention, and her communication, hence—as mentioned earlier—the name of this type, Ego-Stinginess. She doles out little bits of herself when she sees fit, and lives unconsciously in the fear that the rest will be taken from her. This fear of losing the little that she has is the heart of a Five's inner fright and dread and is the reason she is more often than not ungiving and ungenerous. Rather than being consciously withholding, she may project her own reticence to desire things and may believe that others, like her, do not want anything.

She withholds from herself as well as others, often having few material possessions so that she has little to become attached to and thus little that she would miss if it were lost or stolen. Her needs are few, even physical ones, and she tends to parcel out to herself limited quantities of food and drink, preferring an empty belly to a full one. One Five I know refers to this tendency of his as "living lightly on the earth," an expression borrowed from the conservation/ecology movement. Rather than depend on anyone else, Fives prefer to supply and use their own resources. As Horney says in this regard:

> He is particularly anxious not to get attached to anything to the extent of really needing it. Nothing should be so important for him that he could not do without it. It is all right to like a woman, a place in the country, or certain drinks, but one should not become dependent upon them. As soon as he becomes aware that a place, a person, or a group of people means so much to him that its loss would be painful he tends to extract his feelings. No other person should ever have the feeling of being necessary to him or take the relationship for granted. If he suspects the existence of either attitude he tends to withdraw.[6]

Not all Fives are materially stingy with themselves, but many are. If a Five withholds from herself in this way, it is so that she does not have to experience attachment to anything and fear its loss. Most are frugal and tend to be stingy with others, keeping close track of what they give and what they are owed. It rarely occurs to many Fives to be extravagant with gifts, since that frequently seems frivolous, wasteful, and definitely imprudent to them.

This hoarding and withholding lead to the passion of this type, avarice, which we see at Point Five on the Enneagram of Passions in Diagram 2. Avarice means greediness, a powerful desire to acquire. The drive, then, for a Five is to collect, accumulate, and save resources, based on her internal sense of deficient emptiness. It is important to understand that this is a drive to *have* rather than to *consume*. As Naranjo says, "This is a fearful grasping, implying a fantasy that letting go would result in catastrophic depletion. Behind the hoarding impulse there is, we may say, an experience of impending impoverishment."[7] This is the anal retentive stance, the soul holding on to things rather than letting them pass through.[8] The internal logic is that if she squirrels enough away, she will not feel empty anymore, but as with all attempts to fill holes in our souls that result from disconnection with Being, no amount of reserves ever obviates her inner experience of scarcity.

The squirrel, by the way, is one of the animals associated with Ennea-type Five. The other is the mongoose, a small creature who relies on its agility and speed, darting after its prey.

Some Fives are materially avaricious, miserly with their money, spending little in order to amass savings so that they can pore over their stock portfolios and retirement funds in an effort to gain some inner sense of security. Not all Fives express their avarice in this way. Whether materially avaricious or not, most Fives are avaricious about knowledge, believing as they do that it is what will save them and serves to a great extent as a substitute for a more active participation in life, as we have seen. For a Five, avarice is really an attachment to the *idea* of what she has, so ultimately it is knowledge—knowing what she has—rather than any possession that she is really hoarding.

For those who are fearful of having anything lest it be taken from them, which would remind them of their fundamental and primal pain of the loss of Being, their avarice manifests more energetically: protecting and hanging on to what little vitality and emotionality they have. Quoting Naranjo again, "Because of an excessive resignation in regard to love and people, precisely, there is a compensatory clutching at oneself—which may or may not manifest in a grasping onto possessions, but involves a much more generalized hold over one's inner life as well as an economy of effort and resources."[9]

Fives are characteristically afraid of being swallowed up by another and of the demands and expectations others might place upon them, and so withhold from wholehearted engagement in personal relationships. For many Fives, being alone seems preferable to the risk of losing their sense of who they are by being engulfed by a partner and to risking things being asked of them that they feel unable or reluctant to give. What little of themselves they feel they have, they want to hold on to. For this reason, many Fives have difficulty entering into intimate relationships, while others do so readily but often with partners who give them ample independence and autonomy. In the latter case, they choose partners who make few demands upon them either materially or emotionally in terms of contact. In such cases, having someone who will take care of the mundane details of life like buying the groceries and taking out the garbage is often worth the danger of being overwhelmed by her partner.

At the beginning of inner work, a Five's avarice is usually fairly unconscious to her. As we have seen, this is true of the passions of most of the ennea-types. To feel consciously her greed, possessiveness, and boundary-setting distancing flies in the face of her superego, the inner critic. Feeling her avarice would lead to feeling her inner arid and desiccated emptiness, and her superego attempts to make sure this does not happen. Her superego is mocking and disdainful, arrogant and superior, berating her for her inner sense of impoverishment, her lack of emotion, and her fear of life. She is at the mercy of her superego rather than identified with it as an Ennea-type One is, and its attacks create and exacerbate her feeling just plain shitty inside.

Her response to the demands of her superego as well as to any external demands is often simply to stonewall. Often it is even more important to her *not* to comply and in that way to preserve a sense of independence than to do things that she knows are in her best interest. Naranjo says that Fives actually want to subvert perceived demands, whether internal or external, and this may indeed be the case. Whenever anything is perceived by a Five to be something that she is expected or that she ought to do, she tends to go into quiet resistance. She will, for example, refuse to give gifts just because they are expected, or not do the dishes simply because her husband wants her to, or she might procrastinate about doing her taxes, turning them in only after all the allowable extensions have been filed. She may say that she has every intention of doing things that are expected of her, but somehow they just don't get done.

A Five's hostility, then, is expressed indirectly in passively aggressive behavior. With her docile and accommodating self-presentation, she will agree to do things and make commitments only to placate the other, with no intention of actually following through. She tends to procrastinate, postpone, forget, and find all sorts of reasons why she must fulfill her obligations later. She is rarely in touch with the hostility she is expressing in this backhanded way, and is usually quite surprised at the frustration and rage such behavior evokes in others, who are simply feeling the anger that she is not expressing directly and perhaps not even conscious of. She does not feel she can say no directly because she does not feel she has the inner strength to stand behind it. Like a hollow twig, she is afraid she would snap. So she demurs, acting out her aggression silently and not risking a confrontation with anyone. Rarely asserting herself, she appears to go along with another's flow, while quietly in the background going her own way, as we saw earlier.

Her hostility is also expressed in her movement away from life. It is a very loud unspoken "No!"—a silent rejection. Her aloofness is often laden with arrogance, superiority, and disdain—she claims that she does not want to be involved anyway. The world is so imperfect, why should she participate? People are such animals, why would she want to get involved with them? Strong emotions are so messy, why should she want to sully herself by feeling, much less expressing, them?

Another reason that experiencing her avarice directly is so difficult for her is that it is an expression of profound attachment. The avarice, as we have seen, is a drive to acquire, hold on to, and hoard, and expresses an extreme concern with what she has. It runs completely counter to her attempt at appearing and being detached. She idealizes her independence, autonomy, and detachment since caring about others and about things means that if she loses them, she will feel loss and the dreaded emptiness. She does not want to be too attached to anything, as we have seen, and this is behind her dampening of any drive outward, toward anything. So her libidinal energy dries up, reinforcing the inner aridity. She becomes cut off from her vibrancy, her desires, her feelings. She becomes cool and detached, remote and indifferent, unfeeling and uncaring. Others appear like slaves to their desires, and she has little empathy or sympathy for them, only a great sense of relief that she is not caught in the same trap. She does not want to be hemmed in, constrained, or imprisoned by anything, and so does not want to be pinned down or committed to anything she can't get out of. While she may on occasion feel somewhat robotlike and inhuman, it seems a small price to pay for the safety she has gained by not getting too attached.

The detachment of a Five is not freedom at all, as she would like to believe. It is compulsive—she has little choice *not* to respond by moving away. And it is based on fear of involvement. Moving away from something you are afraid of is not freedom at all; it is a reaction that keeps you very much in relationship with what you are frightened of.

Although Ichazo uses the word *detachment* to describe the virtue of Point Five, what he describes might best be conveyed by the word *nonattachment.* We find this on the Enneagram of Virtues in Diagram 1. Of the virtue he says, "It is the precise understanding of the body's needs; a detached being takes in exactly what he needs and lets everything else go. Detachment is the position which allows the energy of life to flow easily through the body." While Ichazo speaks of detachment relative to the body, we can just as easily and perhaps more revealingly substitute the word *soul.* What is implied, then, is a sense of permeability that allows the fullness of Essence to fill the Five's soul and reconnect her with her True Nature. When this happens, there is no need for avarice since she knows herself to be an unseverable part of the Whole, partaking of its plenitude and its riches.

Since the virtue of each type is a quality that both develops in the course of one's work on oneself and is necessary for traversing one's inner terrain, a Five's path necessitates and fosters an inner attitude of nonattachment. This means letting go of the need to hold on to anything. First and foremost for a Five, this means letting go of her distance from herself. She will have to be willing to connect with herself in an experiential way, with her mind following her direct experience rather than taking the lead. In order to do this, she needs to confront her attachment to knowing before she can actually contact her direct bodily and emotional experience. As we have seen, Fives scout the territory ahead and try to think their way across it rather than actually traveling through it. In terms of their inner world, this translates as mentally trying to figure out what they are experiencing and where it might take them before actually experientially contacting it.

Although some Fives attempt to do it, inner transformation that is fully embodied and lived cannot be achieved through the mind alone. No amount of information about the various states of consciousness possible for the human soul can substitute for directly experiencing and integrating them. Nor can knowledge—no matter how accurate—about the contents of a Five's consciousness or even consciousness in general, the nature of her ego structure, or of all of the dimensions of Being ever substitute for touching them with her soul. Such information may be very useful and helpful as a way of clarifying the terrain through cognitively grasping it, but it alone will not bring about inner transformation. This is because our souls are imprinted by what touches them directly, so just as the events of early childhood shaped our souls into personality structures, Being also must directly touch us for our souls to be informed by It.

Like most people, a Five will first encounter her superego as she settles into herself and begins experientially to contact the state and contents of her consciousness. Primarily she will have to defend against her inner attacks on herself about being so wimpy, so empty, and so ineffective in life. As we have seen, her superego is trying to protect her from experiencing her inner emptiness and gives her a very hard time about it, which keeps her from directly experiencing it and thus being able to digest and move through it. If a Five has done or is doing psychological or spiritual work, her superego most likely measures her against the models used in these systems. She will therefore have to go through a process of letting go of the cognitive frames that she has learned from these methodologies so that she can experience herself as she is.

Many Fives are attracted to meditative paths, especially those in which contact with others and the world is kept to a minimum. While this lack of external engagement cuts down on outer stimulus, allowing a profound inner confrontation with oneself, such practices can be misused in the service of a false detachment. For a Five, this can occur through pushing away rather than working through inner contents that do not fit her spiritual superego's idea of what she ought to be experiencing. By turning her attention away from any troublesome direct experience, she can transcend it and become very skilled at detaching rather than truly moving through it. In conditions of minimal input and engagement, she can remain in a fairly serene state. This dependency upon external conditions to support her state, however, is not true detachment, and can become a spiritual cul-de-sac for her.

In order to let go of needing foreknowledge about her inner process, and of the tendency to detach from it and transcend it, a Five will have to confront the fear that drives this need, the fear of experiencing herself exactly as she is. She will see that what she is really frightened of is experiencing her fundamental state of deficiency, the arid emptiness at the core of her personality. She is afraid that if she feels it, it will swallow her up and there will be nothing left, and this is ultimately the source of her fear of engulfment. She has believed that she can conceal this sense of inner poverty from others and from herself by camouflaging it and simply not exposing it, but sooner or later she will have to confront it directly.

As she is gradually more and more able to let go of the need to withdraw from this parched emptiness, an attitude of nonattachment will help move her through this huge hole in her soul. The more she can experience it directly, the less she will be attached to it. While this may sound paradoxical, as we have discussed earlier, we hold on to what we are afraid of experiencing. We perpetuate our attachment to contents of our consciousness by rejecting them, since in this way we remain engaged with them, albeit in a negative way. Our understanding and awareness cannot penetrate such places in our souls, and so they remain encapsulated and undigested within our consciousness.

The more a Five is able to allow and fully experience her emptiness, the more she will see that the only thing she loses is her fear and her distance from herself. She will feel more and more in contact with herself as she makes this inner confrontation, and she will feel stronger and more alive. She will find that the less she holds on to, the more she has, since all she is letting go of are mental structures and internal images of self and other. The arid inner desert will gradually become a spaciousness and a fullness, revealing all of the inner treasures of the realm of Being.

There will, of course, be many more nuances to her process—there will be many other inner contents that she will need to digest and resolve, and her soul will be touched by the various Aspects of Essence whose associated issues she will have to move through—but experiencing and moving through her deficient emptiness is central. She will probably have to approach and move through it over and over again until her soul shifts its primary identification from her personality to Being. Like all core issues, the emptiness will become eventually more and more transparent—less real and final—to her.

In time, if she hangs in with her inner journey, her life will also be transformed. Rather than a life lived from a distance, within conceptualizations and abstractions, she will little by little become more and more touched by and in contact with reality. And rather than the realms of True Nature simply being bits of knowledge to be collected, she will experience them directly, her soul permeable and open. Her quest for knowledge will gradually be replaced by direct understanding, embodied and integrated in her consciousness, and the thirst in her soul, which she may have only been dimly conscious of, will at long last be quenched.

ENNEA-TYPE
SEVEN:
EGO-PLANNING

Sevens are buoyant, perky, optimistic, curious, interested in everything, youthful in spirit, futuristic, and seem always to be one step ahead of themselves. Seemingly more carefree and positive than the other types, Sevens use these very qualities as their biggest defense. They need the stimulation of new ideas, experiences, entertainments, and other pursuits, and get easily bored and dissatisfied when things become repetitious. Lacking an inner trust in the natural unfoldment of things, they believe that they have to figure out how things work and plot where things are going and try to make them conform to this plan. Because this mapping and planning are so central to this type, it is called Ego-Planning. They value being able to grasp the big picture, and once they have a sense of it, they care little for the details. They like to synthesize information, figuring out how one thing relates to the other, and how everything fits together. Inclined to generate schemas about how things work, they frequently get so caught up in the representation that they lose sight of the actual territory. Once they can see where things are going, they have little patience for the actual work it takes to get there. As a result, Sevens have a tendency to be dilettantes, leaving things when the going gets tough and perseverance is required. Also, because they can envision the goal and confuse what they visualize for reality, they berate themselves for not already being there.

Above all, Sevens strive to feel okay about everything, and this is part of the reason it is difficult for them to land fully in their experience. Eternal idealists, they stay focused on the positive that they are sure is just beyond the next corner. They tend to be tolerant and open-minded and can become quite rigid in their demand that this is how others should be as well.

These personality traits stem from a Seven's loss of the particular vantage point about reality, his Holy Idea. There are three names for the enlightened perspective associated with Point Seven: Holy Work, Holy Plan, and Holy Wisdom. Like the Holy Ideas of Points Two and Three, particularly Holy Will and Holy Law respectively, the focus here is on the dynamic aspect of Being—the dimension of Being responsible for all manifestation. Holy Law concentrates on the fact of this ceaseless unfoldment—the reality that the universe as one whole organism moves and changes and that each of our personal changes is part of its continuous evolution. Holy Will centers on the force and directionality behind the universe's dynamism. The overarching focus of the Holy Idea of Point Seven is on the nature of this dynamism, what time means in relation to it, and how to live a life and pursue personal development in a way that is in synch with the characteristics of this movement of Being. Holy Wisdom, Almaas tells us, is the wisdom of egoless living, which can only develop through directly experiencing the perceptions of reality indicated by Holy Work and Holy Plan.

Holy Work is the perception that all of manifestation, from the subtlest spiritual dimensions to the physical world, is the handiwork of Being, and so it is God's Holy Work. A less anthropomorphic and dualistic way of expressing this is that all of creation is an outpouring of Being—Its manifestation and embodiment. When exploring Holy Truth, the Holy Idea of Point Eight, we saw that the enlightened perception there is that all of reality is pure Being, whose central characteristic is presence. The substantiality and reality of this presence can only be perceived by being fully present, fully inhabiting our consciousness and experiencing ourselves in the now. When our consciousness is veiled by thoughts of the past or the future or when we are experiencing ourselves and the world around us through a screen of mental structures, we cannot experience the presence that we are. Free of these constructs, our souls are touched and affected by the presence of our True Nature, and we see that one of its characteristics is its nowness. The very substance of Being is an immediacy. When fully present, we also see that this presence is not static but changes, and that this movement gives rise to our notion of time. Time is how we measure change, and it is a concept that only makes sense if we are a little removed from fully inhabiting the present moment. When we are fully here in the now, time seems to stop. We have the sense that we are stepping out of time. We experience ourselves in an eternal now, in which changes and movement take place. Many of us have felt this in peak experiences, which may arise through close contact with another person, a physical crisis like being in a car accident or fire, or in moments of deep spiritual experience. Our familiar orientation in time ceases, and we feel ourselves living in a world in which that concept isn't relevant.

So within the now, Being unfolds, and this is the unfoldment of our universe. All change takes place in the present, and this change is the continuous arising of forms that nonetheless remain fundamentally Being. As Almaas says, "The whole universe is like a fountain, always unfolding, always pouring out in different forms—but always remaining water, that is, remaining Being or presence."[1] A further step in this understanding is that this flow of presence that is the universe is a constant arising, a continuous act of creation. Creation of the universe, then, did not occur at some moment in the distant past, since time is not relevant on this level of things. Creation is a constant; the universe is constantly being created in the immediacy of the now. What existed a moment ago no longer exists. The world is arising endlessly anew: "The water that pours from the fountain in one moment is not the same water that pours from it in the next."[2] This is a very deep perception, one that may not make any sense at first glance, but I am mentioning it since it may become relevant at some point in one's personal unfoldment.

Movement and change take place in this eternal now, this infinity of presence, and this is the unfoldment of Being. Abiding in this flow of Being is abiding in "real time," and this brings us to the primary implication of this understanding of Holy Work. It is that real work is the endeavor of becoming conscious of our True Nature as Being. This is the holiest work a human being can engage in. It is probably for this reason that Gurdjieff called spiritual development "the Work." This work of real transformation only takes place when we are living in real time, which is another way of saying when we are present, fully existing in the now. Gurdjieff titled one of his books *Life Is Real Only Then, When "I Am,"* and as Almaas says, a person's real age is measured by how much time they have spent in real time, since this indicates the maturity of their soul.

Holy Plan is the perception that the unfoldment of reality is not arbitrary or chaotic but instead follows a kind of cosmic blueprint. The universe has a fundamental intelligence, and so its movements reflect that. Natural laws and order are at work, and all that occurs and comes into existence is a result of the working of this intelligence. The word *plan* is not used here in the sense of things being planned out, preordained, or predetermined but rather in the sense that there is a meaningful design and pattern to how things unfold. Our genetic code or plan, for instance, is contained in our DNA so when a human sperm and ova unite, an embryo that in time becomes a human infant develops, instead of a tree or a spider. Likewise it is possible to plot stages of human physical, perceptual, and psychological development because of the inherent order or plan to our development. And it is possible to chart general maps of spiritual development and to anticipate that certain kinds of practices will lead to certain results. For instance, if we meditate focusing on one point or on our breath, our consciousness will develop more concentration. If we consistently sense into our bodies, we will feel more embodied and more present.

We are recognizing this natural order when we see that if we behave in hurtful and hateful ways toward others, they will probably dislike and tend to avoid us. Or when we notice that if our heart is open to another, we feel the presence of love and compassion in our consciousness, and our relationship with that person feels harmonious. Obviously the way these things and all of reality unfold is not accidental. It follows and reveals a logic and an intelligence that are not linear.

The way our souls and the rest of reality work can never be fully plotted or predicted because of the nature of this intelligence operating within them. The intelligence of the universe is alive and responds to its changing circumstances. As microcosms of the universe, all organisms inherently share this vital intelligence. Species adapt, for instance, in ways that do not necessarily make linear sense, but these adaptations have a kind of organic logic to them whose function is to help the species survive. It is likely that many of the mysteries of our world will never be fully understood by science. Apparent paradoxes reveal themselves the more deeply we understand the physics of matter, as when for example we see that light is both wave and particle. Or on the level of human actions, when something occurs, such as a fatal illness or a death, which we initially consider to be bad, only to recognize many years later that the positive that resulted would not have been possible without that seemingly negative thing happening. Like the Absolute, out of which all of reality arises, and whose other name is the Mystery since it can never be fully understood by the mind, so the workings of things will probably always evade precise formulations.

So we are seeing that there is a natural order to the way things happen in the universe and that this order cannot be definitively understood, foretold, or charted. We have also seen how all change is the unfoldment of Being, which, because Being is presence, takes place as a succession of moments of the present, and that the world we inhabit and we ourselves are part of a constantly arising creation in each moment. These perceptions bring us to Holy Wisdom and the question of what it means to live wisely.

There are many implications contained within an understanding of Holy Work and Holy Plan in terms of how we can conceive of and orient our lives. The first arises from the understanding that Being, whose central characteristic is presence, can only be experienced by being in tune with that characteristic—by being present, in other words. So if we are to make contact with our essential nature, with the depths within us, we can only do so by being fully present each moment of our lives. The second is that the amount of time we spend in Being—in real time—contributes to the maturation of our souls. As Being is a constant arising, all prior knowledge, even memories of past essential experiences, must be left behind for this maturation to ensue. Because our souls follow an organic unfoldment, we cannot plan our development or predict where we are going. The unfoldment of our souls must be greeted on its own terms, as a mystery ready to reveal itself constantly. This unfoldment will be blocked if we try to think our way through it by mapping and charting it according to information we have about the various dimensions and states of Being. If we believe that we know where we are headed and how long it should take us to get there, true unfoldment cannot take place. If we try to make our process conform to a blueprint of inner development, our process loses its aliveness and its immediacy, and the intelligence of our souls cannot lead us to our depths. The Holy Plan of each of our souls can only reveal itself and actualize itself through being continuously present and open to its revelations. These, then, are some of the nuances of Holy Wisdom.

As an Ennea-type Seven loses contact with his essential nature through the vicissitudes of his early holding environment, he also loses the possibility of perceiving reality through this Holy Idea. As will become apparent as a Seven matures, what is lost is contact with the presence of Being and trust in the natural laws of Its unfoldment. There is a deep sense of disorientation left in a Seven's soul in the absence of contact with Being. As Almaas describes it,

> The loss of orientation that is the condition of the ego is due to the absence of adequate holding in childhood, which interrupts the continuity of Being. As a child, one is simply being and our Beingness is unfolding. When the holding environment is not there or is inadequate, one feels a loss of support; and then that Being continues, but disconnected and interrupted from Its unfoldment. When the continuity of your Beingness as a child is interrupted, you experience it as feeling lost if you are experiencing this loss through the sensitivity of this Holy Idea. The loss of holding here is equivalent to the loss of knowing the Holy Work—that reality is unfolding in a way that holds your presence and development.[3]

A Seven feels that he has lost his place in the vast pattern of unfoldment in the universe, and as he matures, the more he loses trust in his
soul's capacity to unfold naturally. With this blind spot, it seems to him
that reality does not support him in naturally developing and fulfilling
his potential. His solution is to take matters in his own hands and to try
to figure out how things work—what the plan is—and to try to make his
process fit into it. Mapping and planning for the future, then, become his
personality's imitation of Holy Plan, and become a substitute for full engagement in the present. Hence, as mentioned earlier, the name Ichazo
gave this type, Ego-Planning. This orientation forms his fixation, his
fixed cognitive view on himself and life, as we see on the Enneagram of
Fixations in Diagram 2.

It is, of course, only much later than early childhood that this future
orientation and planning tendency begins to show itself, and we will return to it later. Focusing on his early childhood, filtered through the
Seven's sensitivity to his Holy Idea, his experience becomes that of a paradise lost. It may be that he never actually experienced blissfulness in his
early months with his mother or that there was a period of fulfilling and
supportive contact, only to be interrupted for one reason or another. If
there was an initial period of closeness, circumstances such as mother returning to work, illness, the birth of another sibling, or a sudden change
in the family's fortune may have severed it. If there was no such period, it
is likely that his soul unconsciously intuited what might have been and so
what was missing. In either case, what remains in a Seven's soul is the imprint of losing the breast—whether actually or metaphorically—and so
losing his source of nourishment, love, warmth, and safety, as though he
has lost the juice of life itself.

This sense of the source of life drying up and disappearing on him
forms an inner desolate wasteland that feels unbearable. Like Fives, this
core state of deficiency feels dry, parched, and empty, an inner wasteland
devoid of life. Emptiness, barrenness, and lifelessness in any form that
they take, whether physical, emotional, or mental, become the primary
things that he avoids since they remind him of his early loss of mother
and, through her, of Being. His whole personality becomes geared toward
avoiding this dry pain. While we find pain on the Enneagram of Avoid-

ances, Diagram 10, at Point Seven, it is really this core sense of barrenness and disconnection from the vibrancy of life that forms a Seven's deepest pain and which his personality is oriented toward not experiencing.

To avoid his inner desert, he envisions, makes real in his mind, and plots his course toward the oasis that he knows is out there somewhere, where he envisions that warmth and emotional lushness await. Mapping and planning, his central preoccupations, can be seen from this vantage point as attempts, albeit unconscious, to plot out his reconnection with Being, the source of true satisfaction. His orientation, then, is toward a future that exists primarily in his imagination, a utopia in which all of his wishes will be fulfilled. Envisioning and imagining what is possible replace facing and being in the present. His lie, then, his way of not facing reality, is false imagination on the Enneagram of Lies, Diagram 12. Reality never conforms to his plan or his imagined sense of what fulfillment looks like, and so he is always disappointed.

In their effort to avoid their dry and bereft core pain, Sevens place a premium on being okay with everything. They give everything a positive spin, looking at the bright side of things and avoiding looking at the darker side. Their inner gaze is focused decisively and tenaciously on seeing things optimistically, since seeing things in their entirety threatens to bring up the avoided desolation and sense of being irretrievably cut off from the flow of life. In some cases, this tendency to focus on the positive was supported in early life by receiving approval for being happy and positive, while showing their pain or fear brought disapproval and even abandonment by parental figures who had little empathy for it.

In their self-presentation, this orientation manifests as compulsively smiling, which often is a cover for pain or hostility. Sevens look cheerful and lighthearted, upbeat and confident, carefree and full of expectation. They tend to have round, wholesome-looking faces, a bright glint in their eyes, and a buoyancy to their walk. They seem energized and enthusiastic, leaning into the future and eager to engage with it.

For a Seven, looking at life from a purely positive vantage point is an attempt to support himself and gain the inner sense of security that he lacks. In this idealism, we see the Seven's strategy for dealing with his fear. Like Ennea-types Five and Six, he is a fear type, although at first glance he appears self-assured and untroubled. It is only as we begin to notice that there is a defensive and compulsive need to be so upbeat that it becomes clear that a Seven's jauntiness is a way of masking his fear. As with the other fear types, the world is a frightening and threatening place to him, one in which he does not feel loved and supported by the universe. Like a child who *must* believe in Santa Claus or the good fairy as a way of avoiding the harsh and painful realities of life, he clings to the positive in an attempt to reframe the source of his fear and so disempower it. This is why idealism is his trap, as we see on Diagram 9.

Clearly much rationalization and justification are necessary to give everything a positive spin, and Sevens are masters at explaining things in such a way that everything comes across as being just fine. To experience anything as not all right is dangerous to them since it threatens to bring up their buried inner pain, and so anything that might be painful or scary is rationalized away. His mind, then, becomes his defensive tool. He removes himself from his wounded heart and inhabits a world lived largely through his ideas and pictures of it. Fully being anchored in his body and feeling the entire range of his emotions, not just the positive ones, is a frightening proposition, and so he creates and lives in a happy, exciting, and promising inner world that is largely a mental construct. Bits are abstracted out of reality to support this inner fantasy world, and the rest is discarded. Rather than fully inhabiting his soul, he relates to it through his mind, and so it becomes an abstraction, symbolic to him rather than real. For this reason, self-symbolizing appears at Point Seven on the Enneagram of Antiself Actions, Diagram 11. His mental picture of himself replaces his experience of his own soul.

Anger and aggression, like emptiness, pain, and fear, are not okay for a Seven to feel or express. Such negative emotions threaten to overwhelm the positive ones—if he feels his anger, his feelings of love and connection might go away, and he also might alienate others. This in turn threatens to bring to consciousness the distance he felt from mother and that he currently feels from Being, and so is scary and something to avoid. To diffuse the potential risk that negative feelings carry for him, he explains them away and talks himself out of them. The negative receives a positive spin. Likewise he uses his charm to diffuse another's aggression, cajoling and beguiling the other into feeling good about him once again. It is also difficult for him to tolerate another person experiencing feelings like hopelessness, depression, grief, and sadness. To these, too, he must give a positive spin, and sets about convincing the other that there really is a silver lining to every cloud. So in his personal relationships, he likes to keep things light and pleasant, tending to avoid a depth of contact.

It is not that his own negative feelings go away. He must constantly distract himself from them. His anger gets channeled into his superego, which becomes righteous and good, advice giving and helpful, constructively critical, all for himself and the other's own good, much like a One. A Seven's aggression becomes something positive in his own mind in this way, since channeling it into his superego protects and supports his sense of doing good and so being okay.

One of the central Seven inner dynamics is that his superego demands that he conform and already have embodied whatever his personal ego ideal happens to be. His ego ideal will match the goal of his dominant internal map, which may for instance chart the path to psychological health according to a particular school of thought or may plot a particular spiritual path whose goal is a particular state of consciousness. His ego ideal might be the envisioned success of a particular kind of industry in which he works or a particular lifestyle that he aspires toward. If he can envision the goal, his superego expects him already to be there, and berates him oh so reasonably for not having achieved it yet.

This in turn leads to hopelessness and a feeling that there is no point in working toward his goal, and so he escapes into pleasure seeking. Like a perpetual adolescent, he has little patience for processes that take time and effort, wanting to be there yesterday, and so has difficulty with long-range commitments and unexciting work in the trenches of life. He is an eternal youth, a *puer aeternus* as the Jungians call this orientation, living in glorious dreams of what tomorrow may bring and refusing to grow up. Behind this tendency is his fear of disappointment, especially in himself.

The defense mechanisms he employs to keep his feet off the ground and to defend against his fear and pain are several. Initially Naranjo gave only sublimation as the Seven's defense mechanism, but in his recent writing he also includes rationalization and idealization. Intellectualization, which he does not include, is another defense mechanism that seems to me even more fundamental than the others are. We can see why it is so relevant to Ennea-type Sevens in the following definition of intellectualization:

> *The psychological binding of the instinctual drives to intellectual activities, especially in order to exert control over anxiety and reduce tension. This mechanism typically occurs in adolescence and is exemplified in abstract discussions and speculations about philosophical and religious topics that tend to avoid concrete bodily sensations or conflictual ideas or feelings.*[4]

Rationalization, which I have mentioned above, is defined as "a process by which an individual employs subjectively 'reasonable,' conscious explanations to justify certain actions or attitudes, while unconsciously concealing other unacceptable motivations."[5]

Sublimation is a defense in which instinctual drive energy is channeled and altered into socially acceptable forms. Raw sexuality becomes transformed into artistic expression, for instance, or aggression becomes transformed into witty repartee. As Naranjo says, sublimation is the process by which a Seven "has become blind to his neediness and instinctiveness while remaining conscious only of his altruistic and generous motivation."[6] He goes on to say that it also explains the Seven's proclivity for fantasy and for planning, as his true impulsive goals become lost through this transformation.

Idealization certainly has a place in the modus operandi of a Seven, not so much as a function of narcissism, as Naranjo suggests, in which self or other are held in exaggerated esteem. As I see it, narcissism is not central to this ennea-type in particular, so neither is idealization in the strict sense in which it is used clinically. Any ennea-type can have a narcissistic tendency, just as any type can have a predominantly schizoid or borderline skew to his structure, no matter how healthy his ego happens to be. Those with schizoid leanings are shy and timid, and tend to isolate themselves from close contact behind distancing boundaries. Those with borderline tendencies feel amorphous and undifferentiated, have difficulty setting boundaries, and tend to fall apart under pressure. While the former may sound Five-ish and the latter Nine-ish, anyone of any ennea-type can have these structural orientations. Idealization in Sevens appears more globally, as a predisposition to see things in a positive light and to be idealistic and optimistic about the world and life in general.

In keeping with the Seven's predisposition to use his intellect as his chief defense, then, he lives primarily from his mind rather than from his emotions or his direct experience. His mind is ceaselessly active, exemplifying what the Buddhists call "monkey mind"—the mind in constant activity, swinging from branch to branch, as it were—well above the ground. The monkey, fittingly enough, is the animal associated with Point Seven.

Cognition to a great extent replaces action for him, and he is constantly generating ideas and plans. These ideas and plans far outstrip any concrete manifestation. For everything that he actually accomplishes, there are a multitude of other plans and other options going on inside of him. Afraid of reality, he finds his intellectual world far safer. If something does not work out, there are always other contingency plans, and better just to think and talk about them than to take the chance of something not working out commendably.

We have seen how mapping and planning are the result of a Seven's loss of a sense of the natural unfoldment of the universe of which he is a part—the loss of the perception of Holy Work—and that in response to his disorientation regarding what to do arising from this loss, he believes that he can and must plan and direct his own life and unfoldment. For most of us, this makes sense. It is a huge leap to contemplate not attempting to direct our lives and instead attuning ourselves to the natural unfoldment of the Holy Work, and so the fallacy of a Seven's orientation may be difficult to grasp. It might become more apparent if we discuss how a Seven characteristically operates in terms of personal unfoldment.

He first of all tries to understand the plan of the psychological or spiritual model that he is working with, and gets a sense of where he is heading according to that model. Then he figures out what issues he needs to address and what states of consciousness need to arise and when and in what order, and tries to bring this about within his consciousness. Obviously no real transformation is possible since such an "unfoldment" arises from a mental construct and is not in tune with how the soul unfolds, which must follow each soul's unique and inherent inner pattern. This pattern cannot be anticipated or forced to conform to our ideas about how it ought to be or when changes ought to take place. Real transformation is only possible through attunement to the laws of Being, and not those of the personality.

The world of the intellect becomes so real for Sevens that battles are won and lost within it, if only in their imagination. They love to theorize and generalize; have a fascination with words, symbols, and analogies; and talk *about* things rather than fully experiencing them. They often end up confusing the map for the territory, and the fine points of the map's symbols often come to replace what they represent. For instance, in studying the enneagram, a Seven might get so involved with the theory and the interconnections possible that he forgets about the actual lived experience of each type. Or a Seven might become a spiritual commentator, critiquing the work of others and measuring it against his own mental map of states of consciousness and spiritual development, and in so doing lose sight of how things really unfold experientially, while at the same time finding an outlet for his aggression and hostility.

His is the realm of intellectual debate in which the talk itself becomes the activity, as, for example, in Talmudic discourse over the many possible interpretations and nuances of biblical words and phrases. Words to him are as real as action, and so frequently replace it for him. Sevens, in this respect, are often described as being windbags, all talk, full of hot air, or all show and no go.

Unlike Ones, who might be likened to grammarians, Sevens are perpetual scholars, loving to gather ever more bits of information. They love fitting concepts together, synthesizing data and generating a systematized grand schema of things. The work of Joseph Campbell comes to mind in this respect, as does that of Carl Jung, the great psychologist whose work centered on the archetypal world and the symbols representing it.

With a Seven's skill at weaving reality into the story line he wants it to conform to, he is a great storyteller, often highly entertaining and amusing. He loves to talk and loves being the center of attention, bringing his tales to life with the help of a group's energy. The comedian Robin

Williams is an excellent example of this capacity to talk about almost anything and turn it into something hugely entertaining and hilarious. On the other hand, Sevens can also be flimflammers, charming and conning you into believing that something quite ordinary and mundane is your ticket to bliss. For this reason, and also because of their tendency to become instant experts at things they know little about, Ichazo's original name for this type was Ego-Charlatan.

Sevens have a proclivity for going to one workshop and then turning around and teaching a whole course in the subject, or taking one bit of data and expanding it into a whole discourse. Some Sevens are dilettantes, as mentioned earlier, knowing a little about a lot of things, and rarely hanging in with anything long enough to master it really thoroughly. For this type of Seven, part of the difficulty is that when things cease to be exciting and they have to get down to the tedious work required for mastery in any arena, they get bored and lose interest. The other reason they tend to remain on the surface of things is that going into them more deeply threatens to bring up their personal limits and difficulties, and this in turn threatens their sense of being up to par. Other Sevens do get deeply involved with one thing, like mastering a musical instrument or becoming a master programmer, but have numerous other interests as well. They do not want to be pinned down to this one thing and defined by it, since with their lack of faith in how things unfold, something might go wrong and they would be stuck.

In spiritual work, this tendency to skate on the surface or to have an alternative in mind when the going gets tough is particularly problematic, and many Sevens leave just when their suffering and their sense of deficiency begin to surface. They tend to move on at that point to the latest and quickest path to enlightenment and are particularly attracted to paths that emphasize transcendence rather than transformation and that promise rapid attainment with little work—receiving enlightenment through direct transmission from a guru, reciting affirmations, visualizing how you want your life to be, weekend courses that promise enlightenment, and the like.

Sevens love to be fonts of knowledge and sources of information, and in this we see the personality's simulation of Holy Wisdom. Many Sevens feel a sense of intellectual superiority and delight in exhibiting how much they know. So in addition to being perpetual scholars, they also like to educate and teach others, displaying their wealth of information. They can be motherly or fatherly in this respect, generously and magnanimously giving advice and support, but beneath their appearance of warm and loving benevolence is a sense of attention seeking and a feeling of emotional dryness and distance.

As a side note, the curious Seven mix of emotional dryness and coolness, criticality, and thrift, juxtaposed with permissiveness, magnanimity, staunch individualism, a live-and-let-live attitude is exemplified in the Dutch culture. Amsterdam, the capital of the Netherlands, with its laid-back feel and its legalized drugs and prostitution make it a mecca for hedonists and escapists, while strict standards actually govern the enforcement of its pleasures.

Sevens love to be influential and are very persuasive regarding their point of view. They have, after all, persuaded themselves that life is not really so scary and that they are not really suffering. If they can also influence others and convince them of their knowledge and expertise, this supports their attempt to be okay and forestalls their fear. The more manipulative and self-serving side to their persuasiveness is clear in the following quote from Naranjo:

> A charlatan is of course one who is able to persuade others of the usefulness of what he sells. However, beyond the intellectual activity of explanation, which can become a narcissistic vice in type VII, persuasiveness rests in one's own belief in one's wisdom, superiority, respectability, and goodness of intentions. . . .
>
> The qualities of being a persuader and a knowledge source usually find expression in type VII in becoming an adviser at times in a professional capacity. Charlatans like to influence others through advice. We may see not only narcissistic satisfaction and the expression of helpfulness in charlatanism but also an interest in manipulating through words: "laying trips" on people and having them implement the persuader's projects.[7]

On the other hand, no matter how persuasive they are at convincing others about their knowledge and expertise, because these rely primarily on mental rather than embodied knowing, they never feel fully secure. By definition, the Seven's attempt to emulate Holy Wisdom cannot work, and so deep down, a lack of confidence and fear of being unmasked as a fraud haunt most Sevens.

Likewise, beneath a Seven's optimism and idealization of himself, others, and life in general lies a great fear of disaster or ruin that seems to loom right over the horizon. Many Sevens have catastrophic expectations, believing in some impending doom that they must help forestall—like the "millennium bug"—which their overactive minds extrapolate into huge global cataclysms. This tendency arises to the extent that a Seven is afraid of life and so lives in an inner idealized world that will be realized sometime in the future. His fear of the painful and frightening within becomes projected onto the world outside, which in turn supports his resolution to maintain his inner utopia. What is most painful and frightening to him is his largely unconscious conviction—his fixed mental belief—that he is irreparably severed from the flow of life, and to that deep place in his psyche, catastrophe seems just ahead.

Because the inner world of a Seven is primarily mental, there is little life in it. His sense of vitality needs constant refueling, so he ceaselessly stimulates himself with new ideas, new sensory impressions, and new tastes. This brings us to the passion of this type: gluttony, as we see on the Enneagram of Passions on Diagram 2. Gluttony has an oral and greedy quality to it. In its usual usage, gluttony means overindulging in food, but in the case of a Seven, the overindulging is not limited to what he eats. His voracious appetite could be for ideas, stories, books, drugs, food, drink, or anything else that turns him on. It could also be for attention, since for some that is a particular kind of turn-on. If he is involved in spiritual work, it could manifest as gluttony for good experiences and high states, for more and different tastes of True Nature.

It is not that he wants to gorge himself on a lot of one thing, especially one ordinary and accessible thing. What he wants is a taste of all sorts of different things, and the more unusual, novel, offbeat, and extraordinary, the better. It is like going into Baskin-Robbins and wanting a taste of each of the many flavors of ice cream. He wants the excitement, the new-ness of something different. Like their hyperactive "monkey minds," Sevens rush through life charged with their quest for new and different stimuli and riding on a high of expectations fueled by their idealistic and overly optimistic dreams and plans. Energetically, Sevens are frequently "wired"—full of excitement and adrenaline about life or, more accurately, about their idea of it—and fittingly, the adrenals are the body part associated with them. They are rocket propelled into the future, a future that seems to hold the promise of more and more interesting things.

Gluttony is really an attachment to consumption. It is a need to be constantly taking something in, chewing and tasting rather than fully digesting anything. Gaps in stimuli bring up anxiety for a Seven, the anxiety that signals his inner hunger threatening to arise in consciousness. Behind the hunger is the pain and angst of his inner dry barrenness, the sense of empty deficiency at the core of his personality. So he hungers for good experiences, high, transcendent, and blissful ones. At root, his gluttony is an unconscious attempt to regain the lost paradise within—connection with mother and, beyond her personification of it, with Being Itself.

We see his idealized Aspect manifesting most pronouncedly in this pursuit of the lost bliss of infancy. The state of consciousness he is trying to emulate is that of the Yellow or Joy Aspect of Essence in the language of the Diamond Approach. The Yellow is the state of joy in the soul that arises from contact with what we love. It may manifest as a bubbly ebullience or a very quiet and deep delight. The teaching of the Yellow is about discovering what we really want, what it is that will truly make us happy. The more we inquire into what it is that brings us joy through listening closely to our hearts, we will see that joy arises the more we are real and the more we face our truth, because this takes us one step closer to our depths. We also see that joy arises as we perceive the unfoldment of Being—the Holy Work—in all of the forms it takes in our universe. Understanding the Yellow reveals to us that we love the people and things that we do because they are manifestations of and remind us of the deepest love of the hearts, our True Nature. Joy is a celebration of Being and a celebration of participating in Its unfoldment. Joy arises the more our hearts are open, spontaneous, and unshackled by fear. The Seven's pursuit of stimulation and engagement is really an attempt to find the happiness that can only come when we are united with the true Beloved of our hearts, True Nature.

Most spiritual teachings tell us that desire is the root of all suffering. The Yellow refines that understanding and shows us that if we desire things out of love for them, we feel joy in our hearts and actually lose any attachment to having them. Our desire, then, if fully felt and allowed, transforms into selfless love. We experience this when we deeply love another person and lose all self-reference in our wish for the best for that person. If our desire arises out of deficiency and wanting to fill our emptiness, we feel only desperation. So it might be truer to say that if our suffering is the root of our desire, only more suffering will result.

The Seven personality style is an imitation of the Yellow. We see this in the Seven's emphasis on being unfettered and spontaneous, his compulsive need to be cheerful and to avoid any pain, and most clearly in his gluttony, which is really a facsimile of spiritual longing for union with the Beloved. A Seven's somewhat manic buoyancy is the soul's attempt to connect with the exuberance of true joy, the Yellow.

Unlike Eights, whose lust is directed toward the most primitive and "dirty," Sevens want a diversion, an escape, a good time, an avoidance of reality and of their fear, pain, and sense of deficiency. So rather than wanting to get down as Eights do, Sevens want to get high. The problem with getting high—whether on drugs, alcohol, or just adrenaline—is that sooner or later you have to come down, not a happy prospect for a Seven. The dilemma is articulated beautifully below in a section from Ram Dass's seminal book of the early seventies, *Be Here Now,* in which he describes his disappointment that all of the insights he had under the influence of LSD could not prevent him from returning to his ordinary state of consciousness:

In these few years we had gotten over the feeling that one experience was going to make you enlightened forever. We saw that it wasn't going to be that simple. . . . And for five years I dealt with the matter of "coming down." . . . Because after the six{th} year, I realized that no matter how ingenious my experimental designs were, and how high I got, I came down. . . . And it was a terribly frustrating experience, as if you came into the kingdom of heaven and you saw how it all was and you felt these new states of awareness, and then you got cast out again, and after 200 or 300 times of this, began to feel an extraordinary kind of depression set in—a very gentle depression that whatever I knew still wasn't enough![8]

Ram Dass's dilemma personifies that of the hippie movement of the sixties and early seventies, which bears all the marks of a Seven-ish phenomenon. Bypassing the personality with the chemical help of psychedelic drugs, many members of the baby boom generation had their eyes opened to their depths. What they saw was what many of the spiritual traditions have been teaching for thousands of years: that our basic nature is love and that we are part of a Oneness. The problem is that the truths the hippies got in touch with when high were not integrated when they came down. It was not enough to give flowers to soldiers and share one's food, home, and body. The defenses of the personality were skipped over rather than worked through, and so the inevitable result was that the undigested shadow aspects of the personality arose unconsciously—such as greed, selfishness, materiality, and so on.

The Beatles sang that "all you need is love," that you should "give peace a chance," that "the love you take is equal to the love you make," and headed by John Lennon, who was probably a Seven, they expressed perfectly that generation's point of view. Peace and love became the movement's motto, but any behavior that did not conform to this axiom was rejected. The emphasis was on personal freedom and rebellion against all cultural norms and constraints, but the pressure to be *only* peaceful, loving, and generous left no room for setting limits, sexually or otherwise, and a kind of tyranny of goodness and hipness took over. Trying to live in an enlightened way could not substitute for one's soul actually being transformed. More and harder drugs were needed to stay high, heroin addiction became rampant, and some of the most gifted musicians of the era who were the voices of a generation died prematurely from overdoses. While many boomers retired their tie-dyed clothing and beads, put on shoes and bras, and abandoned hippie values, others went on to pursue spiritual work seriously and realize the depths within, which drugs had opened the door to.

"Don't worry, be happy" is easier said than done. The lesson of the era may well be that, in the end, Holy Wisdom cannot be faked. For a Seven, living a life that is in accord with Being requires following a long and arduous path in which the guiding force ceases to be his gluttony and becomes instead the virtue of sobriety. We find this on the Enneagram of Virtues, Diagram 1. Ichazo says of sobriety: "It gives the body its sense of proportion. A being in the state of sobriety is firmly grounded in the moment, taking in no more and no less than it needs, expending precisely as much energy as necessary."

There are a number of nuances to the word *sobriety*. It means first of all not being intoxicated. It also means temperance, moderation, self-restraint, seriousness, staidness, and soundness of reason and judgment. It means being unhurried and calm, with no trace of impatience or haste, facing reality and not being fanciful, as well as not being showy. If the virtue indicates an attitude each type develops in the course of spiritual development, as well as one that needs to be cultivated in relation to their inner process for unfoldment to result, what, then, does it mean for a Seven to approach his inner process with an attitude of sobriety?

First of all, as we see in Ichazo's description, sobriety necessitates being fully in the present. For a Seven, as for all of the ennea-types, being fully in the moment means being fully in his body. For a Seven to do that, he must face and work through his mental orientation as well as his future orientation. So he needs to see and confront how much he lives in his mind and how much of his mental activity is devoted to mapping things out and planning his way to what he sees as the goal according to his diagram. His confusion of the symbol for what it represents and of the concept for the reality to which it refers will need to be seen, and he will need to understand that he actually must traverse his inner terrain experientially rather than just having knowledge about it. To understand this, he will need to see that all of his information has gotten him nothing more than a very thorough map of himself and perhaps of consciousness in general, but has not brought him real personal transformation. For most Sevens, this will not happen until they have exhausted numerous instant enlightenment possibilities and have soberly faced the fact that a multitude of peak experiences has had no permanent impact on them.

At the risk of oversimplifying, a Seven will have to move through the following inner territory as he seriously engages in the work of spiritual transformation—not necessarily in this order. Considering letting go of his futuristic and goal-oriented mentality will most likely bring up his fear of directly experiencing what is going on within him in the moment. He will have to confront his fear of emptiness and barrenness, and be willing to see and experience his truth as it is, rather than as he wishes it to be. To do this requires an understanding that the Work is a matter of seeing the truth about oneself, not about having wonderful experiences. There is a Sufi story in which a monkey grabs a delicious cherry inside a bottle but cannot get his hand out of the bottle without letting go of the cherry. (This is, in fact, how monkeys are trapped.) Likewise, our monkey, the Seven, cannot be free without releasing his attachment to something yummy outside of himself. A Seven, then, needs to have the conceptual understanding that excitement and boredom, stimulation and vacuity, the negative and the positive, must be welcomed equally.

He will have to confront his reasonable, rational, and nonetheless profoundly critical and shaming superego to tolerate experiencing things inside that don't fit into his picture of being all right. And his interest in the truth must be stronger than his desire for a positive experience of himself. Probably he will have to process and make peace with a lot of childhood material that instilled his belief that he needs to be cheery all the time, and he will need to see the roots of his fear that he will be abandoned and not loved if he shows or expresses his pain and fear. A reality-based soberness about his process will show him that while this may have been the case in the distant past, it need not be so in the present. The real issue is that currently he, more than anyone else, abandons and rejects himself when he is not feeling positive.

He will see that his aversion to any inner contents that are painful or frightening is anything but the laissez-faire, open attitude that he tries to manifest. His decided bias toward the positive reveals itself to be as imprisoning as the monkey's paw caught in the bottle, since he is not free to experience anything else. In time he will see that this orientation is creating far greater suffering than any inner pain or fear that he might encounter. Facing his inner reality, then, with sobriety will mean experiencing both the positive and the negative fully, but without amplifying or exaggerating these contents.

It also means being patient with himself, and not expecting that he already ought to be where he can envision himself arriving. We have seen how his superego demands that if he can see the goal, he ought to have already attained it, and he must defend against this kind of self-attack so that he has the space to realize that the quality of his inner journey is really the goal itself. In other words, the way in which he relates to himself and his inner contents moment to moment is what transformation is all about. The more open to all of his experience he becomes, and the more time and space he gives himself for his unfoldment to manifest on its own terms—without being pushed, hurried, defined, or anticipated—the more true satisfaction he will find that he is experiencing. He will realize that true happiness and joy arise from experiencing his truth without preferences.

As his experiential contact with himself deepens, he will have to be willing to let go of his models and pictures of what his inner process and its unfoldment should look like. This will bring up his lack of trust in his soul's inherent capacity to unfold naturally, without his mind directing it. His conviction that he is outside of the Holy Plan will be revealed, and his inner sense of desolation and lack of self-arising momentum will be exposed. This is perhaps his deepest pain and what he is most afraid of experiencing.

The sense of feeling disconnected from Being and so from Its dynamism and perpetual unfoldment has left him feeling empty and bereft of natural inner movement, and this huge hole in his consciousness will gradually need to be felt. The more he allows himself to explore and move through this hole of contact with Being, the more he will experience directly all of the extraordinary hues and tastes of Being as It reveals Itself within him. As he integrates these qualities of Being into his sense of who he is, he will find that the oasis his soul has hungered for has been within him all along. He will in time find that the joy he has been seeking is really the glow of the truth as it reveals itself in his soul.

The
INNER FLOW
and the CHILD
WITHIN

The order in which I have presented the ennea-types has been according to what is called the inner flow of the enneagram—the movement from one point to another, indicated by the arrows on Diagram 5. The point following another, moving in the direction of the arrows, is a further elaboration, result, and reaction to the original one. The inner flow follows what can perhaps best be described as the logic of the soul, in its evolving of the various ego types, a logic that may have become apparent if you read the types in the order presented. What follows is a brief summary of the unfoldment of the types following the inner flow. Beginning with the loss of contact with Essence at Point Nine, we will see how each point is an attempt to resolve the soul's predicament in her estrangement from her depths and how each point's conundrum is a natural consequence of the resolution arrived at by the type preceding it. The resolution each ennea-type arrives at is inherently unsatisfying, since this predicament cannot be resolved on the level of the personality,

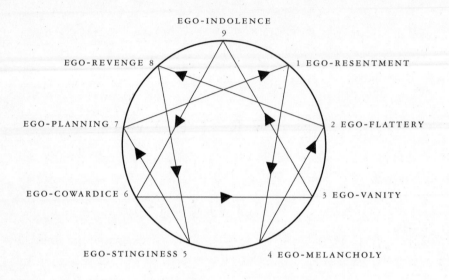

Diagram 5

THE INNER FLOW

and so the search for resolution continues around the enneagram of personality in a kind of vicious cycle.

We saw in our discussion of the inner triangle how losing contact with Essence, represented by Point Nine, leads to the existential fear of Point Six. With no inner foundation of Being, the soul is left insecure and frightened, which in turn leads to developing a false personality—represented by Point Three—in order to be able to survive and function. With nothing more to us than our animal instincts and drives, the world is one of survival of the fittest at Point Six; and with the movement to Point Three, you feel that you must pull yourself up by your own bootstraps, constructing a sense of self and a life, and in effect becoming a demigod. The more you take yourself to be this shell and live on the outer surface of yourself, and the more you identify with what you do and achieve, the more you in turn support the forgetting of your depths, as the movement of the inner flow takes us back to Point Nine. All that is left is to make yourself comfortable and distract yourself, focusing on irrelevancies and the inconsequential in a mechanical and somnambulant way.

So in the movement from one point to the next along the inner triangle, we see the building blocks or layers of the soul's development of a personality structure. As we have seen, the ennea-types surrounding those on the triangle can be viewed as elaborations or variations of this archetypal process. Beginning with Point One (which is arbitrary, we could start with any point on the outer circle), we see that in response to the sense of being imperfect, damaged, or flawed, the natural movement is toward longing for a perfect source, represented by Point Four. From another angle, the attempt of Point One to make yourself and others perfect—which is doomed to failure since what is wrong is losing sight of the soul's inherent perfection—leads to the tragic sense of hopeless yearning of Point Four. Or, from still another angle, the inner sense of sinfulness of Point One leads to Point Four, that of being abandoned and cast out by Being.

Unable to connect with an inner wellspring at Point Four, the soul naturally moves outward, toward others for that connection, represented by Point Two. Becoming dependent upon the love of another for fulfillment looks like the obvious solution when you have decided that your own estrangement from your depths is unresolvable. Attaching yourself to someone who epitomizes what you desire looks like the ticket at Point Two, and romantic love seems to hold the promise of satisfaction. But after playing to others and becoming a flattering doormat at Point Two, the soul has enough of that kind of humiliation, and fulfillment through relationship doesn't fill the inner emptiness anyway.

So the next step in the inner flow is toward Point Eight, opting for dominance and revenge for all the degradation you have suffered at Point Two. The focus becomes getting even and on being tough rather than weak. Rather than surrendering to another's will and becoming powerless as at Point Two, being in charge looks like the answer. Enough of being a victim, no matter how innocent—and enough of love, which doesn't solve everything in the end. Instead of manipulating others to get what you want and waiting around for them to respond, which they never do quite correctly anyway, it's time to take control and grab what you want without concerning yourself with anyone else.

When this solution fails to bring the desired fulfillment, the next movement of the soul is toward withdrawal, represented by moving to Point Five. Taking one's marbles and going home might be the best punishment after all, and these marbles look pretty valuable anyway, and so the focus shifts here to hoarding them at a safe distance from all impingements and demands. Passionate engagement in life has left only emptiness, so observing from a safe distance seems the best solution at Point Five. Knowledge looks as if it might bring fulfillment, which in turn leads to the escape into abstractions and schemas of Point Seven. The quest for stimulating mental engagements looks better than the desiccated emptiness that has become focal at Point Five. Charting your course to fulfillment seems, with the movement to Point Seven, more promising than staying isolated at Point Five.

The mapping and planning of Point Seven lead in turn to getting a sense of how things could be, and with the additional sense that this is how they ought to be, the inner flow takes us back to Point One. The need to be positive at Point Seven leads to a kind of militant do-gooder tendency at Point One, shored up by the defensive conviction of rightness. Out of the idealized plan developed at Point Seven, the criticism of others who don't adhere to it follows at Point One.

—◈— The point preceding one's own in the inner flow (the one directly before, moving backward along the inner flow) is called the heart point of each type. This is because it is the heart of the following enneatype in the sense that it psychodynamically forms a deeper layer in the soul. Each type can be seen as a response and a reaction within the soul to its heart point. We will develop this idea in more detail shortly.

The point following one's own has been called by some enneagram writers the stress point. The idea is that under stressful situations, we move into the perspective of this point, taking on its mind-set, its emotional tone, and adopting its behavioral style. This concept was not part of Naranjo's original teaching, and in my experience it is not totally accurate. Moving with the arrows to the point following one's own might more correctly be thought of as following the line of least resistance in the personality. It is a more defensive position, and so takes us further from our inner depths. Our egoic position is more fortified here, and so we become more impregnable to any deeper truth filtering through our soul. So rather than questioning our position, we become more entrenched when moving into the mentality denoted by this point.

While we often become more defended when under stress, this is not always the case. Situations that are extremely difficult may instead crack through our defenses, bringing us closer to ourselves rather than further away. For many of us, events such as the death of a loved one, an accident, or a serious illness may actually be turning points in our lives in which we open up to something deeper inside and get closer to our inner truth, since we are more open and transparent to it. My personal experience and observation of others is that in times of tension and distress, we are as likely to move to the heart point of our type as to the following point. Defendedness versus openness to inner exploration seems to be the variable rather than stress itself or even its degree. For these reasons, it is more accurate to refer to these points as the heart point and the defensive point.

Focusing on the heart point, what does it mean and what are the implications of it forming a layer underlying our ennea-type? The understanding developed by Almaas in the Diamond Approach is that the characteristics of our heart point correlate to one of the most problematic structures in our soul, which he has named the soul child. Our soul child is a part of our consciousness that was arrested in its development when we were very young, and so it did not mature with the rest of us and therefore feels experientially like a part of us that is a child. It is not simply a younger version of ourselves as we are now; it is the part of us that was not held, fully allowed, and supported as children. Its qualities—which as we shall see are those of our heart point—were not acceptable for one reason or another within our childhood environment, and so we learned to suppress these aspects of ourselves. Our personality developed around this sealed-off part of us, largely in reaction to it. Since its characteristics were not accepted, we developed other ones that were—those of the following point moving along the inner flow of the enneagram—our ennea-type. These parts of ourselves that were acceptable to our parents and supported by the environment matured, while the soul child remained behind, gradually becoming hidden away in our unconscious.

We become aware of the presence of our soul child when the adult part of us knows that we need to do something, and we find ourselves procrastinating or even forgetting about it altogether. We notice it when we need to lose some weight or get more exercise, and instead find ourselves eating bonbons or taking a nap. We notice it when we need to file our taxes, and somehow end up waiting until the last possible moment, despite our best intentions. We notice it, in short, when our actions don't correspond to our objective perception of what's needed, and so we feel divided and at odds with ourselves. We find ourselves doing the challenging things in our lives in spite of our soul child, and much of our energy goes into overcoming its drag on our adult aspirations.

Like all children, the soul child is driven by the pleasure principle, and it wants only to do things that are fun and enjoyable—to a child. Because of this, adult pleasures like solving a difficult problem, assuming a responsibility at work that tests our mettle, clearing things up with a friend that involves saying some difficult things, and so on, are not things that look very interesting to our soul child. So it throws a tantrum inside or simply refuses to budge, and the adult part of us ends up exasperated and at wit's end about taking care of what we need to.

Because our soul child is a deeper layer within our personality structure, it feels more like who we really are. We are more deeply identified with it than we are with the layers that developed around it. This explains another situation in which we become aware of our soul child: when we have accomplished something or are given recognition for some talent or ability. Often we don't feel pride in what we have done and feel untouched by the recognition, as though it were not really us who did it. When this happens, it is because our soul child, who we are more deeply identified with, was not involved. So skills that developed after our soul child was sealed off from consciousness more often than not do not really feel like they belong to us, and we derive little true satisfaction and fulfillment from them.

Our soul child feels more alive and vital than the rest of our personality, since it still retains access to Essence. Like all children, this inner child is a mix of primitive and animalistic tendencies, nascent ego structures, as well as pure qualities of Being. It might be most accurate to picture it as a formed structure in the soul whose inner core is Essence, with more mature personality structures layered on top of it. So as we penetrate through our soul child with our awareness, we inevitably contact all of the essential qualities that were available to us as children—the joy, aliveness, curiosity, strength, and love of life that we felt then. One particular quality of Being will emerge most strongly—the idealized Aspect of our heart point—and we will return to this in a few moments.

Even though when we first get in touch with our soul child, we contact the most childish and negative qualities of the ennea-type that forms our heart point, if our soul child is not part of our ongoing conscious life, we feel that part of us is missing. Because our soul child feels like who we really are, when we are not in touch with it we may be able to do all of the adult things that life requires but we feel that our heart isn't in them. Our heart feels discontented, and our soul child feels like an obstacle and a barrier. Our lives feel dull and boring, mechanical and devoid of real enjoyment and enthusiasm. If our work on ourselves does not involve making our soul child conscious and integrating it, then it too becomes lifeless and unfulfilling. Our soul child then ends up pulling away from our efforts to develop ourselves and can become the biggest impediment to our growth. Although the soul child is not discussed in spiritual teachings to my knowledge, without this structure being integrated within our consciousness, we cannot really speak of true transformation. Without it being brought into awareness and digested, we remain identified with this child within and never fully mature.

On the other hand, experiencing our soul child often feels dangerous and threatening to the adult parts of us. In the curious childlike magical thinking of our souls, we frequently believe that if we allow ourselves to become conscious of our soul child, its reality will suddenly come true. It is as though we believe that keeping it in the closet, cut off from consciousness, also keeps its reality from informing our lives. In fact, quite the reverse is the case: the less conscious we are of our soul child, the more it is running the show, manifesting in all sorts of behaviors and hidden motivations that make life problematic in one way or another for us. Instead of pushing it aside or trying to get rid of it, our soul child, like all children, needs to be held and accepted, given attention and lovingly guided so that it can unfold and develop. It needs the holding that it did not receive in childhood, which now only we ourselves can provide in a way that makes a difference in our soul. This does not mean indulging or reifying it, but instead being present to it and thus integrating it into our adult consciousness. Our soul child does not really grow up; rather, if allowed and accepted but not acted upon, this inner structure in time becomes thinner and more diffuse in our consciousness, allowing us to access the essential qualities at its core. Like all structures in the soul, which are in the end mental constructs, it is not a matter of the structure changing but of it becoming more permeable and porous, so that we become more in touch with the reality it has obscured.

Our soul child has the qualities and characteristics of the heart point of our ennea-type, and its core is the idealized Aspect of that point. In other words, the qualities of the idealized Aspect of each type's heart point are those that we had as children and that were not supported. Because these qualities were not allowed or encouraged, we suppressed them and developed our ennea-type in counterpoint to them. In developing our ennea-type, we tried, albeit unconsciously, to embody the characteristics of the idealized Aspect of our ennea-type, even though those of our heart point's idealized Aspect were closer to our core. Our type, then, functions in such a way as to suppress our heart point. The characteristics of our heart point are really the crucial ones to bring to consciousness, since they bring us closer to our deeper truth. They are also the qualities most missing in our soul. So, for each type, the working through described at the end of each of the chapters on the nine types also needs to include work on the soul child and the heart point. In what follows, I will briefly describe the soul child of each type and the process of establishing our heart point's idealized Aspect as a station—a state that is continuously available to consciousness—and how that transforms one's soul.

When we first get in touch with our soul child, it is usually through experiencing the negative qualities of the heart point, mostly the passion in its most infantile and exaggerated form. Because the soul child is a part of us that has been hidden away in the darkness of unconsciousness, like any living thing that is shut away for a long time, it gets a little twisted. Because of this, we often do not want to sink more deeply into ourselves for fear of encountering our soul child's negativity, which we usually experience as more truthfully what is going on with us, and also more final and unchanging. The sense of it being unchanging and unchangeable arises to the extent that we have closed the door on this part of ourselves—and so it indeed has not changed and so we infer that it never will. The more this part of us is brought out into the light of consciousness, however, the more the kinks get straightened out and its negativity transforms. Again, we might think of the outer part of the soul child being all of its darkest and most troublesome qualities, and the deeper we penetrate into it with our awareness, the more essential its qualities become. Finally, at its core, we experience the essential state associated with our type's heart point.

In the exploration that follows, we will progress backward from the order the types were presented in the preceding chapters, moving against the arrows to the heart points of each. We will begin as we did before with the ennea-types on the inner triangle.

THE SOUL CHILD OF
ENNEA-TYPE NINE

The heart point of Ennea-type Nine is Point Three, so a Nine's soul child first makes her appearance in a tendency to deceive and lie in order to present to another what will get approval. Like a little child who takes a cookie when mommy has told her not to, or plays hooky from school pretending to be sick, a Nine's soul child pleads that she did not do it and that she really *does* have an upset stomach. Beyond the passion of lying, within every Nine is a young place that wants to be seen, wants to shine, and wants to be the center of attention. So there is a little show-off, wanting to do her dance and be applauded. Behind a Nine's self-abnegating tendency lies a drivenness and often a ruthlessness about succeeding—usually well hidden and pushed out of consciousness. Nines are often afraid of appearing too pushy and taking up too much space, which is the shadow of their soul child falling across their consciousness. The focus on doing underlies a Nine's inertia, and often Nines are afraid that if they start an activity, they will become driven and not be able to stop.

As a Nine allows herself to get in touch with this structure inside and its qualities, she will progressively experience herself as a more complete person. Exhibitionist tendencies will transform into a sincere recognition of her personhood. She will see that being a person in her own right was not supported during her childhood, and so she became accommodating and self-absenting in ordered to get approval. Reclaiming herself as personally valuable and lovable will lead her toward the realization of herself as a personal embodiment of Being, the Pearl Beyond Price, a radiant and luminous presence independent from the constraints of her conditioning. She will gradually become free of any self-image or mental construct defining who she is, and be able to contact and interact in the world liberated from the sleep of the personality.

THE SOUL CHILD OF ENNEA-TYPE THREE

Six is the heart point of Ennea-type Three, so behind the efficient and composed veneer of a Three lies a very frightened child. Shy, timid, self-doubting, and insecure, this soul child experiences the world as a hostile and malevolent place. Others appear threatening, sometimes to the point that he may develop paranoia that they are out to get him, and no matter how many achievements a Three has accomplished and how much outer success he has created, he still experiences himself deep down as one of the weaklings in the struggle for survival. In fact, all of a Three's efforts at attainment can be seen as a reaction to his fearful soul child—an attempt to overcome and counter this part of himself. This explains why no amount of success is ever enough for him. Without digesting and integrating his soul child, the inner fear and insecurity cannot be resolved by any amount of status and power. From the perspective of the soul child, a Three's image is an attempt to camouflage this scared and immature part of himself.

Coming to grips with this child who experiences the ground beneath him as inherently shaky and unsupportive is necessary for the development of a Three. As he increasingly acknowledges his fear and sees how much of a driving force it is within his psyche, his anxious inner child will feel held and thus more secure. The allowing itself will in time transform his fear into an inner confidence, support, and ease, and a Three will understand how these very qualities that he had as a young child were not tolerated or supported by his early environment. It may be that family circumstances challenged and eventually eroded his original embodiment of essential Will, or that the ease with which he could do things made him a target of envy and hatred by parents or siblings, and undermined his self-confidence. Regardless of the psychodynamics, as a Three's soul child is integrated into his consciousness, the more his inner ground will feel secure and solid. Through the sense of Essence as his true foundation, his soul will relax into the support of Being. His drivenness, fueled by his anxious soul child, will in time transform into the inner calm and effort-lessness of true Will.

THE SOUL CHILD OF
ENNEA-TYPE SIX

Within every Six is a lazy little one—very Nine-ish—who just wants to stay under the covers, doesn't want to go out and face the world, wants only to be comfortable and entertained. Because of this, Sixes are often afraid that if they relax into themselves, they will become inert, never moving or bestirring themselves again; and they fear that they will ne-glect what they need to in their lives. This is, of course, because hidden from consciousness is this young part that does not want to do anything at all except luxuriate in pleasures and distractions. This inner indolence is really the heart of a Six's fear—she is perhaps more afraid of this ten-dency in herself than of anything else, fearing that if she stops pushing herself with her false will, all will be lost and she will sink into a swamp of laziness. If she is not making efforts, she is afraid that nothing will hap-pen and that her life will go down the tubes.

When a Six courageously allows herself to stop striving and lets herself be, she may initially experience an immobility or lack of desire to do any-thing at all. In time, the inertia and indolence of her soul child will trans-form into what it is replicating: the loving holding of Being, a sense of being held in the embrace of the Divine, knowing herself to be made up of love and one with all of existence. The sweetness and benevolence of the universe—the dimension of Living Daylight—will become part of her sense of self, and the fear in her soul will gradually subside as she realizes more and more completely her inextricable connection to Being. Eventually the whole mind-set of being frightened of others will disappear as she recognizes that her nature is the same as all that exists, and that all sense of self and other is illusory. With Being as her inner ground and her perception of its continuity in all outer forms, she has indeed found the rock she can truly stand on.

THE SOUL CHILD OF
ENNEA-TYPE ONE

Inside of the moralistic, righteous, and upstanding stance of a One is a young child who cares nothing about being good or doing the right thing. He only wants to play and have a good time and to take in all of the wonderful things that life has to offer—a little Seven. A One's soul child wants to sample every piece of chocolate and have a bite out of all of the other children's cookies. He is a little glutton, wanting to grab exciting tidbits of everything he can get his hands on, and wanting to have three different activities going on so that he can jump from one to another whenever things get monotonous. His gluttony may reach hedonistic levels, in which the suppressed essential quality of the Yellow or Joy makes its distorted appearance as indulgent pleasure seeking. The all-too-familiar Moral Majority spokesperson or evangelical Christian who gets caught with his hand in the till or his pants down is the leaking through of this sensualist and bon vivant soul child.

As a One moves beyond his judgments and self-criticism, and is able to allow this pleasure-seeking young part of himself, the distorted manifestations will gradually transform. He will understand that behind his condemnations of the sinfulness and imperfections of others is an attempt to defend against his own soul child. He tries so hard to be good because he got the message early on that his desire to have fun and play was not acceptable. Enjoyment itself was something that seemed taboo, and so life became hard work and a matter of shouldering a heavy burden. The more he penetrates his soul child's desires, the more he will get in touch with the love and delight in life itself that underlie them. Joy in the creation, the handiwork and manifestation of Being, will suffuse his heart, and he will turn his focus away from what is wrong with everything to how wonderful it all is.

THE SOUL CHILD OF ENNEA-TYPE SEVEN

Within every seemingly magnanimous and happy-go-lucky Seven is a very miserly, withholding, and withdrawing soul child—a little Five. She holds on to what she has tenaciously, storing all of her candy and her toys away so that the other kids cannot get at them and take them from her. Driven by fear of loss and an inner sense of scarcity, she feels empty inside and afraid that no more sustenance will come her way. For all of a Seven's apparent gregariousness, optimism, and interest in life, this young place inside wants to hide from life and connect with it from a distance. This soul child can also be a nerdy little know-it-all who relies primarily on her intellect. It is likely that in a Seven's childhood, her reclusive, self-enclosing, and solitary tendencies were not allowed, and that she got the message that she needed to be more externally oriented and buoyant. It is also likely that her mental skills got supported and developed at the expense of a more innate and intuitive understanding, turning her into a little egghead who felt disconnected from the other kids. A Seven's sunniness became a way of masking and defending against her inner sense of scarcity and of not belonging, not feeling part of the group or family, and not fitting in.

It is very difficult for a Seven, with her need to be cheery, optimistic, and enthusiastic about things, to acknowledge this withdrawn, frightened, and reclusive young part of herself. What feels the most difficult is the sense of scarcity that drives her soul child—the parched inner emptiness and dryness—which initially feels life threatening for a Seven to make contact with. The more she does not judge and reject this part of herself, the more the avaricious and isolating tendencies will transform, especially as her sense of being an ultimately separate entity—and thus one who is cut off from the rest of existence—is challenged. Her geeky, nebbishy, and bookish qualities will transmute into true and embodied knowing, that of the Diamond Consciousness. As her sense of ultimate separation from Being and from others comes into question, and her inner desert blooms with all of the flowers of Essence, her soul will truly know directly. She will feel part of the Whole, understanding experientially that separation is impossible, and her okayness will be real rather than reactive.

THE SOUL CHILD OF
ENNEA-TYPE FIVE

Inside of every self-enclosed, withdrawn, and quiet Five lives a little Eight-ish soul child who dreams of getting even and of devouring endless pints of ice cream. This soul child delights in getting down and dirty, slogging it out with the other kids, and lustfully immersing himself in life. His soul child may show up as a Five curses the other drivers within the isolation of his own car, as he screams at the referee while watching a football game on TV, or as he condemns all of the politicians as crooks while listening to the evening news. A Five's soul child can be a little bully and a little bigot, convinced that he is right and closed to any other possibilities. He may be defensive and denying about any perceived weakness, reacting with aggression when challenged. He can be punitive and vindictive, wanting to get even with others who he feels have wronged him.

For a Five, these tendencies of his soul child can be challenging to acknowledge and allow, since they betoken a zesty and gutsy engagement with life that appears very threatening. As a child, his wholehearted and passionate engagement in life for one reason or another was not supported. His vibrancy and aliveness, his strength and his courage—his embodiment of the Essential Aspect of the Red—was damped down. The vindictive and self-avenging tendencies of his soul child when it first appears may well be his soul's response to this stifling. In reaction to his Red not having been allowed, a Five withdrew and cut himself off from his own vitality. As he allows his lusty and dynamic soul child to surface, a Five will gradually reconnect with his aliveness and will progressively feel more part of life itself. As he integrates his soul child, his knowing becomes more embodied and inclusive since his heart and his belly also become involved. As he contacts the courage to face the unknown, his life becomes more and more of an exciting and engaging adventure that he is fully and heartily immersed in.

THE SOUL CHILD OF ENNEA-TYPE EIGHT

Within the tough and no-nonsense Eight who delights in testing her grit and that of others, dominating and controlling life, and triumphing over any adversity lies a needy, clingy, and lonely little Two-ish soul child who is desperate to be loved and held. An Eight's soul child wants to snuggle up to others, getting as close as possible, and can be pretty insistent and demanding about it. Beneath an Eight's show of strength is this soul child who is filled with all of the emotions that she considers weak—needing others, fearing rejection, insecurity, and a deep sense of sadness and loneliness. With the sense that her contactful and loving qualities were not wanted as a child, an Eight reacted by essentially saying "Fuck you!" to everyone she felt dependent upon, and set out to prove that she didn't need anyone or anything. She hid what felt like her vulnerable soft underbelly behind a veneer of callousness and in the process closed down her openness and receptivity.

As an Eight contacts the defensiveness behind her pride and the sense of rejection and neediness that underlie it, it may feel as though her whole world will collapse. She has done everything she can to not experience these "weak" places in her soul and often feels that she will not survive if she allows them to emerge. As she lets herself contact her neediness and pain, her heart can open again and her soul can become permeable. She can be touched once again, and as she contacts reality with less and less of a thick and defended skin, she will gradually feel more and more connected with life. Instead of trying to wrestle life for what she needs, she will find her soul relaxing, melting, and merging with her essential nature, whose honeylike nectar fills her soul in the form of Merging Gold.

Instead of fighting with reality, she will be united with it; and as she progressively surrenders more and more fully to his Being, she will find fulfillment and loving union rather than the capitulation she has feared.

THE SOUL CHILD OF
ENNEA-TYPE TWO

Behind the loving, giving, and helpful outer facade of a Two lies a competitive, jealous, and spiteful little Four-ish soul child. Twos try to present themselves as sweet and kind, self-sacrificing, and humble, all of which can be seen as very much a reaction to the darker tendencies of their soul child. This is a little boy inside who wants to scream "I hate you!" to the other little boy who got the teacher or mommy's attention, pull his hair, and tell him how awful he is and how stupid he is, too. He is very observant about who gets how many cookies, tries to grab the most and the best, and reacts with spite and venom if he does not get what he wants. He is filled with envy, believing the other kids have what he lacks and that they are better than he, cuter, and more lovable. He can be bitchy and backbiting, vindictive and huffy.

For a Two, the negativity and pettiness of his soul child are often initially difficult to acknowledge and tolerate. It threatens all of his pretense of open-heartedness and harmlessness; but most of all, it puts him first. This is, in fact, the very thing necessary for a Two's unfoldment—getting in touch with himself as central. As a Two contacts his soul child and, instead of rejecting him, judging him, and pushing him away, opens his heart to him, he will become primary in his own consciousness. This is very taboo for a Two, who learned that being self-centered set him up for parental disapproval. He will find that as he focuses more on himself—listening to and filling his own needs, responding to his own impulses and taking his own initiative, recognizing his limits and setting them with others—he indeed becomes more centered within himself. This is not the negative thing he had feared, signifying loss of love and becoming more selfish to him, but rather is a doorway into his personal connection with Being. The more he takes care of himself instead of others, in other words, the more he connects with the spark of the Divine within, realizing himself as the Point. Instead of having others be the point of his existence, around whom he orbits, he finds himself one with Being, a star in his own universe.

THE SOUL CHILD OF ENNEA-TYPE FOUR

Within the dramatic, intense, and emotional façade of a Four is a bossy and pushy little One-ish soul child who is intent on all the other little kids' behaving properly—seeing to it that none of them jumps the line, that their clothes are tidy, and that their manners are good. This soul child is a Goody Two-shoes, prim and proper, and critical of all those who don't follow the rules. She is a stickler for fairness and correctness and gets quite angry when the other kids are bad. They are the problem children who need to be straightened out, and in this we see the Four's tendency to blame others for their problems, as well as their defensiveness when an "imperfection" about them is pointed out.

Acknowledging this self-righteous and resentful little soul child is difficult for a Four, since it feels like her biggest flaw, opening her up to tremendous self-attack and self-hatred. Rather than imploding her aggression and directing it toward herself, bringing her soul child to consciousness is really a huge part of solving her inner suffering. The more she sees it, the more she can acknowledge her defensiveness and her need to be right, and in so doing, her soul is gradually able to relinquish its control. Understanding her need to control others and make them do what she wants will expose her lack of perception of the perfection of things as they are and, more important, of her own perfection. As she progressively integrates her soul child, she will see how the purity, luminosity, and inherent brilliancy of her soul were not allowed or mirrored in her childhood. Losing touch with the Aspect of Brilliancy, which she most embodied, she felt damaged, and developed in reaction a personality style based on estrangement, abandonment, and longing for connection outside of herself. The more she integrates her soul child, the more the little do-gooder will transform into a shining sense of inner completeness, perfection, and elegance. Instead of living a life based on envy or on mourning and longing from afar for contact, she will find that the completeness she seeks is within and that the grass inside is very brilliant indeed.

—∿∿— These brief descriptions are intended as pointers toward inner exploration and the elaboration of understanding about one's own soul. It is important to remember that the qualities of the heart point are those we are most defended against and usually have the most judgments about. Because of this, our soul child may be a part of ourselves that we don't want to see and acknowledge. This may have made the preceding material more difficult to take in than even the information on one's own type. In my experience, it takes many years of dedicated work to allow ourselves really to perceive—much less integrate—our soul child. Our biggest obstacle is our judgments and self-criticism about this part of ourselves, and disengagement from our superegos is necessary for this inner exploration. Although this part of our work on ourselves may be a difficult personal confrontation, it is infinitely rewarding, and our development as true adults depends upon it.

THE SUBTYPES

According to the theory of the enneagram as taught by both Ichazo and Naranjo, each of us has one instinct that is a more central preoccupation than the others are, which is referred to as our subtype. There are three instincts, which Ichazo calls conservation, social, and syntony; and which Naranjo calls self-preservation, social, and sexual. We see these depicted in Diagram 2. The conservation or self-preservation instinct is a primary focus on physical survival, maintenance, and sustenance, although Ichazo seems to expand it to include the satisfaction of emotional and intellectual needs as well. The social instinct focuses on our relationship with others as a group and with society as a whole. The sexual, or syntony, instinct has to do with intimate relationships and our need to be syntonic or in tune with others. The theory goes that one of these arenas is more of a central concern for each of us. Just like our ennea-type, our subtype does not change. Because this life area is a focal point for each of us, we are primarily oriented toward its satisfaction. We could say that we are sensitive to this area of life, in much the same way that we are sensitive to our Holy Idea: it is an area we feel vulnerable about and hence much of our energy goes into it.

The particular instinct that we are galvanized around is where the passion associated with our type is most pronounced. In other words, if you are a Social Two, for instance, your pride would be most pronounced around situations or issues that involve your status or social standing. If you are a Social Three, it is in that area that your lying would be most pronounced, and so on. This is one way of determining what your instinctual type is—by noticing where the passion of your ennea-type is most apparent in your life.

As we will see in the following descriptions of each of the instinctual types and in the accompanying diagrams, there is a word or phrase that describes the style and central concern of each subtype. Most of these descriptors are those I learned from Naranjo, although in some cases I am using those of Ichazo, depending upon which seems more accurate.

Another layer of the theory taught by Naranjo is that the descriptors for the two instincts that are not our dominant one are exchanged. For example, if you are a Social Six whose descriptor is duty, your functioning in areas of self-preservation would be characterized by strength or beauty (depending upon your gender), while in the relationship arena your functioning would be characterized by warmth. So, if male, you might approach situations involving self-preservation with machismo, while in intimate relationships, your manner would be warm and friendly. Rather than describing what the results of this switching for each subtype look like, I am simply giving this information here as food for further explorations.

Like the ennea-types themselves, which can all be seen as differentiations of the primary one, Ennea-type Nine, so too each of the subtypes can be seen as differentiations of Point Nine on each of the instinctual enneagrams. All of the self-preservation subtypes, for instance, can be seen as different variations of satisfying survival needs, hungers, and appetites as indicated by the descriptor appetite at Point Nine.

Let us, then, turn to the twenty-seven instinctual subtypes, beginning with those of self-preservation.

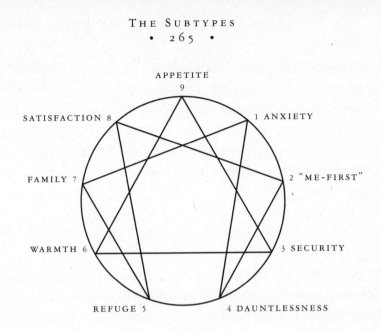

Diagram 6

THE SELF-PRESERVATION SUBTYPES

9 · APPETITE

The focus for a Self-preservation Nine is on satisfying his appetites and hungers. His laziness, in the sense that we have defined it as the passion, manifests here in the substitution of nonessential satisfactions for those that he really needs. At the deepest level, this shows up in substituting material gratifications for those that are really spiritual. An example on a more superficial level of this substitution of the nonessential would be eating a chocolate bar when what he really needs is a nourishing meal. Also, as the word *appetite* suggests, Self-preservation Nines tend to overindulge, ingesting and acquiring far more than they actually need out of insecurity about receiving sustenance.

1 · ANXIETY

The satisfaction of their basic needs becomes fraught with anxiety for Self-preservation Ones. They have an underlying belief that they are not good enough to merit their needs being met, and because of this they worry in anticipation that something will go wrong and their survival will be endangered. This can become a self-fulfilling prophecy, causing them to take action preemptively or to do things badly out of their anxiety. Their passion of anger gets triggered if someone threatens their survival, a reflection of their deeper anger at themselves for not being perfect and so being unworthy of survival.

2 · "ME FIRST"

Self-preservation Twos are afraid of being neglected and not having their needs met, so out of their survival anxiety, they take care of others so that others will take care of them. They have a self-sacrificing facade: this is the proverbial Jewish mother syndrome in which she appears to be thinking of others first and putting them ahead of herself, but in fact is really manipulating them in this way on her own behalf. The passion of pride manifests here as a hidden sense of entitlement and privilege—a conviction that others must take care of them in compensation for their martyrdom, and that they deserve to keep the best bits in the kitchen for themselves.

3 · SECURITY

Self-preservation Threes equate inner security with having enough money and a reliable position in the world. To this end, they strive relentlessly to assure their survival, which feels perpetually in jeopardy to them. This is the subtype of the workaholic who cannot take a break, and the self-made man who accumulates a fortune and yet feels that his survival is still precarious. The passion of lying arises here as deceiving oneself that amassing huge amounts of wealth will give the soul the security it lacks. Lying is also used by Self-preservation Threes to get what they think will give them the security they hunger for.

4 · DAUNTLESSNESS

The term given by Ichazo for Self-preservation Fours is *defensive action,* as opposed to *dauntlessness,* which Naranjo associated with this subtype. Ichazo, quoted by John Lilly and Joseph Hart, defines defensive action as "protecting one's dream of the future."[1] Rather than be limited by their circumstances, they will rashly go after what they want and feel that they must have to survive. They take action to preserve themselves but do not consider the consequences, and actually put their survival in peril. A Self-preservation Four, might, for instance, buy herself all sorts of beautiful things that she feels she can't live without, and end up sliding deeply into debt. Or, feeling unable to bear the constraints of a boring job, she might throw caution to the wind and on the spur of the moment buy herself a ticket to some exotic island. The passion of envy manifests here as wanting the security and material gratifications others seem to possess, and recklessly striking out to get them.

5 · REFUGE

In this case, I am using Ichazo's term for the Self-preservation Five subtype—*refuge,* rather than the one Naranjo gave, *home*—as I think it conveys more of the feeling of what a Self-preservation Five seeks. Self-preservation Fives want to ensure their survival by finding a safe place that they can withdraw to and within which they can insulate themselves from the world. So they are preoccupied with the creation of and vigilance over a personal refuge. They guard their space and their privacy, retreating from others and the world as a way of taking care of themselves. The passion of avarice manifests within this subtype in this reclusive squirreling away of themselves, as well as in stockpiling their resources, especially money.

6 · WARMTH

Warmth describes the style of Self-preservation Sixes. They are warm, friendly, and affable, making themselves likable to others as a way of ensuring their survival. The term Ichazo used for this subtype is *affection,* indicating that this is what they see as key to preserving themselves. Perceiving others as a threat to their survival, Self-preservation Sixes use their geniality to befriend and align themselves with others to offset the possibility of others turning against them. The passion of fear manifests here in this apprehensiveness around their self-protection.

7 · FAMILY

Naranjo originally used the term *family* for Self-preservation Seven. Ichazo's term, *defenders,* captures a different nuance of the same style: Self-preservation Sevens try to assure their survival through banding together and taking care of others who they feel an affinity or connection with. They become patriarchs, taking care of their extended family. Self-preservation Sevens share the amicability of their Six neighbors, appearing magnanimous, supportive, and fatherly. The passion of gluttony appears here as a hunger for tastes of anything that seems to promise survival, whether ideas, theories, nutritional support, plans to get rich quick, and so on.

8 · SATISFACTION

Self-preservation Eights are fixated on what they believe will bring them satisfaction of their needs, and they gobble up what they think they need, often at the expense of filling their real needs. So the drive for satisfaction leaves little room to figure out what it is that they really require. Their insecurity about self-preservation manifests in dominating and controlling behaviors around what they consider their turf, and around sustenance and support—keeping watch over what and how much is eaten out of the refrigerator, for instance, or where exactly her husband is spending their money. The passion of lust manifests in the voracity of their drive for satisfaction.

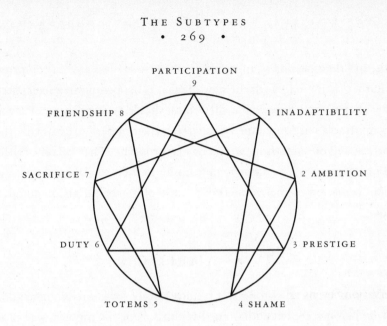

PARTICIPATION
9

FRIENDSHIP 8

1 INADAPTIBILITY

SACRIFICE 7

2 AMBITION

DUTY 6

3 PRESTIGE

TOTEMS 5

4 SHAME

Diagram 7
THE SOCIAL SUBTYPES

9 · PARTICIPATION

Social Nines have a drive to belong, lacking the certainty that they actually do. They lack a sense of ease in social situations, because of their sensitivity to whether they are really welcome or not. They often feel that they don't know how to become part of the group, and, rather than being themselves, they try to fit in by emulating socially acceptable forms of behavior and communication. Inevitably this leaves them feeling that they are not really making contact, and so reinforces their sense of being left out. This attempt to participate through social conventions is how the passion of laziness manifests here, and in their resulting tendency to make superficial contact with others.

1 · INADAPTABILITY

Social Ones express their social awkwardness and insecurity in stiffness. They have rigid ideas about how both they and others should behave socially, and their passion of anger arises when these ideas are not conformed to. Rather than going with the flow of what is happening in a social gathering, they try to impose what they think should be happening. They are uncomfortable with spontaneity, reflecting their underlying fear that they or others will do something wrong or inappropriate. They become critical and make others wrong for not conforming to their social standards, a reaction formation to their underlying sense of not being good enough to belong.

2 · AMBITION

Social Twos are social climbers, very conscious of social hierarchies and intent on being accepted and aligned with those at the top as a way of resolving their sense of not belonging. Who they are associated with and how important those people are gives them their sense of social standing. The passion of pride manifests here in the self-validation and sense of being worthwhile that arise when they have achieved the position and status that they are after. It also manifests in their refusal to be seen as unimportant or ordinary, rather than special and stellar in whatever group they are part of or aspire to be connected with.

3 · PRESTIGE

The way Social Threes feel they can relate to others is through having a prestigious image. The description of this subtype given by Ichazo (via Lilly and Hart) is "the need for a good public image."[2] For Social Threes, then, the focus is on how they are seen, and they will change their image to fit the values of a particular social group in order to be seen in a good light. Like Social Twos, they want to be socially important; but unlike Twos, they want to be important in their own right rather than through those with whom they are associated. The passion of lying manifests here in doing whatever they need to do to create their prestigious image. Their deepest lie is that this image is who they are.

4 · SHAME

Social Fours have the notion that there is a right way to be, and they are perpetually ashamed because they are not that way. They have a fundamental sense of not fitting in and of not being able to do things properly in order to fit in. Social Fours tend to be formal and a bit stiff, paying a lot of attention to their manners. Behaving properly is very important to them, since it is an attempt to cover their deeper sense of social inadequacy. Others appear to Social Fours to match the standard they have for themselves, and so they experience the passion of envy toward them and turn their hatred toward themselves in the form of shame.

5 · TOTEMS

Social Fives have, as Lilly and Hart relate of Ichazo's definition, "heroes to live up to."[3] They are very conscious of social hierarchies, and as the word *totems* implies, they want to be one of the faces on the totem pole. A totem is a symbol or emblem representing a family or social group, and this is what a Social Five lives in the shadow of and also wants to be. He is very aware of social archetypes and wants to embody them, becoming an exemplar or a fount of knowledge. He may develop expertise in a specialized field in which he wishes to be next in the lineage, and wants to be seen as such. His passion of avarice manifests as a holding on to whatever he considers gives him his social standing.

6 · DUTY

To a Social Six, fulfilling what she sees as her social role dutifully is the only way to be. She attempts to resolve her social insecurity by giving authority to a belief, a group, or a leader whom she considers more powerful, and becoming faithful, deferential, accommodating, malleable, and obedient to it or him. She is loyal, devoted, even fawning and obsequious in the carrying out of her mission on behalf of the authority, whatever she considers that to be. Her passion of fear appears here as being afraid of crossing her authority figure and being afraid of breaking social norms and obligations.

7 · SACRIFICE

Social Sevens are characterized by relinquishing their personal freedom and aspirations for social ideals. They have a profound sense of obligation toward others and feel that they must sacrifice themselves to fulfill what they see as their responsibilities. Their sacrifices are in the service of a future that they imagine and make plans to realize—a future that promises to give them the sense of belonging, social acceptance, and social standing that they lack. The passion of gluttony manifests here as a hunger for this sense of social ease and for all of the things that they believe will give it to them. Ichazo (per Lilly and Hart) uses the descriptor *social limitations* and describes this subtype as "predetermining his social activities,"[4] which highlights a different nuance of this subtype. It points the Social Seven's tendency to map and plan his social involvements to resolve his social insecurity.

8 · FRIENDSHIP

Social Eights attempt to resolve their sense of not belonging by maintaining friendly social relationships. Being a "buddy" is what Social Eights see as key to resolving their social insecurity. Friendship here is a very deep bond, one implying undying trust and loyalty, a sense of fraternity and being part of the same gang. An Eight's domineering and controlling tendencies manifest in the arena of social relationships for a Social Eight. Breeches of trust or friendship might result in a vendetta and are not easy for a Social Eight ever to forgive. The passion of lust manifests here in the passionate and possessive nature of these bonds with others.

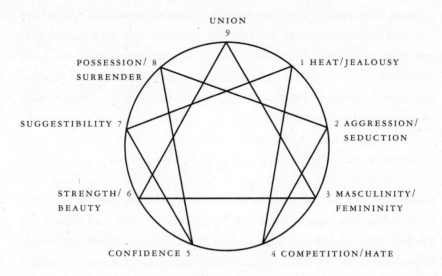

Diagram 8

THE SEXUAL SUBTYPES

9 · UNION

Sexual Nines are driven by a desire for the love of another and for total union, which appears to them as the key to their happiness. Total merging with another is seen by Sexual Nines to be what they need to be whole. They tend to merge easily with others, losing touch with themselves in the process. This substitution of another for what they really need to merge with—their essential nature—is the heart of a Sexual Nine's passion of laziness. Since this is the archetype of all of the sexual types, this attempt to fill the hole left by loss of contact with Being with the love of another is shared by all of the subtypes that follow.

1 · HEAT/JEALOUSY

Sexual Ones have a vivacious, gushy, hyperanimated, and effusive style of behavior. This constant sense of being impassioned is a leaking of their sexual "heat" into their personality style. They are perpetually afraid that someone more perfect will come along and steal their partner, if they have one, and so are always on the alert for signs that their partner desires someone else. If they don't have a mate, they are convinced deep down that another, better person will be more desirable to their object of affection than they are. As Ichazo says, "Union with another is always threatened by someone more perfect."[5]

2 · AGGRESSION/SEDUCTION

Ichazo gave only *aggression* as the descriptor of this subtype,[6] and Naranjo distinguished between a female Two's seductive style and a male Two's aggressive one. Because of their insecurity about their desirability, Sexual Twos either seduce or force the other into relationship, depending on their gender. Once in a relationship, Sexual Twos also either entice or push their partner into doing what they desire, again depending on gender. Sexual Twos of both genders usually have a tenacious attraction to an elusive partner. Female Twos are obsessed with the desire to be wanted, and male Twos are obsessed with overcoming all obstacles to union. In both cases, they are attempting to find personal value through love. The passion of pride manifests here in an extreme sensitivity about being desired or not, and sometimes as a pride in the number of sexual conquests one has made.

3 · MASCULINITY/FEMININITY

To Sexual Threes, physical and sexual appeal seems like the key to being desired, so they emphasize their gender characteristics. As a general style, the males exaggerate their virility and masculinity, and the women intensify their femininity. When attracted to someone, they take on the attributes of that person's inner masculine or feminine ideal—in Jungian terms, shaping themselves into the other's animus or anima. They are competitive with others about being seen as the most attractive, and being successful is measured by being desired. The passion of lying manifests here in deceiving themselves that love is the answer, that they must shape themselves into their beloved's ideal to be loved, and ultimately that they *are* that image. It also appears in their use of duplicity to out-maneuver their rivals and win over the object of their desire.

4 · COMPETITION/HATE

Sexual Fours compete with others of their own sex in their attempt to find love. Their competitiveness is based on a sense that love is scarce and so it needs to be fought for. They try to convince their rivals and the object of their affection that they are better than the competition, and their wish to "disappear" their challengers is a form of hatred. The choice of object of desire is determined by how many other people want that person, so that, too, arises out of competition. Sexual Fours are not only competitive in the relationship arena—competition is their dominant behavioral charac-teristic—but it is there that it is most pronounced. The passion of envy manifests here as wanting someone another has or desires and in their underlying hatred of their rivals.

5 · CONFIDENCE

Sexual Fives lack confidence in their attractiveness, capacity for relation-ship, and sexual performance. This makes it difficult for them to follow through on their attractions, despite the false confidence that they mani-fest as a compensation for their sense of inadequacy or undesirability. As Ichazo says, a Sexual Five "needs someone he feels safe with—a refuge"[7] in order to overcome his inhibitions. The passion of avarice manifests here as a holding back of his affection for fear of being rejected and a holding on to his love object once he has set his sights on her.

6 · STRENGTH/BEAUTY

Sexual Sixes have an underlying attitude of self-doubt regarding their sex-ual attractiveness and their desirability. Fundamentally they are afraid that they will not be loved, and this is where their passion of fear shows up most strongly. They are afraid to make intimate contact with another, and try to hide their fear behind exaggerating their strength (in the males) or their beauty (in the females). Male Sexual Sixes emphasize their machismo, attempting to appear virile, manly, and tough. Emotionally they may appear callous and arrogant. Female Sexual Sixes play up their attractiveness, using their capacity to attract as a way of stilling their fear about really connecting with another.

7 · SUGGESTIBILITY

Sexual Sevens tend to merge with whatever ideas, plans, or people they come into contact with. So they are easily influenced, especially by their partner or someone they are attracted to. The prospect of a relationship with someone sets off their mapping and planning, and the relationship gets projected well into the future, with infinite possibilities appearing just over the horizon. So they are suggestible in the sense of being easily swayed and impacted, as well as in the sense of being easily propelled into myriad fantasies by or about a relationship. The passion of gluttony appears here in the many attractions that Sexual Sevens tend to have and in their difficulty in forming deep, long-term contact with one person.

8 · POSSESSION/SURRENDER

Both male and female Sexual Eights try to possess and control their mates. While Sexual Eights can be overtly domineering, it is an attempt to cover their insecurity about being loved and desired. Both male and female Sexual Eights see relationship as a conquest and want to hold the power in the relationship so that they don't have to be vulnerable and dependent. Female Sexual Eights want to surrender control to a partner who they see as worthy, and may make a passionate appearance of surrender while staying very much in control. The passion of lust manifests here as the desire to possess the body and soul of an Eight's beloved.

THE WINGS

The wings, in the language of the enneagram, are the two points on either side of an ennea-type. The theory, as originally presented by Naranjo, is that each ennea-type is the midpoint between its wings. So in addition to other ways of understanding them, each ennea-type can be seen as a blend of its two adjacent points. Among enneagram authors, Don Riso in particular has written extensively about the wings. Rather than seeing one's ennea-type as a mixture of the wings, he says that one wing is the strongest, and so he has developed a schema of subtypes based on the dominant wing. His approach to the wings, then, uses two points rather than three. This is an intriguing way of looking at the ennea-types and shows us once again how multidimensional a symbol the enneagram is, allowing for many levels of interpretation. What I am presenting has a different slant, and I am mentioning Riso's approach so that the reader will not be confused about the different ways the wings have been understood and described.

Looking at each ennea-type as the interaction of its wings is an illuminating way of understanding some of our inner dynamics—the play of forces, pushes and pulls within the psyche that result in the beliefs, attitudes, behaviors, and emotions connected with our ennea-type. One nuance of Naranjo's presentation of the wings is that the point "behind" an ennea-type falls into the point "ahead" of it, moving clockwise around the periphery of the enneagram; so, for instance, if you are a Seven, Point Six falls into Point Eight, and the result would be Ennea-type Seven. As with much about the wings, I will not elaborate or develop this point but leave it as an idea to be tried on and experimented with.

Understanding the wings may also give us useful insights into our psychodynamics—the forces at work within each of us during our formative years, which shaped our soul in a particular way. Looking back over your childhood and adolescent years, you may notice that there were periods when one of the wings of your type was dominant and other periods when the other was more so. It may even seem as if your type *was* each of the wings at these various junctures. Some people's experience is that they seemed to bounce back and forth between the wings as they were growing up, until their identity solidified in their ennea-type. As adults, many people still feel the pulls in their psyche to one wing and then the other.

The brief descriptions of the interplay of the wings of each type that follow are intentionally sketchy, since my purpose is not to concretize things too much. Rather, what I hope to convey is a way of looking at and exploring the wings for yourself. Looking at each type as the midpoint where the mental fixations, core deficiency states, and the passions meet is especially fertile. In the following, we will look at the intersections of various facets and levels of the wings, and how they result in certain characteristics of each ennea-type. Referring to Diagram 3, which shows the ennea-types, might be helpful as we move around the circle.

THE WINGS OF ENNEA-TYPE NINE

With Ego-Revenge (Eight) as one wing and Ego-Resentment (One) as the other, a Nine is caught between the bad boy of the enneagram on one side and the good boy on the other. Strong instinctual drives arise at Point Eight and meet strong superego prohibitions at Point One. Of necessity, what results is a deadening of impulse and stalling of movement. These are very strong pulls in two different directions—what often feels like a hopeless conflict—so Ennea-type Nine goes numb to his inner life and becomes outer rather than inner directed. Because of the profound and mostly unconscious inner discord, Nines set about trying to make and keep things harmonious, avoiding conflicts as much as possible.

THE WINGS OF ENNEA-TYPE ONE

As the midpoint between Ego-Indolence (Nine) and Ego-Flattery (Two), a One has as a wing going to sleep on her essential nature on the one hand, and pride on the other. On the Nine side, there is a profound inner sense of worthlessness and resignation about oneself; and on the Two side, there is self-inflation and grandiosity. So there is the sense of valuelessness on the one hand, and an overvaluation of self on the other. What results is the One's sense of being basically flawed, but with the deadening to self and outer directedness of Nine plus the pride of Two, the badness gets projected outward—others are bad and need to be fixed.

Also, caught between the Nine's demand of herself to be universally loving and holding, and the Two's demand of herself to be someone who loves others and whom others love, Ones inevitably must identify with their superego and try to be perfect. And just as inevitably, they must also feel fundamentally not good enough at meeting these ultraloving demands. The sense of not being perfect also comes from the intersection of the Nine's sense of insufficiency and worthlessness, meeting the Two's fundamental sense of rejection.

THE WINGS OF ENNEA-TYPE TWO

With the wings of Ego-Resentment (One) on one side and Ego-Vanity (Three) on the other, Twos have the inner demand to be a perfect person while feeling basically flawed on the one hand, and the demand to present a perfect image on the other hand. These requirements to be perfect inside and out are impossible to meet, so a Two feels hopeless about himself and turns to others for salvation, and hence he becomes dependent upon them. From another angle, the high morality of One meets the duplicity and amorality of Three, and the result is that Twos constantly feel guilty. And from another perspective, the One-ish drive to be a good person plus the Three-ish drive to impress others leads to the Two's pattern of looking to others for approval and recognition as being a lovable person. Additionally, the Three's drive to create himself as a person, plus One's need to be good, equals the Two's drive to present and shape himself into the image of a really good and lovable person.

THE WINGS OF ENNEA-TYPE THREE

With Ego-Flattery (Two) on one side and Ego-Melancholy (Four) on the other, Threes lack an inherent sense of direction and momentum, and at the same time feel cut off and abandoned by Being. The result is that they feel cut off from any natural inner sense of depth and dynamism, and so they feel that they must live their life on the surface of themselves, in image. They also end up feeling that they must become little gods, creating themselves and their lives and maintaining them. Also, caught between the Two's dependency on others and the Four's sense of abandonment, Threes give up on counting on or turning toward others and experience themselves as totally self-reliant and self-determined. From an emotional angle, caught between the two most emotive ennea-types, both prone to depression and hopelessness, Threes swing into action and immerse themselves in doing, losing touch with what they feel in their focus on accomplishment.

THE WINGS OF ENNEA-TYPE FOUR

As the midpoint between Ego-Vanity (Three) and Ego-Stinginess (Five), Four is the place where the sense of being an independent operator creating her own laws and universe meets the sense of being an ultimately separate entity. The result is a profound sense of estrangement from the dynamism of life and from other people. The drive, then, for Fours is to connect, to make contact with something authentic both in themselves and others. And the emotional state, resulting from the interaction of the dry emptiness of Five and the sense of inner nothingness of Three that characterizes the core of both, is the isolated despair and hopelessness of Four.

From another angle, the achievement and goal orientation of Three plus the sense of isolation and lack of connection of Five result in the striving of Four for reconnection with an authentic inner source. A Four's image, then, becomes that of someone who is longing for the real.

THE WINGS OF ENNEA-TYPE FIVE

With Ego-Melancholy (Four) on one side and Ego-Cowardice (Six) on the other, Five is the blend of longing for an authentic connection with a source on the one hand, and fear, self-doubt, and insecurity on the other. The result is the Five's attempt to know, to scout the territory ahead and connect with it through knowledge, while staying at a safe distance from everything experientially. Also, with the Four's sense of being cut off and abandoned and the Six's survival anxiety, the result is the Five's avarice—the hoarding and holding on to everything she has out of fear that it will be taken away from her. From another angle, the Four's inner sense of hopelessness and certainty of being forsaken plus the Six's fear of others and the world at large result in the self-enclosure and isolation of Fives.

THE WINGS OF ENNEA-TYPE SIX

As the midpoint between Ego-Stinginess (Five) and Ego-Planning (Seven), Six is the uneasy intersection of the Five's movement away from others and the world and the Seven's gluttonous movement toward them. Fives hide, while Sevens are drawn outward to taste everything in life, and Sixes end up vacillating and stuttering in doubt, unsure whether to move forward or back, to reach out or to withdraw. The inner sense of emptiness and barrenness of Fives plus the need of Sevens to be and feel upbeat leaves Sixes unsure about what they are feeling.

From another angle, the inner sense of desiccated emptiness of Five plus the optimism of Seven results in the main object relation into which Sixes fall: idealizing an authority figure on whom high hopes are projected from a one-down position.

THE WINGS OF ENNEA-TYPE SEVEN

At Seven, the doubt of Ego-Cowardice (Six) meets the lust for life of Ego-Revenge (Eight). The result is the Seven's wanting a little taste of everything in life but, because of her fear and doubt, not fully immersing herself in anything. Like Eights, Sevens are stimulated and excited by all the things of the world, but because of their fear, the contact stays primarily mental and thus presumably safe. Eights are sensory oriented, and Sixes doubt their experience, so Sevens end up sampling a lot of things but questioning everything.

Also, the Six's self-doubt, lack of confidence, and insecurity plus the Eight's drive to be the top dog, dominating and triumphing over others, result in the Seven's characteristic visions and grand plans for what she is going to achieve, a fraction of which she takes the chance to try to realize.

THE WINGS OF ENNEA-TYPE EIGHT

Here, the need to be all right of Ego-Planning (Seven) meets the inner deadness of Ego-Indolence (Nine). The result is Ennea-type Eight's characteristic denial of anything that smacks of weakness or deficiency within himself. The utopian plans and dreams of Seven meet the inertia of Nine, resulting in the Eight's characteristic prejudice toward whatever he encounters—he sees what he wants to see, in other words, in a very entrenched sort of way. Also, with his vision of how things could be, coming from Seven, and his external focus, coming from Nine, he demands that things conform to the way he thinks they ought to be, wanting all the wrongs he sees to be righted.

From another angle, the Seven's hunger for stimulation plus the deadness to the essential realm of Nine leads to the Eight's lust for material gratifications and his focus on sensory satisfactions.

EPILOGUE

May God stand between you and harm
in all the empty places where you must walk.

—OLD EGYPTIAN BLESSING,
QUOTED ON THE TV SERIES *BABYLON 5*

In conclusion, I would like to return to Gurdjieff's notion, discussed at the beginning of this book, that the enneagram is a multidimensional symbol, encompassing "as many different meanings as there are levels of men." This feels important to me to reiterate, so that no one is left with the impression that what I have conveyed in this book is the last word on its various nuances. To the contrary, I feel that I will have achieved my aim if I have given readers food for thought and avenues of inquiry to deepen both their understanding of the enneagram and of themselves. The enneagram is a bit like a code, and we need entryways in order to gain access and open it up so that its wisdom can be revealed to us, and that is how I've seen my job in this book.

Second, as Gurdjieff also taught, the enneagram gives us great power. The information it contains can deeply affect and even unsettle us, and so I would like to repeat what I said at the end of the Introduction to this book: be careful how you use it, both in terms of yourself and with others. I have seen many people feel objectified when others have bandied about their various characteristics in attempting to figure out the person's type. Also, analyzing another without their asking you to do so can be wounding, and bringing something unsolicited to another's awareness of which they are not conscious can feel like an attack. Most of all, using the enneagram as ammunition to criticize or judge another person is definitely a misuse. With yourself, remember that it is not meant as fuel for your superego. It is meant to help you understand yourself more deeply and, through that understanding, to open your heart to compassion for yourself and for others.

Third, the enneagram is only a map. The enneagram and the information about the human soul and its evolution that it reveals are not ends in and of themselves. No matter how fascinating it may seem to pick apart and decipher more understanding from the enneagram, unless this information is secondary to our direct experience and fulfills the function of enhancing our personal unfoldment, it will do us little ultimate good. On its own, the information contained within the enneagram and within this book is not a panacea—it will not solve our problems, resolve our issues, or connect us with our depths. It is only information, whose function is to orient and guide us in our inner work, and unless that knowledge is put to use, we do not benefit from it. If it only remains intellectual, it may stimulate our minds and provide interesting diversion and entertainment, but this should not be mistaken for the actual work of transformation.

That endeavor is neither rapid nor is it easy. The directions that I have pointed toward regarding the inner work that each of the types needs for real personal transformation are easily summarized in a few pages. On the other hand, the actual working through of the personality such that our souls are progressively less occluded and so that they become increasingly transparent takes many years, no matter how dedicated we are and how much we apply ourselves. It is also work not easily done alone. Since true transformation requires overcoming the inertial pull of identification with the personality, support in the form of a spiritual school or a Work group is usually necessary. Because becoming conscious means seeing what we are blind to, the guidance of a teacher is often required for our Journey to be successful.

This Journey requires facing painful and sometimes deeply frightening aspects of ourselves, tucked away in the recesses of our souls. Things definitely feel as if they get worse before they get better, as we get closer and closer to some of the deep strata of the personality, with abysses and primitive energies that sometimes feel as though they will sweep us away. It is not an easy journey and it requires a degree of honesty with ourselves only possible if we are personally driven to know who we really are and if getting in touch with the truth—no matter how uncomfortable—brings joy to our hearts.

For those who choose to undertake it, it is infinitely rewarding. A whole universe awaits within us, complete with its infinite vastness and its paradoxes, its strangeness and its exquisiteness. While we will sometimes encounter black holes and vast empty places, all the beauty of the cosmos is there to unfurl itself. As we take this Journey, we increasingly understand what being human is all about: becoming transparent windows of the Divine, traveling through all of the limitless beauty of the creation, and living lives informed by Being, lives filled with profundity, contentment, and meaningful expression and contribution. It is my sincere hope that this book has shed light on the terrain and that it will continue to support your Journey Home.

DETERMINING
YOUR ENNEA-TYPE

Figuring out what your ennea-type is can be a tricky matter. Some people recognize their type immediately by reading or hearing the descriptions; some people's type is obvious to one who knows the enneagram by looking at them, while others are more difficult for themselves or anyone else to type. Why one's type is clear-cut with some people and indiscernible with others seems to be one of those mysteries about the enneagram and the soul. There are many different ways of determining someone's type: in Ichazo's Arica Training, facial characteristics are used, since specific regions of the face seem to correspond to each type. I have run across useful inventories and questionnaires, and there are probably a vast number of other surveys and methods that I'm not aware of. Because we are dealing with a gestalt—a complex interaction of beliefs, emotional states, behavioral patterns, and other factors—determining one's type is not as simple as pointing to one particular characteristic or physical attribute. Typing is an art that requires stepping out of our own subjective perspective and contacting the feel of another person's soul. It requires seeing another clearly, not as we would want them to be but as they really are. This can be especially difficult with those we are close to. Much experience with people whose type is very clear can sharpen our capacity to tune in to someone's type quickly.

My personal preference is to offer people guidance in determining their own type, rather than imposing my opinion on them, and I think it is always necessary to be open to the possibility of being wrong about someone's type. We are dealing with very powerful information about how someone ticks, and it is important to be very sensitive to the effects it may have on someone, whether we are typing them accurately or not. I have seen many instances of people being mistyped—either by themselves or by others—and because we have all nine types within us, they end up focusing on the one they have been typed as and missing what is more fundamental to their structure. I have also seen instances in which someone has been mistyped and so has been turned off to the enneagram, finding it to be inaccurate.

With this said, what follows are some guidelines that I have found useful in typing others and in helping students determine their own type, as well as some common confusions I've seen people make in typing.

WHICH CORNER IS DOMINANT?

One way to begin the process of determining an ennea-type is to figure out which corner of the enneagram the person belongs to. Does he or she belong to the fear corner—those types on either side and including Ennea-type Six—that are primarily motivated by and oriented around fear? Or is he or she an image type—being either an Ennea-type Three or one of its wings—primarily concerned with their presentation and effect on others? Or is the person's central orientation self-forgetting and an outer-directed focus of attention, which would locate him or her at either Ennea-type Nine or one of its wings?

There are two ways to begin answering this question, both of which come from Naranjo's original teaching. The first is looking at the person's body type, using the somatotype classifications of the American psychologist of the midtwentieth century, W. H. Sheldon.[1] Very generally speaking, those belonging to the indolent corner at the top of the enneagram—Eights, Nines, and Ones—tend to be of mesomorphic body type: solidly built, muscular, and tending toward stockiness. The fear types—Fives, Sixes, and Sevens—tend to be ectomorphs: thin, lanky, and wiry. The image types—Twos, Threes, and Fours—tend to be endomorphs: curvaceous and soft of body type, with thin wrists, ankles, and waists. The correlation between the corners and these body types seems to be true in general or as an average, but there are many exceptions to these broad trends. Because of this, it would be misleading to determine a person's corner based solely on body shape.

The other way of determining which corner someone belongs to has to do with whether self-forgetting, fear, or image dominates the person's concerns and style of behavior. The way Naranjo helped us zero in on this central orientation was through an exercise in which we did a continuum-of-awareness monologue in the presence of two other people, voicing whatever was arising within us. Afterward the three of us tried to assess whether the strongest tendency of the speaker was to be fearful—speaking and then holding back, being afraid he couldn't do what was required of him, blocking his impulses and doubting what he was saying, with suspiciousness or feelings of persecution in his content; or was it to be indolent—getting lost in the story, rambling on and forgetting the main point of what he was saying, becoming absorbed in the petty details of the content, and focusing on the others and not on his inner experience; or whether the main tendency was to be image conscious—being pretentious, concerned with how he was coming across or about what the others thought of him, presenting an image or a show, with a feeling of phoniness. Doing an exercise like this might not be conclusive, but it may give you a general sense of predisposition toward one of the corners. A variation on this exercise would be to write for twenty minutes or so without stopping, and afterward look at the content and the feeling tone, to see whether one of these three tendencies dominates.

THE IDEALIZED ASPECT

A way to begin pinpointing your type is to identify which of the idealized Aspects is the one you most try to emulate, as well as the one that seems to you to be the answer to your problems. Below is a brief description of each of the Aspects and some of the ways each of the ennea-types tries to embody them.

ENNEA-TYPE NINE · LIVING DAYLIGHT

Living Daylight is the experience of everything in the universe being made of love. It is the recognition of Being as what sustains and supports all of manifestation, and that our nature is inseparable from It. It gives us the sense of being held by a warm and benevolent presence and connects us with the goodness of life and of ourselves. Nines believe that these qualities are missing and are what they need. So they want to be included, noticed, loved, and appreciated by others, and want to contact the goodness of life and feel that they are included in its bounty. They emulate this quality by being supportive, giving, and loving toward others. They fade into the background, harmonizing with others and rarely asserting themselves. They avoid conflict and try to keep things pleasant and comfortable both for themselves and others. Their focus is outward, on others and on the events in their lives. They are sensitive and open to the perspectives and points of view of others, and so mediate well. At the same time, they have difficulty determining what they think, feel, and believe. They tend to have a fuzzy, amorphous, or slightly out-of-focus feeling about them.

ENNEA-TYPE ONE · BRILLIANCY

The state of Brilliancy is one of completeness, wholeness, perfection, and purity. Ones attempt to embody these qualities and to impose them on others and the world around them. Ones have a very clear sense of what they consider right and wrong, and believe that if others behaved correctly in accordance with these standards, all would be well. So the dominant quality of Ones is an eye for imperfection, frequently accompanied by criticality and faultfinding, and trying to make things conform to what they consider to be right and good. Like Nines, their focus is outward, but here it is with resentment that things are not perfect and with the agenda of making them so. Ones are firmly identified with their superegos and have difficulty understanding that whatever is happening is right. Chaos and disorder are difficult for Ones to tolerate, so they often are fastidious and tidy both in their personal appearance and in how they keep their various environments. They try to be what they consider good, and push out of consciousness what isn't. Energetically they feel sharp and crisp, and often have a pristine and clean quality.

ENNEA-TYPE TWO · MERGING GOLD

The state of Merging Gold is one of blissful, ecstatic union. It is a dissolving of the separating boundaries of the personality, resulting in a sense of oneness with another or Being Itself. It is the state of being in love, merging and melting into oneness with one's beloved. Twos long for this kind of union, believing intimate contact, either physical or emotional, is the thing that they most need. Being loved and connected to that special other is a Two's deepest desire. Twos emulate the characteristics of Merging Gold by attempting to be someone others will love and consider special. They are sensitive to the emotional states and needs of others and try to be there for them so that they will be loved in return. Twos are acutely attuned to any sense of rejection by others and will go to great lengths to be loved and accepted. While it is difficult for them to ask for attention directly, they become quite demanding and prideful if they feel that they are being ignored or overlooked. Twos often feel to others sticky, clingy, and needy, as well as filled with their own self-importance.

ENNEA-TYPE THREE · THE PEARL

The Pearl, or Personal Essence, is the state of being a person whose consciousness, life, and interactions are informed by Being. It is the state of being truly autonomous, free of all object relations and mental constructs defining who you are, and so it is the state of being a real person—an individuated embodiment of True Nature. Threes want to fulfill their potential and fully realize themselves, but this gets translated by the personality into cultural, material, and sometimes spiritual success rather than into actual unfoldment. They imitate the characteristics of the Personal Essence by believing they are functioning independently, while they are actually being shaped by and conforming to prevailing cultural images. They transform themselves into the image others want to see, and focus on their activities and accomplishments. Their sense of value is determined by how successful their performance is, and so they have difficulty not being active. Getting the job done is the most important thing to them, and so they overexert and subordinate physical needs, feelings, and inner experience in that pursuit. Focusing on their presentation, they deceive themselves and others to fulfill the image they are trying to present. Threes often seem slick and polished, as well as slippery, disingenuous, and sometimes just plain fake.

ENNEA-TYPE FOUR · THE POINT

The experience of the Point is of self-realization—it is the recognition that who you are is Essence. The actual experience is sometimes of being a shining star emerging out of the vast blackness of space, luminous and radiant, with a sense of meaning, value, importance, and appreciation for our individual uniqueness. Fours want to be seen as unique, original, and authentic, since they lack this sense of identity with Being. Because of their estrangement from Being, they often feel lonely and disconnected, and long for a sense of relatedness with others. They are acutely sensitive to being abandoned and neglected, and tend to dramatize their emotions and often feel dissatisfied and melancholic. Others seem to Fours to have what they lack, and what they have and who they are never seems quite enough. They seem to suffer more than others, and their longing for authenticity makes them controlling of themselves and of others. Fours may seem sad or depressed, but this is not always the case. Some seem happy enough although somewhat dissatisfied, with an air of vacancy despite the apparent strength of their emotions.

ENNEA-TYPE FIVE · DIAMOND GUIDANCE

The experience of Diamond Guidance is that of understanding and knowing in a deeply embodied and experiential way. It is the capacity to analyze and synthesize information from the present and the past instantaneously and to grasp something in an all-inclusive manner. Fives feel that what they need is knowledge, and they imitate this intuitive understanding through trying to make sense of life by observing it from a distance. They substitute detachment for objectivity, mental knowledge for active engagement in life, and tend to be loners who spend a lot of time by themselves and resent intrusions by others into their solitude. They live in their own bubble, feeling and maintaining a sense of isolation, which protects them from the impingements and demands that they fear. Dogged by an inner sense of impoverishment and insubstantiality, Fives seem empty, dry, and weak. They often seem withdrawn, pulled into themselves, withholding their vitality and engagement with others and with life in general. They tend to live simply and frugally, rarely wasting energy or resources.

ENNEA-TYPE SIX · WILL

Essential Will is the experience of inner support, which gives us a sense of confidence in our ability to persevere and bounce back when faced with difficulties. Will infuses us with a sense of steadfastness, definiteness, groundedness, solidity, commitment, persistence, and indestructibility. Out of touch with Will, Sixes lack faith in their capacity to defend and protect themselves, so they are frightened, unconsciously feeling always at risk of not surviving. Plagued by self-doubt, uncertainty, indecisiveness, and insecurity, Sixes think that their fear will be resolved if they can find something or someone who will give them confidence and who can dispel their doubt. To resolve their fear, phobic Sixes want a person or a cause they can believe in and become blindly loyal to, and counterphobic Sixes try to become that for others. Subordinating their will or, conversely, imposing their will on others, becomes the personality's imitation of real Will. Likewise, being suspicious of authority and either covertly or overtly being defiant of it become a Six's way of having his own will. Energetically Sixes feel to others frightened and suspicious.

ENNEA-TYPE SEVEN · THE YELLOW

The Essential Aspect of the Yellow is the experience of joy, delight, appreciation, and simple happiness. It is a warmth in the heart, which might be ebullient and bubbly or calm and deep. Sevens want to feel this gentle happiness rather than their parched and dry inner emptiness. So they look for stimulating ideas and things to get excited about, and their style is one of appearing optimistic, enlivened, enthusiastic, and above all, okay. They try to plot their course toward whatever holds the promise of joy, and so mapping and planning are central to their process. Lacking trust in their natural unfoldment, they try to make their inner process conform to their mental map, which they hope will lead them to the treasure that will finally bring them happiness. Driven by fear of how things will unfold, they always have backup maps and plans. They usually have many different things they are interested in and can get excited about, and lose their motivation when things get repetitive and difficult. Sevens often seem wired and mental, charming and talkative, but sometimes leaving you wondering where the substance is.

ENNEA-TYPE EIGHT · THE RED

The Essential Aspect of the Red gives us a sense of aliveness, vitality, vibrancy, strength, and capacity. It gives us initiative and forcefulness, boldness and daring. Eights believe that strength is the answer, and so they attempt to control and dominate, to bully and overwhelm to gain a sense of it. They have little tolerance for what they consider weakness or deficiency, and so have difficulty with "soft" feelings, especially pain and fear, both in themselves and others. Imitating the Red, they engage life with gusto and passion, forcefully and aggressively going after what they want. With the need to be in charge and take the lead, they have difficulty not being the boss and going along with someone else's wishes. They are fighters for what they believe in, and just as the Red is the power to defend what is real, Eights are fierce defenders of what they consider to be the truth. They seem to others large in energy, with a strong and powerful presence even when they aren't saying a word. Some Eights seem to have a perpetual chip on their shoulders, meeting life with belligerence and bluster. They have difficulty being vulnerable and receptive, tend to stay very much in control and in charge, and often feel energetically hard.

COMMON CONFUSIONS

Frequently people have difficulty distinguishing the heart point from a person's actual ennea-type. This can be especially true for those who have done a lot of inner work, since they may have become more conscious of and integrated more of their soul child. Some people also spend more time in the defensive point, that of further externalization, and so have difficulty telling which type is the most fundamental. In such cases, asking questions like which Holy Idea seems the most lacking in that person's consciousness and which of the passions seems the most prevalent may help clarify the person's ennea-type.

There are also some types that people frequently confuse, and in the following brief comparisons, I will discuss the basis of the confusion and give some pointers to help distinguish between the types.

NINE AND FIVE

The tendency to fade into the background, not drawing attention to oneself, and being reticent in groups is shared by both Nines and Fives. One of the main ways of discriminating a Nine from a Five is looking at their eyes: Nines tend to have a deadened or sleepy quality to their eyes, while Fives have a brightness and sharpness to their gaze, relying as they do on observation for safety. Body type also usually differs, with Nines tending toward largeness, heaviness, and roundness, while Fives are typically lean and sinewy. Nines feel that they do not deserve attention, while Fives usually don't want it. Nines incline toward clutter and collections of things, while Fives lean toward simplicity and sparsity.

NINE AND TWO

The common thread here is self-abnegating behavior, giving to and taking care of others—a mothering tendency. The main difference is that Twos give to get, so if you do not reciprocate or acknowledge what they do for you and how generous they are, you will incite their wrath; and Twos usually feel unappreciated or underappreciated by others. Nines, on the other hand, tend to become flustered and embarrassed when given acknowledgment. Nines also lack the feeling of specialness and pride that Twos have. If a Nine is ignored or overlooked, this is what they expect, while a Two will quietly or loudly kick up a fuss about it.

ONE AND FOUR

Both of these types share a tendency toward criticality and judgmentalness, as well as controlling behaviors and often a striving to be good. One of the key distinguishing factors is that Ones are identified with their superego, while Fours are at the mercy of theirs. In other words, Ones feel righteous and justified in pointing out the imperfections of others and deflect their own being pointed out, while Fours experience a great deal of shame and self-hatred when seen as bad and not measuring up to their own perfectionistic standards. Fours are typically more emotionally dramatic, in touch with their pain, aesthetically inclined, and more desirous of contact than Ones.

ONE AND SIX

The shared focus here is authoritarian tendencies as well as anxiety. Ones are very clear about what is right and what is wrong, and set themselves up as authorities who try to make others conform to their standards. Sixes are devotedly loyal to their chosen doctrine or authority figure and can be fanatically evangelical. Both Ones and Sixes may be anxious and doubtful, but what distinguishes them is the motivation: Ones are afraid of being wrong or of not doing something well enough, while Sixes are not driven by these perfectionistic concerns. They are simply doubtful and frightened, lacking faith in their internal discernment and abilities.

TWO AND FOUR

The shared tendencies here are emotive intensity, drama, envy, competitiveness, and a preoccupation with relationship. One of the main differences is that Fours tend to isolate themselves when they are in pain, since they are ashamed of their feelings, while Twos usually move toward those they are close to at such times. Fours long from afar for contact and intimacy, while Twos actively pursue getting it. Most Twos are more spontaneous and shameless than Fours, although there are some pretty reserved Twos and some very expressive Fours. Fours as a rule derive a sense of depth and beauty from their suffering, while Twos mostly do not. Twos focus on what they can do for others and how they will be loved in return, while Fours are not primarily oriented toward giving.

THREE AND SEVEN

Threes and Sevens are sometimes confused with each other, since both are active, energized, cheerful, buoyant, and positive. The difference is that Sevens tend to have a wide variety of interests and areas of expertise, not liking to be pinned down or defined by one pursuit. Threes, on the other hand, easily stick to one thing, wanting to take it to the greatest level of success possible. To Sevens, their plans for what they will do are far more interesting than the actual doing, and they accomplish a fraction of the things they imagine and fantasize about. Threes derive their sense of value from what they actually produce and achieve, and their plans are secondary to the finished product. Threes are pragmatic and practical; Sevens are idealistic and visionary.

FOUR AND FIVE

Sometimes it is difficult to tell whether someone is a Four or a Five, since both tend to be retiring and self-enclosing. One of the main differences is that Fours long for contact from their isolation, while Fives are grateful for the lack of impingement, interruption, and demands. Another is the emotive wetness of Fours, in contrast to the dry emptiness of Fives. Fives lack the sense of tragedy, suffering, and melancholy of Fours, although both may feel impoverished and deprived. Fives become indifferent, while Fours become envious and spiteful in difficult situations with others.

SIX AND EIGHT

It is sometimes difficult to discern whether someone is a counterphobic Six or an Eight, since both share a tough style and an emphasis on proving how strong they are. Both can be aggressive and combative, on the offensive rather than the defensive. One of the main differences is that the machismo of Sixes is driven by fear, which you can frequently see in their eyes, while that of Eights is based on a compulsion to be dominant. Sixes are trying to overcome their fear, while Eights are trying to overcome their weakness. Eights are controlling and domineering in their relationships, while Sixes are not.

DIAGRAMS

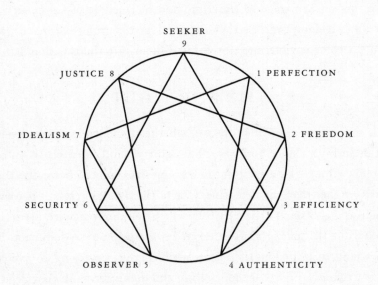

Diagram 9

THE ENNEAGRAM OF TRAPS

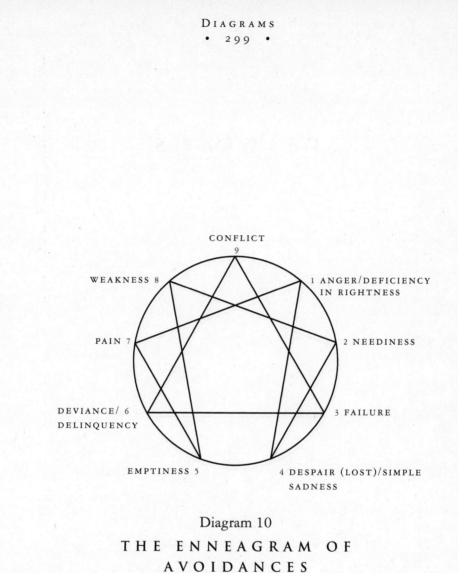

Diagram 10

THE ENNEAGRAM OF
AVOIDANCES

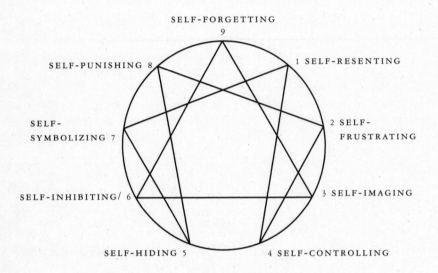

Diagram 11

THE ENNEAGRAM OF ANTISELF ACTIONS

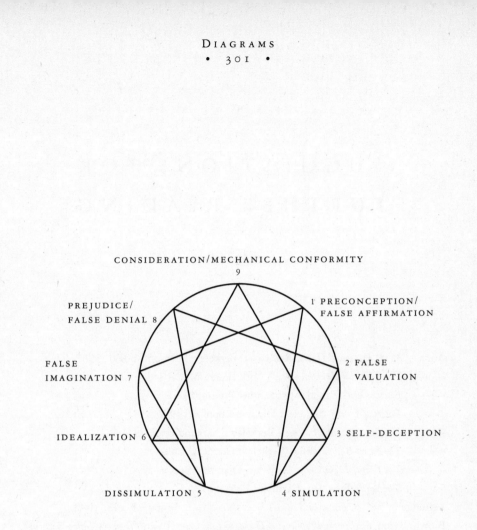

CONSIDERATION/MECHANICAL CONFORMITY
9

PREJUDICE/
FALSE DENIAL 8

1 PRECONCEPTION/
FALSE AFFIRMATION

FALSE
IMAGINATION 7

2 FALSE
VALUATION

IDEALIZATION 6

3 SELF-DECEPTION

DISSIMULATION 5

4 SIMULATION

Diagram 12

THE ENNEAGRAM OF LIES

SUGGESTIONS FOR FURTHER READING

Almaas, A. H. *Diamond Heart, Books 1–4.* Berkeley: Diamond Books, 1987–97.

———. *The Elixir of Enlightenment.* York Beach, Me.: Samuel Weiser, 1984.

———. *Essence.* York Beach, Me.: Samuel Weiser, 1986.

———. *Facets of Unity.* Berkeley: Diamond Books, 1998.

———. *Luminous Night's Journey.* Berkeley: Diamond Books, 1995.

———. *The Pearl Beyond Price.* Berkeley: Diamond Books, 1988.

———. *The Point of Existence.* Berkeley: Diamond Books, 1996.

———. *The Void.* Berkeley: Diamond Books, 1986.

Bettelheim, Bruno. *Freud and Man's Soul.* New York: Vintage Books, 1982.

Brown, Byron. *Soul without Shame: A Guide to Liberating Yourself from the Judge Within.* Boston and London: Shambhala, 1999.

Davis, John. *The Diamond Approach: An Introduction to the Teachings of A. H. Almaas.* Boston and London: Shambhala, 1999.

Freud, Anna. *The Ego and the Mechanisms of Defense.* New York: International Universities Press, Inc., 1966.

Freud, Sigmund. *The Standard Edition of the Complete Works of Sigmund Freud.* New York: W. W. Norton & Co., 1949.

Greenberg, Jay R., and Stephen A. Mitchell. *Object Relations in Psychoanalytic Theory.* Cambridge, Mass.: Harvard University Press, 1983.

Horney, Karen. *Neurosis and Human Growth.* New York: W. W. Norton & Co., 1950.

———. *Our Inner Conflicts.* New York: W. W. Norton & Co., 1945.

Kaplan, Louise J. *Oneness and Separateness: From Infant to Individual.* New York: Simon & Schuster, 1978.

Mahler, Margaret, Fred Pine, and Anni Bergman. *The Psychological Birth of the Human Infant.* New York: Basic Books, 1975.

Mitchell, Stephen A., and Margaret J. Black. *Freud and Beyond: A History of Modern Psychoanalytic Thought.* New York: Basic Books, 1995.

Moore, James. *Gurdjieff: The Anatomy of a Myth.* Rockport, Mass.: Element, 1991.

Naranjo, Claudio. *Character and Neurosis: An Integrative View.* Nevada City, Calif.: Gateways/IDHHB, Inc., 1994.

Ouspensky, P. D. *In Search of the Miraculous.* New York: Harcourt Brace Jovanovich, Inc., 1949.

Rumi, Jelaluddin. Numerous titles, translations by A. J. Arberry, Coleman Barks, and Reynold Nicholson.

Shah, Idries. *The Sufis.* New York: Anchor Books, 1964.

————. *Tales of the Dervishes.* New York: E. P. Dutton, 1967.

————. *Thinkers of the East.* New York: Penguin Books, 1971.

————. Numerous other titles.

Suzuki, Shunryu. *Zen Mind, Beginner's Mind.* New York and Tokyo: Weatherhill, 1970.

Trungpa, Chögyam. *Cutting Through Spiritual Materialism.* Berkeley: Shambhala, 1973.

Winnicott, D. W. *The Maturational Processes and the Facilitating Environment.* New York: International Universities Press, Inc., 1965.

Zimmer, Heinrich. *Philosophies of India.* Princeton, N.J.: Bollingen Series/Princeton University Press, 1951.

NOTES

INTRODUCTION

1. See James Moore, *Gurdjieff: The Anatomy of a Myth* (Rockport, Mass.: Element, Inc., 1991).

2. See James Webb, *The Harmonious Circle: The Lives and Work of G. I. Gurdjieff, P. D. Ouspensky, and Their Followers* (New York: G. P. Putnam's Sons, 1980).

3. Quoted in P. D. Ouspensky, *In Search of the Miraculous* (New York: Harcourt Brace & Co., 1949), p. 294.

4. Gurdjieff used the term *personality* to designate this part of ourselves, which encompasses but is a much larger structure than one's persona or outer presentation, the common meaning of the word *personality*. In the psychological usage of the word, *ego* indicates the conscious self (in contrast to the unconscious), as well as a set of functions basic to human behavior, such as memory, cognition, speech, and defensive functions, to name a few. Because of these different meanings of the word *ego*, I prefer to use the term *personality* to refer to our conditioned sense of self.

5. Naranjo taught that the enneagram and the Tarot came out of the same tradition and that the Tarot is fundamentally a diagram of stages on the path of realization, a teaching passed on to us by one of Ichazo's students.

6. Claudio Naranjo, M.D., *Ennea-type Structures: Self-Analysis for the Seeker* (Nevada City, Calif.: Gateways/IDHHB, Inc., 1990).

7. Ibid., p. 333.

8. While the understanding of how the loss of each Holy Idea gives rise to a whole personality type is crucial to our study, an in-depth study of each Holy Idea is not. The Holy Ideas are the focus of Almaas's book *Facets of Unity: The Enneagram of Holy Ideas* (Berkeley: Diamond Books, 1999), and these two books can be seen as complementary.

9. John C. Lilly and Joseph E. Hart, "The Arica Training," in *Transpersonal Psychologies,* ed. Charles T. Tart (New York: Harper & Row, 1975), p. 334.

CHAPTER 1. THE INNER TRIANGLE

1. Sigmund Freud, "The Ego and the Id," *Standard Edition of the Complete Psychological Works of Sigmund Freud,* ed. James Strachey (London: Hogarth Press and the Institute of Psycho-Analysis, 1953–74), vol. 19, p. 26.

2. See the work of D. W. Winnicott and Almaas's *Facets of Unity: The Enneagram of Holy Ideas* for more detailed information on the concept of the holding environment.

3. Ibid., pp. 43–44.

4. Margaret Mahler, "On Human Symbiosis and the Vicissitudes of Individuation," *Journal of the American Psychoanalytic Association* 15:740–63. (1967), p. 750. Emphasis in original.

5. Freud, "An Outline of Psycho-Analysis" (1940), *Standard Edition of the Complete Psychological Works of Sigmund Freud,* 23:144–207, p. 145.

6. Some believe that Freud worked with Kabbalistic teachings and did indeed have an understanding of spiritual realms, but there is nothing in his writings to substantiate that assertion definitively.

7. A. H. Almaas, *Essence: The Diamond Approach to Inner Realization* (York Beach, Me.: Samuel Weiser, 1986), pp. 97–98.

8. For more on working with the superego, see Byron Brown's book, *Soul Without Shame: A Guide to Liberating Yourself from the Judge Within* (Boston and London: Shambhala Publications, 1999).

9. *The Essential Rumi,* trans. by Coleman Barks (HarperSanFrancisco, 1995), p. 153.

CHAPTER 2.
ENNEA-TYPE NINE: EGO-INDOLENCE

1. Almaas, *Facets of Unity,* pp. 211–12.

2. Ibid., p. 210.

3. *The American Heritage Dictionary, Second College Edition,* Boston: Houghton Mifflin Co., 1985.

4. Soviet culture tends more toward the Eight side of Nine; and the Chinese, to the One side; but the ideology is Nine-ish in both cases in the sense of subordinating individuality to the functioning of the state.

5. "Eisenhower, Dwight D." Britannica. CD 99 Standard Edition © Encyclopaedia Britannica, Inc.

6. This and all subsequent definitions of the virtues by Oscar Ichazo are from an unpublished document from the Arica Institute.

CHAPTER 3.
ENNEA-TYPE SIX: EGO-COWARDICE

1. Almaas, *Facets of Unity,* p. 235.

2. For more on the genital hole, see Almaas's *The Void—A Pyschodynamic Investigation of the Relationship between Mind and Space* (Berkeley: Diamond Books, 1987).

3. There is dispute about whether he was a Five or a Six. Because of the Five's focus on knowing, the penetrating intelligence with which Freud broadened our understanding of how the psyche functions makes the case for his having been a Five, while the content of his discoveries speak directly to issues especially germane to Sixes, e.g., his focus on the instinctual drives, the oedipal complex, and his understanding of anxiety.

4. Charles Brenner, M.D., *An Elementary Textbook of Psychoanalysis* (New York: Anchor Books, 1974), p. 72.

5. Burness E. Moore, M.D., and Bernard D. Fine, M.D., *Psychoanalytic Terms and Concepts* (New Haven and London: The American Psychoanalytic Association and Yale University Press, 1990), p. 149.

6. *Webster's Third New International Dictionary,* s.v. *paranoia.*

7. David Shapiro, *Neurotic Styles* (New York: Basic Books, Inc., 1965), p. 56.

8. Ursula Hegi, *Stones from the River* (New York: Simon & Schuster, 1994), p. 207.

9. Quoted in George Stephanopoulos, *All Too Human: A Political Education* (Boston, New York, and London: Little, Brown & Company, 1999), p. 69.

10. Quote from "The Core of the Teachings" on the Krishnamurti Foundation Web site.

11. For more on the Aspect of will, see A. H. Almaas's *The Pearl Beyond Price—Integration of Personality into Being: An Object Relations Approach* (Berkeley: Diamond Books, 1988), pp. 299–308.

CHAPTER 4.
ENNEA-TYPE THREE: EGO-VANITY

1. Almaas, *Facets of Unity,* p. 265.

2. For more on the Pearl, see Almaas's *The Pearl Beyond Price.*

3. *Webster's Third New International Dictionary of the English Language Unabridged,* s.v. *vain.*

4. Ibid., s.v. *vanity.*

5. Moore and Fine, *Psychoanalytic Terms and Concepts,* p. 103.

CHAPTER 5.
ENNEA-TYPE ONE: EGO-RESENTMENT

1. D. T. Suzuki, "A Few Statements about Zen," in *The World of Zen: An East-West Anthology,* ed. Nancy Wilson Ross (New York: Random House, 1960), p. 30.

2. Almaas, *Facets of Unity*, p. 141.

3. Naranjo, *Character and Neurosis*, p. 40.

4. Brenner, *An Elementary Textbook of Psychoanalysis*, p. 85.

CHAPTER 6.
ENNEA-TYPE FOUR: EGO-MELANCHOLY

1. Integrating and living this realization is another matter, related more directly to the Pearl, or Personal Essence, discussed in Chapter Four.

2. Jay R. Greenberg and Stephen A. Mitchell, *Object Relations in Psychoanalytic Theory* (Cambridge, Mass.: Harvard University Press, 1983), p. 121.

3. Ibid., pp. 128–29.

4. Naranjo, *Character and Neurosis*, p. 97.

5. Ibid., p. 117.

6. Freud, *Mourning and Melancholia*, Vol. 14 of the *Standard Edition*, 1957, p. 249.

7. Gertrude Blanck and Rubin Blanck, *Ego Psychology: Theory and Practice, Vol. 1* (New York: Columbia University, 1974), p. 260.

8. Moore and Fine, *Psychoanalytic Terms and Concepts*, p. 53.

9. Ibid., p. 181.

10. Naranjo, *Character and Neurosis*, pp. 115–16.

11. Ibid., p. 116.

12. For more information about this transformation, see A. H. Almaas, *The Point of Existence: Transformations of Narcissism in Self-Realization* (Berkeley: Diamond Books, 1996).

CHAPTER 7.
ENNEA-TYPE TWO: EGO-FLATTERY

1. Almaas, *Facets of Unity*, p. 121.

2. Ibid., p. 130.

3. In contrast to experiencing that all of existence is made up of love—which is the experience of Living Daylight, the idealized Aspect of Point Nine—the focus here is on the experience of a blissful union that dissolves all sense of the separate self.

4. Karen Horney, M.D., *Neurosis and Human Growth: The Struggle toward Self-Realization* (New York: W. W. Norton & Co., 1950), pp. 239–40.

5. Ibid., pp. 243–44.

6. Karen Horney, M.D., *Our Inner Conflicts* (New York: W. W. Norton & Co., 1945), pp. 51–52.

7. Moore and Fine, *Psychoanalytic Terms and Concepts*, p. 90.

8. Elsworth F. Baker, M.D., *Man in the Trap* (New York: Collier Books, 1967), p. 109.

9. Naranjo, *Character and Neurosis*, p. 186.

10. Horney, *Our Inner Conflicts,* p. 54.

11. Eric Berne, M.D., *Games People Play* (New York: Ballantine Books, 1964), pp. 116–22.

CHAPTER 8.
ENNEA-TYPE EIGHT: EGO-REVENGE

1. See Sogyal Rinpoche, *Dzongchen and Padmasambhava* (Berkeley: Rigpa Fellowship, 1989).

2. Heinrich Zimmer, *Philosophies of India* (Princeton: Bolligen Foundation, 1951), p. 456.

3. The Muslim religious obligation to engage in a holy war against infidels.

4. Horney, *Neurosis and Human Growth,* pp. 210–11.

5. Horney, *Our Inner Conflicts,* pp. 68–69.

6. Ibid., p. 68.

7. *Newsweek,* Dec. 21, 1998, p. 65.

8. Horney, *Neurosis and Human Growth,* p. 200.

9. Fritz Perls, M.D., Ph.D., *Gestalt Therapy Verbatim* (Lafayette: Real People Press, 1969), p. 1.

10. Naranjo, *Character and Neurosis,* p. 140. Emphasis in original.

11. Ibid., p. 140.

CHAPTER 9.
ENNEA-TYPE FIVE: EGO-STINGINESS

1. Horney, *Neurosis and Human Growth,* pp. 263–64.

2. Ibid., pp. 260–61. Emphasis in original.

3. Horney, *Our Inner Conflicts,* pp. 91–92.

4. Almaas, *The Pearl Beyond Price,* pp. 188–89.

5. Naranjo, *Character and Neurosis,* p. 86.

6. Horney, *Neurosis and Human Growth,* p. 264.

7. Ibid., p. 66.

8. Ennea-type Ones have a different kind of anality, which manifests in obsessive-compulsive types of behavior such as an exaggerated need for order or cleanliness.

9. Ibid., p. 66.

CHAPTER 10.
ENNEA-TYPE SEVEN: EGO-PLANNING

1. Almaas, *Facets of Unity,* p. 170.

2. Ibid.

3. From the unedited transcript of A. H. Almaas's *Facets of Unity*.

4. Moore and Fine, *Psychoanalytic Terms and Concepts*, pp. 101–2.

5. Ibid., p. 160.

6. Naranjo, *Character and Neurosis*, p. 168.

7. Ibid., pp. 165–66.

8. Baba Ram Dass, *Be Here Now* (San Cristobal, N. Mex.: Lama Foundation, 1971), [unnumbered page].

CHAPTER 12.
THE SUBTYPES

1. Lilly and Hart, "The Arica Training," in *Transpersonal Psychologies*, p. 348.

2. Ibid., p. 347.

3. Ibid.

4. Ibid.

5. Ibid., p. 349.

6. Ibid.

7. Ibid.

APPENDIX A

1. W. H. Sheldon and S. S. Stevens, *The Varieties of Temperament: A Psychology of Constitutional Differences* (New York: Harper & Brothers, 1942).

ACKNOWLEDGMENTS

I would like to express my gratitude first of all to Hameed Ali (A. H. Almaas) for his generosity with his material, his time and advice given to me during the course of writing this book. My personal debt to him for the effect his work has had on my life is beyond measure. I would also like to thank Claudio Naranjo for his teachings, including those on the enneagram contained in this book, which changed the course of my life. Although I have never met Oscar Ichazo, he is the ultimate source of much of this material, and to him I also express my thanks. My chance meeting with Karen Johnson over three decades ago led to my interest in spiritual work, and years later she introduced me to the Diamond Approach, and to her I am also grateful.

Many years ago now, Rhodora Mouskos and Rennie Moran suggested that I write this book, and that was the seed out of which this book eventually grew. It might not have been published without Sherry Anderson's inspired assistance in helping me find my wonderful agent, Thomas Grady, whose unerring and generous guidance has been invaluable. I am also grateful to Sherry for her encouragement, her careful reading of the manuscript, and her guidance, suggestions, and comments. Geneen Roth has been a great birth coach for this book, and I am deeply grateful to her for offering to write the Foreword and for her unswervingly enthusiastic support, her eagerness to read each chapter, and her feedback and guidance throughout this process. Mitch Horowitz, my editor at Tarcher, has helped shape this book into its final form, and I want to express my thanks to him for his many questions that made me search more deeply and explain more clearly, even when I thought things were perfectly obvious; for his vision and belief in the importance of this project; and for his patience and graciousness with this first-time author; I am also grateful to Deborah Miller, who copyedited this book, for her careful attention to all of its details and her suggestions which have made it a stronger book, and also for her appreciation of it. I would also like to thank Tony Schwartz for his encouragement and guidance during the early stages of this process, and Marjorie Nathanson, who helped me contextualize this project and its place in my personal unfoldment.

The insights and perceptions of my fellow teachers of the Diamond Approach, based on their own inner experience and their years of work with others, are inextricably woven into the fabric of this book. In particular I would like to thank Marie Ali, who co-led groups on the enneagram with me for years and helped develop some of this material. I would also like to thank her for her feedback and comments on the chapter on her ennea-type, as well as the following friends and colleagues who did the same: Kristina Bear, Jessica Britt, Byron Brown, Janet Green, Jeanne Hay, Linda Krier, Scott Layton, Deborah Ussery Letofsky, Morton Letofsky, Joyce Lyke, David Silverstein, Mary Ellen Stanke, and Patty Willis. I would like to thank Rosanne Annoni, Kristina Bear, and Sara Norwood Hurley for their careful reading of the entire manuscript and for their comments and suggestions. Also, my appreciation to Paul Rosenblum for his elephantine contribution, and for his and Jeanne Hay's celebratory support.

To all my students, whose sincerity and dedication to the truth make it an honor to work with them, I also want to express my thankfulness. Without my having been a witness and guide for their inner explorations, the material in this book would not have emerged. The questions I was pondering about the material always were miraculously answered by what was revealed as we explored their inner terrain together, as I worked with them when I was not writing. Indirectly they are all present in this book, and I am grateful to them for what they have taught me and for their understanding during my absences because of this project.

Even though they have not completely understood what I've been up to all these decades, the members of my family have been unfailingly supportive of my pursuing what I felt I had to, and I am grateful to them all for that.

Finally, I would like to express my endless gratitude to Bob Rosenbush who became my husband during the writing of this book. His initial encouragement about this project was crucial to this book's inception, and his sustained belief in its importance, his encouragement and unstinting willingness to be a sounding board and to give me advice and feedback throughout have been invaluable to me, and most of all, our relationship has been a continual source of revelation.

INDEX

ABOUT THE AUTHOR

⸺⧉⸺

SANDRA MAITRI was a member of the first group of students to whom the Chilean psychiatrist Claudio Naranjo presented the enneagram system in the United States almost three decades ago. Throughout her many years of studying and teaching it, Maitri has preserved the legacy of this original transmission. As one of the principal teachers of the Diamond Approach, she teaches the enneagram as part of the larger work of personal transformation, working with hundreds of students each year in the United States and Europe. She lives in Marin County, California. You can visit her website at www.sandramaitri.com.